EVIDEN

What You May Not Know About Columbine

EVIDENCE IGNORED:

What You May Not Know About Columbine

Rita Gleason

EVIDENCE IGNORED: What You May Not Know About Columbine

Copyright © 2018 Rita Gleason

Content Editor: Maddy Drake
Copy Editor: Klancy Hoover
Cover Art: Macario Hernandez
Editor-in-Chief: Kristi King-Morgan
Formatting: Kristi King-Morgan

ISBN- 978-1-947381-18-6

www.dreamingbigpublications.com

Prologue

On April 20, 1999, two young men brutally attacked and murdered twelve fellow students and one teacher before turning their guns upon themselves. Twenty-four other people were wounded, several grievously so. Those individuals, and all who witnessed the horror on that early spring day, bear the emotional and physical scars inflicted upon them by two gunmen filled with an unfathomable rage. Columbine was forever transformed and, for many, will forever be synonymous with school violence.

The question we all ask, and the one for which we will never have an answer, is why? What drove two seemingly bright high school seniors weeks away from graduation to commit such atrocities? At what point did they progress from fantasizing about revenge for perceived wrongs to actively plotting the destruction of the entire Columbine High School student body, and the school itself? Why were signs of trouble ignored or missed entirely and what, if anything, could have prevented the attack?

One wonders if the gunmen could have even addressed these questions adequately themselves—whether they were capable of understanding what drove their anger and hopelessness. Both left behind video diaries in the form of the so-called "Basement Tapes," as well as journals and website postings that seem to be a portrait of contradictions. Their fury is well documented, as is the detailed planning the two undertook to orchestrate their fatal attack. Throughout these words and images, however, we can see glimpses of other sides of these young men. It is far too easy to categorize Eric Harris as the psychopathic, manipulative leader and Dylan Klebold as the hapless, depressive follower. Perhaps there were elements of such in each of their personalities, but to try to wrap things up into a tidy little package seems to belie the true cause of this tragedy and may blind us to important clues that could prevent future mass killing sprees like this one. By the same token, laying the blame at the feet of secularism and the drifting of some away from a belief in, or expression of, faith is also too simple. In the aftermath of the murders, religious leaders decried the separation of church and state, claiming it has led people away from Christ and, by extension, from a life of meaning and principle. Such "lost souls" corrupted by selfish pleasures and struggling to find purpose in the absence of service to the Lord would inevitably, like Eric and Dylan, destroy themselves and others, bringing about the downfall of society. To decree that the majority of non-believers are incapable of upholding a moral standard or of creating lives of consequence and beneficence is to negate the millions of individuals who do just that. The actions of Harris and Klebold are in no way representative of those who do not live their lives through Christ, and such implications appear to be both overreaching and without basis.

The Columbine massacre and the events surrounding it have been explored in reports, books, movies, and even college theses—yet we still struggle to find answers. Some have expressed concern that all of this analysis has given Harris and Klebold what they craved: power, recognition, attention, and infamy. It is true that the boys discussed the impact their actions would have on the world and how they would be remembered. Had they lived, they likely would have enjoyed the tremendous fallout from their crimes. But they did not live. Perhaps Brooks Brown, a friend to both Harris and Klebold, addressed this best when speaking before the House Civil Justice and Judiciary Committee to ask for a state investigation into the massacre. He said, *"Eric and Dylan are dead. They lost. They died that day. And if you're religious, they are in hell. Having a bad time. They did not win."*[1] To stifle the conversation and the search for understanding would only further add to the tragedy of April 20, 1999.

Chapter One

Trench Coat Mafia

When news of trouble at Columbine High School broke, it was not long before the media was relaying stories about the Trench Coat Mafia. As the day wore on, the tales about the TCM grew increasingly more bizarre. The group was a far-reaching syndicate of dispossessed misfits bent on world domination and revenge for past mistreatment. They were a gang of Satan- worshiping bisexuals and homosexuals with an X-rated initiation ritual. None of this was true, of course, but it would be months before some, including the news media, came to that conclusion. Even today, there are many who are still unclear as to the workings of the Trench Coat Mafia and what, if any, relationship the group had to the Columbine killers Eric Harris and Dylan Klebold.

While it would be easy to blame the media for disseminating this misinformation, the seeds for this story came from within the walls of Columbine High School. Students were familiar, in varying degrees, with the kids who dressed mostly in black and kept to themselves at the table under the stairs in the cafeteria. Rumors floated around about these kids: their beliefs, their activities, and what one had to do to join the group. No one was really sure exactly who belonged to the TCM. Even amongst the students who had been part of the group there was disagreement over whether Harris and Klebold were mere associates or full-fledged members. As far as the general student population was concerned, if a kid wore black, a trench coat or duster, or hung around with known members of the clique, then that kid was as good as a member. The only fact that was fairly universally well-known was that the students in the Trench Coat Mafia were outcasts.

As the first wave of kids were streaming out of the school during the initial gunfire and explosions, the survivors relayed bits and pieces of information about who was responsible for the attack to the police and those assisting victims. The Sports and Athletics Supervisor at nearby Clement Park helped shelter some of the fleeing students in the park's maintenance facility. He relayed to police that "*A majority of the students* [he] *helped informed him there had been a TRENCH COAT MAFIA (TCM) gang shooting over at the high school.*"[2] The Clement Park Supervisor transported a police officer, via golf cart, over to obtain first impressions from kids taking refuge at the park. These observations were confirmed by a second individual, a salesman who had been taking a scheduled tour of Clement with the park's maintenance man. In his interview, he *"advised that the only thing he had heard the juveniles say was, 'The Trench Coat Mafia did it.'"*[3] The salesman left the park area shortly after noon on that day, roughly 40 minutes after the attack began. It makes him among the first to receive information about what was transpiring at the school.

Officer Gallego of the Jefferson County Sheriff's Office was responsible for several witness interviews the day of the massacre. In his report, he relayed the information he received from faculty and students in the initial hours after the incident began. Of the thirteen individuals he interviewed, five people—including Columbine High School's Campus Supervisor—indicated that the shooters were members of the Trench Coat Mafia.[4] A teacher still holed up in the English wing of the school reported events to police by telephone. Among the things he relayed were that it was his understanding that the shooters were Columbine students. *"He also reported that he has heard of the group calling themselves the Trench Coat Mafia."*[5] Even one of the first shooting victims, interviewed in his hospital bed shortly after coming out of surgery that afternoon, told police that the gunmen were dressed in black trench coats *"and referred to them as 'Trench Coat Mafia.'"*[6] Several other witness accounts in those early hours, to both law enforcement and the media, also pointed the finger squarely at the TCM.[7,8,9,10,11,12] The police were so inundated with leads as to the TCM's involvement that they devoted quite a few resources, including an investigator from the FBI, to look into the group.[13] A questionnaire entitled *Team Four Interview Guideline Minimal Questions To Be Asked*, which was filled out by many of the witnesses, included the questions: *"Did you see or talk to any of the Trench Coat Mafia members on Monday? Tuesday? How about the prior week or weekend?"* and *"Can you provide any further information on the members of the Trench Coat Mafia?"*[14] While it may be convenient to claim that the media created the legend of the TCM in the days and weeks after the incident, the police were taking the group very seriously based upon information received from victims of the attack. The limited scope of the TCM was evident fairly early on, as eight days after the massacre police reported, *"we had no information that the TCM was anything other than a small group of associates at this one school."*[15] It would take several more months before law enforcement officials were confident that no one else in the clique participated in the planning or orchestration of the Columbine attack.

Early reports of the TCM were fueled by many misconceptions that had swirled around the group at Columbine High School. The myths surrounding the Trench Coat Mafia were introduced to the school community early on. Many students at the school told police that they had been warned away from the group before they ever reached Columbine. In an interview with a boy shot by Dylan Klebold, he stated that in the previous year—while he was still in middle school—he *"heard rumors that you need to stay away from those guys.* "[16] His statement was echoed by another student who relayed to investigators that when she was an eighth grader at Ken Caryl Middle School, her class was visited by Columbine High School student representatives who "*told the Ken Caryl Middle School students to avoid any of the Trench Coat Mafia students.*"[17] The girl reported that she heeded this advice. A third student, a freshman, reported a similar warning but admitted that she was not sure who was actually in the TCM.[18] One boy was told by a friend "*that he should never have anything to do with them and that he should never look them in the eyes, and just avoid them at all costs.*"[19]

A prevalent belief was that the members of the Trench Coat Mafia were either gay or bisexual[9,20,21,22,23,24,25,26] and that those in the group all had sexual intercourse with one another.[27] Other students thought that the TCM required new recruits to be sexually "jumped in" to the gang. A Columbine senior told investigators that it was her belief that anyone interested in joining the TCM "*had to do strange sexual things to become a member*"[28] and another girl stated she had heard that girls wishing to join the group "*had to sleep with an unknown guy who wore a beanie hat with a propeller.*"[29] The rumor was completely baseless. A former student, and one of the group's founding members, told police that the only requirement for joining the clique was to be liked by the other members.[30] The question about the sexual identity of those in the TCM may have originated from the tendency of members to exchange friendly greetings. According to one associate of the group, they "*treated each other as 'family,' often hugging each other when departing company.*"[31] A former TCM member was known to say hello to both his male and female friends by kissing them on the lips.[23,32,33] It was that behavior, in part, that resulted in some abusive name-calling by other students. Some kids felt that the hugging and kissing was done for attention and to stir controversy. *"When this happened everyone would call them names like 'fag' or 'faggots'.*"[34] In one particular incident, a year before the attack by Harris and Klebold, some TCM members responded to the name-calling by escalating the behavior to groping and *"physically 'making out' in front of the 'jocks.'*"[35] School officials felt that this was done to harass the jocks. The TCM members involved were disciplined and told not to engage in that type of conduct.[32,35] It is unclear whether the jocks were subjected to discipline for hurling derogatory homophobic slurs at the TCM members.[36] Despite the rumors, most of the members of the Trench Coat Mafia were actually heterosexual. While their dating opportunities may have been limited due to their status as social outcasts, most of the members of the group were known to date individuals of the opposite sex. A former TCM member and girlfriend of someone still within the group told police she was aware of the student body's perception that TCM members were gay. *"She heard the guys sleep with the guys, the girls sleep with the girls and then they trade.*"[37] She confirmed that this was, in fact, untrue.

Another widespread misconception was that all of the Trench Coat Mafia members worshiped the devil. In the Christian community of Littleton, this belief engendered fear and mistrust of the group.[38,39,40,41] The idea likely took hold because TCM members were known to wear black clothing and play card games like Magic in the cafeteria. Magic is a trading card game that involves battles between wizards called planeswalkers. Some students felt that this game was associated with Satanism, with one student telling police that he *"thought the 'magic cards' were cards about the devil and about power."*[42] Many in the TCM listened to music with darker themes that would not be classified as mainstream. On occasion, some male members of the group would also wear white or black makeup and black nail polish.[23,34,43] One student reported to police that early on in her attendance at Columbine she was warned to avoid the Trench Coat Mafia because they *"were satanic, they used drugs together, and 'they all have sex together.' "*[27] In police interviews, the TCM were described as satanic[27,40,43] devil worshipers[38] and devilish.[39] Trench Coat Mafia members did nothing to help allay these impressions with some of their behaviors. Following the incident when the TCM members were reprimanded for groping one another in the cafeteria, one of them then approached a table and began telling each occupant of the table that *"Satan loves you."*[36] Another member would carry a book he referred to as *"The Devil's Bible"*[44] while discussing with others why he did not believe in God.[44,45] Many TCM members and associates professed varying beliefs of atheism, agnosticism, Wiccanism, and even Satanism. Such associations were individual, however, and Satanism did not represent the group as a whole.

Whether Eric Harris and Dylan Klebold were members of the Trench Coat Mafia has been a hotly debated topic for years. By their senior year, it is widely believed that the TCM was a less noticeable part of the Columbine landscape. Some felt that the group had largely disbanded after some of the founding members graduated the previous year.[41,46,47] A dedication to the Trench Coat Mafia that was supposed to appear in the 1998-1999 yearbook, however, indicates that there were still some students who identified themselves as TCM. The dedication, which was pulled by Columbine staff after the massacre, read: *"Ode to the TCM- From hacking and bowling to a downtown day at a certain convention, from players and abstainers to certain teachers we won't mention, from learning to sack and wearing black, to last years week of OOS suspension. High school is over so get some coolio's and relieve that built up tension. Have an awesome summer! Robyn."*[48]

Several of the original members of the Trench Coat Mafia, when interviewed by police, indicated that both Harris and Klebold were full members of the group.[49,50,51] A female member echoed the sentiments that the clique had begun to fizzle out, but that Eric and Dylan became more involved around that time.[52] One of the founding members of the group told police that Klebold and Harris joined the TCM in 1997[30] and Robyn Anderson, who was found to have assisted Harris and Klebold in obtaining guns used in the shootings, classified the Trench Coat Mafia as *"a loose knit group of individuals that included Dylan Klebold, Eric*

Harris."[53] These statements, and the belief that Harris and Klebold were part of the TCM, were echoed by quite a few of the known TCM members[54,55] and their close friends.[56,57] Several other individuals outside of the TCM, including Dylan's best friend who was loosely affiliated with the group, indicated to police that Harris and Klebold were, indeed, members.[58,59,60] Yet a few of the boys' acquaintances, including one of the original TCM students,[61] felt that they were not.[62,63] There is no way to know for certain if Eric or Dylan identified themselves as part of the TCM. According to Tom Klebold, Dylan's father, "*he had heard Dylan mention the 'Trench Coat Mafia' and he advised that Dylan told him that the 'jocks' called him and his friends that. Mr. Klebold said that Dylan was kind of amused by the name the 'jocks' had given them.*"[64] The evidence for Eric Harris's involvement is not completely clear either. Harris did not wear his duster often but not all TCM associates had one, nor were they required to in order to be part of the clique. Harris had been good friends with Chris Morris, one of the group's founding members, for a few years and he did submit a video assignment for his Government/Economics class in December 1998 featuring himself and Klebold entitled "Trench Coat Mafia Hit-Men For Hire."[65,66,67] In the paper Harris wrote to accompany the video, he stated that "*The so-called 'Trench Coat Mafia' is a small group of friends who generally wear dark clothes, military fatigues, and long black dusters. Most people usually just stare and whisper when they see us. We don't mind because we generally don't like people anyway.*"[68] When Eric's father found out about the trouble at Columbine, he placed a call to 911 and told the operator that he felt his son might be involved. When the operator questioned him on this involvement, Wayne Harris replied, *"ahhh... he's a member of what they're calling the Trench Coat Mafia."*[69,70] It is not known whether the elder Harris got that information from his son or if he assumed it because Eric was known to wear a duster.

Regardless of what the TCM was or was not, and who did or did not belong, it was universally understood at Columbine High School that Trench Coat Mafia members and their associates existed amongst the bottom-dwellers of the school's social hierarchy. One would have been hard-pressed to find kids that shared a positive opinion of the group, with most viewing them as freaks, outcasts, and jokes.[28,71,72,73,74,75,76,77] The sentiment was shared by many students regardless of whether or not they had personal experience with TCM members. In fact, most kids that were interviewed admitted that while they did not actually know anyone in the group, they were quite definitive in their opinions of the TCM. A male student told police that although he was not personally familiar with anyone in the Trench Coat Mafia, TCM members were *"looked at as a 'joke.'"*[78] A Columbine senior stated, *"he knew the name Trench Coat Mafia. He said it was a nickname for a group of weird kids."*[79] And in a police statement, a female student claimed that even though she did not associate with the group because she and her friends were athletes, *"she knows that TCM type people are mean, strange, and act weird."*[80]

It was common knowledge that TCM members were subjected to bullying, which was often meted out at the hands of the school athletes or "jocks".[81,82] In police interviews, some said that the bullying seemed to extend both ways, with members of each group intentionally antagonizing those of the other.[59,83] Some students and faculty believed that the TCM went out of their way to isolate themselves[24,84] and provoke the name-calling and fights.[32,33,34,35] Many other witnesses claimed that while they observed abuse by the jocks, they never saw retaliation by TCM associates.[43,85,86,87] Even the creation of the term "Trench Coat Mafia" was borne out of this bullying behavior.[88,89,90,91] Members of the group did not select the name, but rather adopted the moniker after they were derisively referred to as such by a group of jocks. In a statement made by a student athlete, who had come to the attention of police as someone Harris and Klebold did not like, the officer wrote:

He told me he never did anything directly to them to harass them but was part of a group of guys who coined the name "The Trench Coat Mafia". I asked him to tell me about this. He said he along with the other guys "jocks" were at their table in the cafeteria in the fall of 1997. It was about 90 degrees outside and everyone in the school was wearing shorts except this group of guys wearing trench coats. When they walked through the cafeteria his group began making comments like look at the trench coats, one person said they look like they are in the mafia, then someone said they are in the Trench Coat Mafia. He said he had made at least one of these comments but

*could not remember what he had said at the
time. Since that date that was their identity.
[He] told me after the term "TCM" was given
to the group there was less harassment than
before they had a name. It seemed they now had
a name and enjoyed the identity.*[92]

Most of the ridicule was not so mild, ranging
from abusive language to physical altercations.
While the TCM was subject to derision by almost
all members of Columbine's student body, the jocks
seemed to be the group that delighted the most in
"giving them 'crap.'"[93,94] The student making this
claim was widely recognized as one of the original
members of the TCM and was pictured in the
Columbine yearbook photo of TCM group
members that circulated following the massacre. A
fellow student, who worked with this boy at a local
movie theater, relayed the following to police:
*"Then one night he came into work and told me he
had been chased in his car by so and so. Well, turns
out so and so were athletes from my school who
don't seem to have anything better to do than
torment this dude. I can see why the fellow I worked
with hated Columbine High School."*[95,96] Other
well-established members of the TCM had similar
experiences, with one reporting that *"members of
the Trench Coat Mafia were daily victims of teasing
and harassment."*[97] He indicated that in response to
the bullying he had been suspended several times
for fighting while a student at the school. Another
former student and TCM member told police that he
felt he was harassed by both Columbine staff and

students, but that the kids were particularly cruel. They called him a "freak" or "faggot" and cornered him in the halls or threw things at him.[87]

A Columbine senior and football player told police that although he had not participated in the bullying, he knew that Harris and Klebold did not like him because he was an athlete. In his statement he said, "*he has seen members of the 'Trench Coat Mafia' harassed on a nearly every day basis by the 'jocks' and especially by the football players at Columbine High School.* [He] *said these 'jocks' would make fun of the 'Trench Coat Mafia' students' clothing, but the 'Trench Coat Mafia' students being harassed would not stand up for themselves.*"[98] The football team's role in the torment was confirmed by a member of the baseball and golf teams. According to his police statement, "[He] *knew that these kids got picked on all the time, and most of the time it was done by the football team. He believed it was just because they were different.*"[99] Most kids at Columbine understood that the TCM members were not fans of the school's athletes and assumed that this attitude was a result of bullying.[98,100] Brooks Brown, a friend to both Harris and Klebold, recalled an incident during which a group of jocks dumped a bag of ice water on a TCM member in the cafeteria. A fight ensued outside. "*When security intervened, the Trench Coat Mafia kids wound up with three-day suspensions. The jocks who had started the fight were never even sent to the office.*"[101] Other kids witnessed physical altercations between the two groups, with one student telling police "*he has seen the 'jocks' call the Trench Coat Mafia students 'dirt bags and stuff' in the hallways at Columbine High School.*

[He] *said during the school year prior to the shooting, when the Trench Coat Mafia students were in his weight lifting class in gym, he had seen fights between the jocks and the Trench Coat students in the locker room."*[23] Another student reported an incident he and his friends had with TCM members in the school parking lot in the year prior to the massacre. He was in a pickup truck exiting the school grounds when a group of Trench Coat Mafia students were blocking the road and would not yield. The student *"yelled at them saying, 'get out of the way you faggots' and the driver of the Bronco came close to running them over."*[102] As they drove away, the boy alleged that Chris Morris, a TCM member and friend of both Eric and Dylan, was swinging a length of chain above his head. The confrontation was reported to school authorities and the boy who made the homophobic remark was talked to, but not reprimanded, for the harassment.[102,103] Morris was also allegedly known to get in physical confrontations and threaten kids with a knife.[104,105,106] It was likely this reputation that helped promote the erroneous belief that he may have been involved in the planning or execution of the massacre.

In what might be viewed as an oddly ironic attempt to explain that bullying was rare at Columbine and did not contribute to the killings, a football player injured by wood splinters after being shot at by Eric Harris in the library told *TIME* magazine:

Columbine is a clean, good place except for those rejects, [he] *says of Klebold and*

Harris and their friends. "Most kids didn't want them there. They were into witchcraft. They were into voodoo dolls. Sure, we teased them. But what do you expect with kids who come to school with weird hairdos and horns on their hats? It's not just jocks; the whole school's disgusted with them. They're a bunch of homos, grabbing each other's private parts. If you want to get rid of someone, usually you tease 'em. So the whole school would call them homos, and when they did something sick, we'd tell them, 'You're sick and that's wrong.'[107]

Several students detailed accounts of other incidents in which members of the TCM were the aggressors. A female athlete told police that she felt intimidated by the group because they would give her dirty looks.[108] Another boy reported that it was this intimidation that caused him to break off his friendship with Eric Harris. He and Eric were acquaintances, but the student distanced himself from Harris in January 1999 because *"Eric Harris and the other Trench Coat Mafia students began picking on people and harassing them."*[109] A Columbine student recounted his run-in with the TCM when he was cleaning up the school grounds as part of his community service. At the time of the incident, the boy's hair had been bleached blond. He told police that a group of kids in trench coats were hanging around a black, older model BMW—a description consistent with Dylan Klebold's car. One of the kids *"called out 'hey look… there's a little punk! Hey, punk rock!'"*[19] Other students also saw TCM members calling kids names in the cafeteria[110,111] and a substitute teacher told police that she had spoken with three African American students after the massacre who alleged that members of the Trench Coat Mafia *"had been calling them 'nigger' and growling at them when they passed in the hallways. The students said the Vice Principal basically told them to turn the other cheek."*[112] A member of the football team recounted an exchange that occurred when he parked his car near some Trench Coat students while on his way to practice. One of the group *"said something to him like 'fuck you, get the hell out of that space.'* [The student] *stated that the guy also said something like 'you stupid jock.'"*[113] When he returned from practice, he found that his car antenna had been broken.[113] A student wrestler also had an argument over a parking spot with TCM members and was warned not to park in their space again.[114]

To many, it appeared that the TCM members stuck together and that if a member of the group got into a fight, then all of the members would become involved.[115] Indeed, Robyn Anderson told police about a big fight that had allegedly taken place behind the pizza parlor where Dylan and Eric worked. The fight was between twenty Trench Coat Mafia members and some freshmen at Columbine.[116] The boys' former boss confirmed this incident and told police he remembered Dylan Klebold and another boy waiting behind the pizza shop for the fight.[117] He also alleged that one year before the massacre Harris, Klebold, and Morris were going to battle another group behind the shops on West Coalmine and South Pierce Streets. *"As*

Harris, Klebold, and Morris walked there from the Blackjack Pizza store donning their trench coats, the other group fled."[118]

The police reports indicate a clear pattern of bullying of TCM members, as well as a mutual dislike between the group and certain factions of the Columbine student body. The reports also indicate quite clearly that despite the bullying, no other members or close associates of the Trench Coat Mafia were involved in the planning or execution of the events perpetrated by Eric Harris and Dylan Klebold. Rumors persist that several TCM members were absent from school because they had prior knowledge of the carnage that was to come. Police reports show definitively that this was not the case. Most of Eric and Dylan's friends attended school that day, and those that left the school grounds prior to the attack during the first lunch session were able to prove that they often did so in the weeks and months before the massacre. Exhaustive interviews with all suspects, analysis of surveillance videos, eyewitness accounts, and crime scene evidence indicate that Harris and Klebold, whether they were truly TCM members or not, were solely responsible for the carnage that day.

Chapter Two

Bullying of Eric Harris and Dylan Klebold

Immediately following the tragedy at Columbine High School, the national spotlight was focused on the problem of bullying and how much of a factor it may have been in the events that took place on April 20, 1999. Eric Harris and Dylan Klebold were described as social misfits, picked on so aggressively by jocks that their feelings of rage and helplessness drove them to strike back at their tormentors. The scenario was supported, in part, by the number of eyewitnesses who came forward to report that the two gunmen made specific reference to killing all the jocks or kids with white hats, a common fashion accessory of the athletes at Columbine.[119,120,121,122,123,124,125,126,127,129,130,131,132]

Many of the same witnesses also told police that Harris and Klebold, upon entering the school library, shouted to their victims that their rampage was due to "*all the shit you've put us through the last four years.*"[120,124,125,128,129,130,132] One of the boys was also heard to exclaim that he had been waiting a long time for the opportunity to get his revenge.[123,124,127,131,132,133,134] The same things were heard in the hall outside the science rooms when Eric or Dylan yelled, "*This is revenge, Fuckers!*"[135]

The notion that these young men had taken a stand and retaliated against their abusers resonated so loudly with many who had suffered abuse themselves that some went so far as to applaud the boys' heinous crime. The *Columbine Report* is littered with interviews of students from Columbine and other area schools who were subsequently turned into police after expressing their belief that Eric and Dylan were pushed too far and that the injured and dead had gotten what they deserved. A bitterly sad example is that of a fourteen-year-old girl who was questioned by police after an altercation with her mother. The girl was found to be in possession of a journal written in tribute to the two killers and told the officer that she had also penned some poems about Eric Harris. When asked about her feelings for Eric she replied, "*I think he's the greatest person in the world... because he had the guts to do something about mean people.*"[136] The misguided youngster confessed that she had fantasized about committing a similar attack but was thwarted by her lack of access to weapons and the Internet. Even today there are countless websites, blogs, vlogs, fangirls, and fanboys dedicated to praising the actions of Eric and Dylan. The killers have been elevated by some to a bastardized form of martyrdom—champions of the dispossessed and downtrodden.

In recent years, some have reversed their opinion on the role of bullying in the Columbine massacre. The prevailing belief in certain circles is that Harris and Klebold were not victims of bullying, at least not significantly, and that bullying did not influence the deadly choices the two made. Examination of available evidence suggests that neither scenario is entirely accurate. Harris and Klebold were bullied, and that bullying did have a considerable impact on their views of both themselves and society. Each young man appeared to have support in the form of friends and family, however, as well as access to professional counseling. Had either boy chosen to avail himself of the aid that might have been offered by those safety nets it could have drastically changed the course of events in that final year.

There is no mistaking the fact that Eric and Dylan were subject to abuse by their fellow students. It was documented by both boys in their individual writings, as well as by countless friends and acquaintances who witnessed the bullying. Even students that never saw evidence of direct harassment of Harris or Klebold told investigators that other kids made a point of staying away from the boys because they were different.[137] A substitute teacher stated that Klebold had once told him that *"he was one of the few people that actually ever talked to him,"*[138] and several students were even warned not to associate with the two boys because they were *"weird."*[139] A friend of Dylan's reported that she was slammed into a locker and called a *"fag lover"* just for talking to Klebold in the hallway.[140] One of the students who was shot at, but was uninjured, told police that *"everyone would pick on the shooters,"*[141] and a friend of the boys revealed that he had seen jocks pick on Harris and Klebold in the hallways at school.[89] A good deal of the harassment was verbal, with kids teasing Eric and Dylan over their style of dress, musical tastes, and athletic ability.[57,90,142,143,144,145,146,147,148,149,150,151,152,153,154,155]

During their "zero hour" bowling class, both boys were taunted by some jocks because *"we jocks thought we could play the game better."*[156] It did not help that each boy had an unusual bowling style with Dylan tossing the ball like a softball and Eric throwing his like a basketball.[142]

In a police interview, a student in Klebold's gym class stated that because Dylan was not very coordinated, *"everybody made fun of Dylan in class. They even called him 'Stretch' because he was so tall."*[157] A female classmate informed investigators that Klebold tried very hard in gym but that the kids still referred to him as *"the Jolly Green Giant."*[158] The teasing over his height was confirmed by yet another student who reported that Klebold seemed to ignore the name-calling.[159] At one point, Dylan mentioned to a female friend that he was having trouble with the jocks but did not go into detail on the matter.[160] One of the jocks admitted to police that he would make fun of Dylan in the cafeteria when he wore his trench coat,[161] which seemed to be fodder for many comments at

Klebold's expense.[162] Dylan's T-shirts were fair game as well. Another student athlete advised police that he had gotten into a verbal altercation with Klebold over a shirt he often wore that read something to the effect of *"AOL-Where Kewl Hackers Hang Out."* It represented Dylan's interest in computer programming and an Internet Instant Messaging group. The disagreement earned the wrestler a place on Dylan's "Shit List".[163] An acquaintance of Klebold's stated to police that Dylan *"was sort of the brunt of jokes"*[164] and while he and his friends did not mock Klebold openly, he believed Dylan may have been aware of what was being said about him. In one instance, according to written statements by Harris, a group of boys shot up Klebold's bicycle.[165]

Robert Perry, a former TCM member, described Eric Harris as angry and bitter. He told investigators that Eric *"had been constantly picked on, taunted, and had food thrown at him by some of the other students at CHS."*[166] A food throwing incident was echoed in the 2001 Governor's Columbine Review Commission report that stated, *"(although school authorities disputed the point), that Harris and Klebold had been the victims of a particularly humiliating incident in which they were surrounded in the cafeteria by other students who squirted them with ketchup, laughed at them, and called them 'faggots', and that teachers were present at the time but did nothing to intervene."*[167] Klebold's mother referenced this incident in the book *Far from The Tree: Parents, Children and the Search for Identity* by Andrew Solomon. Dylan had returned home with spots of ketchup all over his shirt. When Sue Klebold asked him what happened, *"he said he'd had the worst day of his life and didn't want to talk about it."*[168] Even people Harris had considered to be friends would sometimes join in on the teasing,[169,170,171] which was a particular sore spot for Eric and resulted in him placing many of these individuals on a "Shit List" of people he hoped to kill. Also included on this list were associates of any people who had harassed him, Dylan, or friends of theirs, even if those kids had never participated in the harassment themselves.[172] A former student, contacted because his name was found on a similar list entitled *Class of 98 Should Have Died*, said he knew it was because he had spent the majority of his time in gym class making fun of Eric Harris. The boy told police that *"Eric had a big head on a very skinny body so he just teased him all the time."*[148] Another former student on this list admitted that he *"had been relentless in his abuse of Eric during gym"*[173] and that the entire gym class had ridiculed Eric because he was not very good at sports.[173]

The bullying would become physical at times and result in minor injury for the boys, especially Harris. In a police statement, a student who shared a gym class with Harris told investigators that Eric was once the winner in a game of BIFF: an individual form of dodge ball. As a result, during the second game *"some jocks ganged up on him and were hitting him in the face with balls. Then after gym they were pushing him into lockers."*[174] According to a student athlete, both Harris and Klebold had experienced being slammed into lockers.[175] Brooks Brown wrote of an incident he witnessed while he, Dylan, and Eric were having a cigarette outside. A car carrying some Columbine football players drove by yelling at them, *"and threw a glass bottle that shattered near Dylan's feet. I was pissed, but Eric and Dylan didn't even flinch. 'Don't worry about it, man,' Dylan said. 'It happens all the time.'"*[176]

A friend of Harris's told investigators about an incident in which her former boyfriend had punched Eric in the face.[57] The episode, according to Eric, put that kid and his friend in the top five of Harris's "Shit List". When the girl informed Harris in a note passed during German class that this boy was afraid of him and asked how he could get off the list, Eric replied: *"He will always be under the gun and in the sights since he hit me in the face, even though it didn't hurt at all. Until I get to hit him back I will always be pissed at him and his dickhead friend too. If they want 'off' then tell them to show some fuckin respect to their elders (me + dylan) and never make another smart ass remark about us or to us."*[177]

Visual evidence of this type of aggressive behavior was documented in a video production that Harris and others made for a class.[178] In the video, Harris and a friend were being filmed as they walked through the halls of Columbine. As the shoot began, the two were seen talking animatedly, but they spied a group of four jocks coming towards them in the hallway ahead. The talking ceased abruptly and as the boys approached the jocks, Eric dropped his head down low as though bracing for an impact and continued to walk straight ahead. Eric's friend quickly fell in line behind Harris, as did the videographer, and as the jocks walked past them one of them intentionally shouldered the latter boy roughly, causing him to almost drop his video camera. It is clear by the preparatory response of Eric and his friends that this type of event was commonplace. Would the reaction of the jocks have been the same if Eric had willingly gotten out of their way instead of attempting to stand his ground? A female student told police that it was routine for jocks to "*line up across the hall, one next to the other, forcing students to have to go all the way around down another hallway to get around them.*"[179] The video suggests that Eric Harris was loath to give in to the intimidation.

According to several police statements, while Klebold was more likely to appear to try to ignore the bullying,[31,159] Harris had actually stood up for himself on several occasions. In one instance, Eric challenged a student who had repeatedly antagonized him for listening to the band Rammstein. A friend of that student told police that one day in the hallway the student made a snide remark about Rammstein as they passed Harris and Klebold. Eric confronted him, saying: "*Every day you pass me and make fun of me saying Rammstein sucks. Why do you do this crap asshole? What did I do to you?' My friend replied, 'Oh man you're so cool, you're my idol!' Then Eric's friend Dylan approached us seeming to back up his friend.*"[180] The two sides did not come to blows and separated when the bell rang to signify the start of class. Harris narrowly avoided another fight with a wrestler known for mocking him and other members of the Trench Coat Mafia. Eric challenged the jock to a fight in the school parking lot, but when the other boy's friends arrived the battle was called off.[156]

In the same series of notes with his friend in German class, Harris referred to someone he called a *"faggot punk ska skater shitface who always makes fun of my kleid* [style of dress, in German] *so I told him to shut the fuck up about it, and he is such a disrespectful smartass and today he comes up and says 'whats up' in his little smartass tone so I yelled at him."*[177] Police reports also reference a student who claimed that roughly one month prior to the massacre he observed several seniors walking behind Harris, taunting him with statements such as, *"The war is over, you can go home."* Harris responded with, *"Shut up assholes."*[181] In fact, in his final months, Eric seemed ready to challenge anyone. In early 1999, a boy told police that he had accidentally bumped into Harris as he rounded a corner in the hallway. Eric became angry and the two got into a shoving match before going their separate ways. Harris warned the kid that he *"should watch his back."*[182] Eric's confrontational manner increased even further in the weeks leading up to the attack. Chris Morris told police that he was irritated with Harris because he appeared to be picking fights intentionally, expecting the bigger Morris to back him up.[183]

Morris also informed investigators that *"Harris was constantly picked on by the jocks because he was small,"*[184] and *"was depressed about his size and getting picked on."*[146] These statements were reiterated by a female classmate and acquaintance of Eric's.[86] Evidence supports that Harris may have been sensitive about his size because he lied about it. After his arrest for breaking into a van, Eric entered a Juvenile Diversion Program. On the assessment documents for the program he wrote that he was five feet, eleven inches,[185] adding a full two and a half inches to his height.[186] Tom Klebold, Dylan's father, told police that while Dylan denied to him that he was a victim of bullying, "*he did indicate that people picked on Eric (Harris).*"[187] According to Brooks Brown, Harris had also been teased in gym class over a physical deformity. Eric was born with pectus excavatum: a condition that results in inappropriate development of the breastbone and accompanying ribs. As a result of the anomalous growth, the chest assumes a caved in appearance. To correct the condition, Harris underwent surgery in December 1993. A steel strut was placed to push the sternum outward. The strut was removed in a second surgery six months later.[188] Brown wrote that it "*wasn't that noticeable-it was just sunken in a bit-but when Eric would take his shirt off in P.E. class, the bullies were ready and waiting to mock him.*"[189] This type of harassment was confirmed by Eric in a journal entry written five months before the attack. He blamed the bullying for making him seek revenge and expressed his low self-esteem.

> *Everyone is always making fun of me because of how I look, how fucking weak I am and shit, well, I will get you all back, ultimate fucking revenge here. you people could have shown more respect, treated me better, asked for my knowledge or guidence more, treated me more like a senior, and maybe I wouldn't*

have been so ready to tear your fucking heads off. Then again, I have <u>always</u> hated how I looked, I make fun of people who look like me, sometimes without even thinking sometimes just because I want to rip on myself. That's where a lot of my hate grows from, the fact that I have practically no self esteem, especially concerning girls and looks and such. Therefore people make fun of me… constantly… therefore I get no respect and therefore I get fucking PISSED.[190]

A few days later Harris penned, "*If people would give me more compliments all of this might still be avoidable… but probably not. Whatever I do people make fun of me, and sometimes directly to my face. I'll get revenge soon enough. Fuckers shouldn't have ripped on me so much huh! HA! Then again, its human nature to do what you did… so I guess I am also attacking the human race. I can't take it, Its not right… true… correct… perfect. I fucking hate the human equation.*"[191]

In his last journal entry a few weeks before the massacre, Eric wrote: "*I hate you people for leaving me out of so many fun things. And no don't fucking say, 'well that's your fault' because it isnt, you people had my phone # and I asked and all, but no, no no no don't let the wierd looking Eric KID come along, ooh fucking nooo.*"[192]

On April 19, 1999, the day before he would attack his school, Harris got into an argument with a boy who bumped into him in the hallway.

According to the student, he had turned to greet a friend and accidentally collided with Eric. The two quarreled over who should be watching where they were going and as the boys parted ways, Harris allegedly told the other kid to "*have a good day tomorrow.*"[193]

Klebold's personal journal accounts of being bullied and ostracized tended to be more philosophical, sometimes mystical, and more despairing than those of Eric Harris. Dylan often used the term "zombie" to refer to those he felt persecuted him. In a March 31, 1997 entry, Dylan wrote about the thoughts that constantly swirled through his mind, among them "*the asshole* [name redacted] *in Gym class, how he worries me.*"[194] He spoke of release from his torment through suicide and how he felt trapped in the routine of "*go to school, be scared & nervous... hoping that people can accept me... that I can accept them.*"[195] A few weeks later, Klebold detailed all the things wrong in his life, including: "*nobody accepting me even though I want to be accepted*" and "*I dont know what i do wrong with people (mainly women)-its like they all set out to hate and ignore me.*"[196] Dylan's writings on the subject might even be considered a bit paranoid, as illustrated in a March 7, 1997 entry in which he penned, "*I swear-like im an outkast, & everyone is conspiring against me...*"[197] and a notation later that year wherein Klebold opined, "*I have always been hated, by everyone & everything, just never aware...*"[198] Dylan did have a brief relationship with a girl who later dated Harris. A journal item written around the time that he and the girl broke up revealed Klebold's dissatisfaction with this experience. He complained that this type of happiness seemed phony to him and that he was looking for a purer, truer love.[199] It would appear that, in Dylan's mind, his dislike for Columbine's athletes may have played a role in the demise of the relationship as his entry states, *"I get rejected for being honest about fuckin hate for jocks."*[199] In a later missive he noted, *"I didnt want to be a jock... I hated the happiness that they have-& I will have something infinitely better."*[200] When Eric began to date Dylan's ex-girlfriend the following month, Dylan's anguish seemed to deepen because he feared losing Harris, too. Klebold complained that he was alone and appeared philosophical about the unfair dichotomy: *"the meak are trampled on, the assholes prevail."*[201] On this day, Dylan also documented for the first time his desire to not only turn a gun upon himself, but on others as well. *"ill go on my killing spree against anyone I want."*[201]

A few months later, he would make his first known reference to "NBK", the code name for the attack made in homage to one of his favorite movies, *Natural Born Killers*. In an entry dated February 2, 1998, Klebold's writing took on a more condescending tone as he compared himself to a god. He indicated his belief that it was this status that set him apart and that it was also the reason for his mistreatment by others. Dylan repeated his desire for retaliation by stating, *"I know the meaning of each life: To be loved by yer love, & to be happy w. ones self. Only for the gods though (me, [name redacted], etc.). The zombies & their society band together & try to destroy what is superior & what they don't understand & are afraid of. Soon...*

either ill commit suicide, or ill get w. [name redacted] *& it will be NBK for us.*"[202] A few lines down he remarked, "*society is tightening its grip on me, & soon, I &* [name redacted] *will snap. We will have our revenge on society, & then be free*" and "*I am God. [Name redacted] is God. the zombies will pay for their arrogance, hate, fear, abandonment, & distrust.*"[200] Dylan's statements seem to indicate that he considered someone other than Eric his partner for an armed assault, but by the school year's end plans were well underway with Harris. In Eric's yearbook he penned, "*NBK will be the ultimate revenge, to our shitlists, the pigs, everyone! we'll fuckin 'Take care of business' to be sure*"[203] and "*My wrath for january's incident will be godlike. Not to mention our revenge in the commons.*"[204] In the final days before the massacre, Dylan made his last comments about rising above the efforts of the zombies to destroy him by making them pay for all the suffering they had caused. On April 15, 1999, he wrote: "*the zombies will never cause us pain anymore.*"[205] In the final hours, Klebold remarked: "*The little zombie human fags will know their errors, & be forever suffering & mournful, HAHAHA.*"[205] Even Klebold's dress on the day of the incident may be viewed as an expression of his feelings about the zombies. In addition to his black BDU's, black boots, and black duster, Dylan wore a black T-shirt with the word "WRATH" printed in red letters across his chest.[206] Klebold's fury was also mentioned in a police statement by a female student. The girl provided a description of a gunman that seemed to match Dylan Klebold closely. Upon seeing the gunman descend the stairs into the cafeteria, she ran and hid in the girl's bathroom with three other students. The young woman reported that "*The male was very angered, every one was pretty much cleared out except the four of us in the bathroom and he was screaming and yelling, 'I hate you.' Not to anyone in particular he was just yelling it.*"[207]

The killers did not stop at physically hurting Columbine students; they also expressed their hatred by damaging things that represented the students and the school. The cases holding the trophies and awards of Columbine's athletes were shattered with shotgun blasts and pipe bombs.[208,209] On an archway in the entry hall to Columbine was an inscription that read "*Through These Halls Pass the Finest Kids in America. The Students of Columbine High School.*" A video shot by the Columbine Fire Department after the attack showed that the word "finest" had somehow been blurred out.[209] The inscription was restored and referenced when Columbine re-opened its doors to students the following fall.[210]

Harris and Klebold did not limit their bitterness to the students of Columbine High School. Both boys held animosity towards teachers and administrators over what they perceived as favoritism towards certain segments of the student body, particularly the jocks.[211] A manager at Blackjack Pizza told police that the boys "*would gripe about how they did not feel they were being treated fairly and were unjustly persecuted at school.*"[212] The woman felt that both Harris and Klebold were "*somewhat paranoid.*"[212] During the spring of 1998, Dylan was reprimanded for defacing the locker of another student. He was taken to the dean's office and his father was called to come to the school to discuss the matter. While waiting for Mr. Klebold, Dylan became agitated and "*advised that he was very upset with the school system and the way CHS handled people, to include the people that picked on him and others.*"[213] An acquaintance of Harris and Klebold affirmed this to police when he said that teachers would not intervene when the boys were being bullied and did nothing to put a stop to the harassment.[214]

The preferential treatment was noted by other students as well. One girl told police that she had witnessed teachers treating Dylan and Eric unfairly. She felt it was obvious which students were the teachers' favorites and that group did not include Harris or Klebold. The girl further relayed that an employee of the school's computer lab "*picked on Dylan Klebold and Eric Harris unjustifiably. [She] said when this occurred, Dylan Klebold and Eric Harris would glare at this female, however, they would not say anything out loud back to her.*"[215] A friend in Eric's German class revealed to investigators that Eric did not like the German teacher because the teacher "*picked on*" herself, Eric, and another girl in the class.[216] Harris's dislike for this particular teacher was confirmed in a note he gave to the latter girl in which he wrote "*frau sucks.*"[217]

In a puzzling twist, two months before the attack on February 20, 1999, Harris and Klebold visited the Dean to seek help regarding a problem they were having with another student. The boys politely told the Dean that this student "*was parking to close to one of their cars and was 'mouthy' with them.*"[35] The Dean told investigators that he had contacted the other student's counselor about the matter and that the counselor presented the issue to the boy. The ultimate disposition of the complaint is not available in any of the police documents in the Columbine case. It is curious that Harris and Klebold, who by that time would have been far along in the planning of their assault, would bother to lodge a grievance with school officials. Was it an attempt to prove to themselves that the administration's response would be unsatisfactory? If the situation remained unaddressed, would this have strengthened their resolve for the attack? If the matter was handled appropriately, would the boys have stopped to reconsider their plan?

In addition to the structural damage done to the building during the rampage, the boys destroyed computers, televisions, library books, telephones, statues, video equipment, and the Front Office [218,219] — which are all things needed by the teachers and administrators of the school.

The public outcry over the possible role of bullying in the murders was so great that the Governor's Columbine Review Commission held public hearings to learn more about the matter. Regina Huerter, Director of Juvenile Diversion for the Denver District Attorney's Office, also prepared a nine-page report entitled *The Culture of Columbine* for review by the Commission. After interviewing 28 adults and fifteen students, Huerter determined that bullying was commonplace at Columbine High School. Most of those interviewed told Huerter that Harris and Klebold were "*often the brunt of ridicule and bullying,*"[140] which usually involved name-calling or physical aggression (pushing or shoving).[140] The consensus among those whom Huerter consulted was that school officials and staff did not do enough to address the problem and that, in some cases, the favored students would not be disciplined at all. The Commission's summary of their inquiry reads:

Some parents insisted to Commission staff members that bullying was rampant at Columbine High School and that the school's administration did little to control it. One former teacher's aide at Columbine who testified to a serious bullying problem at the school asserted that she had raised the issue of bullying at a faculty meeting but that no one had acted on her complaint. This echoed other complaints that school rules were inconsistently enforced, so that some groups of students were given more lenient treatment than others.

The Commission was told that students at the school were reluctant to come forward at the Commission's public hearings to talk about bullying because they feared peer retribution or embarrassment if they did so. To encourage students to talk candidly about circumstances at Columbine High School, the Commission sent investigators there to interview students in confidence. They spoke with 43 people, of whom 28 were parents and 15 current or former students of Columbine. Those interviewed were strongly critical of the school, felt that a significant amount of bullying had occurred (especially from athletes), and believed that it would have been futile to report bullying to the school administration because no one there would have done anything about it. The investigators' report lists several specific incidents of bullying and similar behaviors.

On the other hand, the school's principal, Frank DeAngelis, testified that bullying was not a problem at Columbine High School, and assured the Commission that the school had acted firmly to punish bullying incidents if they occurred. A number of teachers at Columbine defended strongly the school, its students, and its administration. Some of them had taught at the school for many years, had chosen to teach there because it was an excellent school, and had elected to remain at the school even after the violence there because they believed it deserved their loyalty. They claimed that many of the bullying and other incidents described in the investigators' report either had never happened or had been dealt with appropriately by the school administration. Although they did not claim that bullying had never occurred at the school, they insisted that the Columbine administration had dealt swiftly with it when it surfaced. They insisted that, as faculty members, they had indeed stepped in whenever they observed anything verging on bullying, and that the school's principal had backed them when they had done that.

The county school superintendent also cautioned the Commission that there was indeed another side to some of the reported incidents, but that dictates of confidentiality made it impossible to offer details in support of the appropriateness of the school

*administrators' responses in the form of imposition of
disciplinary sanctions on those involved in bullying.*[220]

Based upon their research, the Commission
concluded that they "*cannot assert that bullying at
Columbine High School caused the homicidal attack
on April 20, 1999. But it received testimony that the
perpetrators had been victims of bullying at the school
and had been taunted and rejected by fellow
students.*"[220] This conclusion is further bolstered by the
testimony of dozens of friends, acquaintances, and
classmates of Harris and Klebold, as well as by the two
killers themselves in their personal writings and video
tapes.

Being mocked, assaulted, and cast aside most
certainly contributed to the twisted view Eric and
Dylan had of themselves and the world. As such,
discounting the effects of bullying on the boys is
blatantly contrary to all available evidence. Just as
their exposure to violent video games, movies, and
explicit song lyrics did not make them kill, bullying—
while a contributing factor—cannot be solely blamed
for the terror that Klebold and Harris wrought upon
Columbine. Far too many children are subjected to
relentless, unprovoked harassment or ostracism from
their peers and do not respond in such a horrendous
manner. Something about Eric and Dylan—their
individual personalities, collective life experiences,
and their ability or inability to constructively process
emotional responses—led them to commit these
terrible crimes. Had they lived and had the capacity to
fully understand what drove them, we might have
found the answers to our questions. But Harris and

Klebold are dead, and we are left to sift through what remains of their lives in order to find understanding. We cannot selectively pick and choose what information we will incorporate into the search. If we are to get to the truth, or as much of the truth as we can reach, then every detail needs to be considered— nothing can be tossed aside because it is too complicated or detracts from a neatly compacted version of events.

Chapter Three

Harris and Klebold as Bullies

There does not seem to be any question that Eric Harris and Dylan Klebold felt mistreated by their peers and the administration at Columbine High School. There also does not seem to be much doubt, given the boys stated as much in their writings, that this perceived mistreatment was a significant factor in their desire to destroy the school and students. It is important to note, however, that while Klebold and Harris were subject to bullying, there is ample evidence that both boys also bullied others and that Klebold in particular had shown a pattern of disrespectful behavior towards teachers, administrators, and authority figures in the years leading up to the massacre.

The earliest documented evidence of Eric and Dylan's harassment of other kids occurred when they were in eighth grade at Ken Caryl Middle School. A girl reported that Harris, Klebold, and several other boys sent her a threatening letter.[221] It was also around this time that Eric told a boy he had met that he did not like him.[222] Additional evidence of the boys' bullying can be found in Harris's "Mission Logs" from 1997. The "Mission Logs" are a series of journal entries that Eric posted on his website detailing the nighttime exploits of himself, Dylan, and another friend. The boys would sneak out of the house after dark and vandalize the homes or property of people they did not like. Harris explained the missions this way: *"Anyone pisses us off, we do a little deed to their house. Eggs, teepee, superglue, busy boxes, large amounts of fireworks, you name it and we will probly or already have done it. We have many enimies in our school, therefor we make many missions."*[223] Eric described one mission taken in revenge of kids that had allegedly shot up Klebold's bicycle. On that particular night, the boys lit off an assortment of crackling balls, thunderbombs, and bottle rockets by one of the kids' homes. The "Rebel Clan", as Harris referred to them, then proceeded to put model putty on Brooks Brown's Mercedes, toilet paper the tree outside a third boy's house, block driveways with large rocks, and tag a fence with the letters 'RC'.[165] Eric portrayed another mission as a hit against a kid that he classified as *"an utter fag,"* "*immature little weakling,*" "*queer,*" and hated by everyone in school.[165] There is no indication that this boy had done anything in particular to Eric or his friends. In fact, Harris had previously been on good terms with the boy. On that mission, Harris, Klebold, and the friend toilet papered two trees in the student's yard, left an egg on the welcome mat, and left two more in some bushes. The Rebel Clan also superglued the house's front door and mailbox flag.[165]

It was around the time of these missions that Eric Harris had a major falling out with Brooks Brown. The two young men got into an argument in early 1997 when Brown told Harris he would no longer drive him to school. After months of Eric complaining that Brooks was always late picking him up, a frustrated Brown told Eric he was not welcome to ride with him anymore.[224] Harris took offense and ended the friendship. A few weeks later in February 1997, Eric dented the trunk of a boy's car and cracked Brown's windshield with snowballs.[225] In retaliation, one of the boys took Eric's backpack and brought it with him to the Browns' house. Wanting to resolve the issue, Brown's mother—Judy—decided to take the matter up with Eric's parents. She alerted Harris that she was in possession of his backpack and was heading over to his house to talk to his mother about the incident. Judy recounted that Eric suddenly became very aggressive and began yelling at her, beating on her car, and yanking on her door handle.[226,227] In addition to informing Harris's parents about the altercation, Judy Brown also contacted the Dean of Students at Columbine to help with conflict resolution and reported the property damage to police. In his journal,

Eric's father—Wayne Harris—listed the things his son was being accused of, including: *"aggression, disrespect, idle threats of physical harm, property damage."*[226] The last entry on the page reads, *"overreaction to minor incident."*[226] It is unclear if the "overreaction" comment represented Mr. Harris's opinion of Eric's behavior or that of the Browns'. Upset because Eric would not pay for the damage to his car, Brooks Brown informed the Dean and Eric's parents about the Rebel Clan's missions and that Eric had been drinking alcohol. Harris denied the latter allegation to his parents[228] but admitted the truth in rants in his online "Mission Logs".[165] Harris told his father that he wanted to talk things over with Brooks and work it out with the help of an adult.[229] Privately, however, Eric fumed over the ordeal. In his take on the incident, he laid all of the blame on Brown. *"This mission was also liquor free as a result of this person named Brooks Brown* [phone # redacted] *who tried to narc on us. Telling my parents that I had booze and shit in my room. I had to ditch every bottle I had and lie like a fuckin salesman to my parents. All because Brooks Brown thought i put a little nik in his windshield from a snowball… BS? yes"*[165] Neither Eric nor his parents ever offered to have the windshield fixed and the Browns eventually paid out of pocket to replace it several months later.[230] Harris managed to avoid legal ramifications over the incident when the Browns decided not to press charges. The mother of the "utter fag"—whose home the Rebel Clan had toilet papered, egged, and superglued—also opted not to involve the police since the damage sustained was minor.[231] Although Eric escaped prosecution, he remained irate over the situation. His anger towards Brooks Brown would bring him to the attention of police a few more times over the next several months.

According to both Wayne Harris's journal and a report compiled by the Colorado Attorney General, the Browns contacted authorities again in April 1997 with reports of harassing phone calls and damage to a tree on their property. They suspected it was the work of Eric Harris.[232,233] In his journal, Harris's father wrote that he believed Eric was being accused of things because Brooks Brown was *"out to get Eric"* and that Brooks was *"Manipulative & Con Artist."*[232] Mr. Harris's notations show a level of frustration with events as he wrote, *"We feel victimized, too"* and *"We don't want to be accused everytime something supposedly happens. Eric* ~~learned his lesson~~ *is not at fault."*[232] The elder Harris spoke with a deputy by phone in late April and made the following entry: *"If Future problems-mediator? Lawyer? (Abortration) 'mediation services' thru Jeffco County."*[232] He also noted a follow-up phone call he placed to the Browns three days later. Wayne Harris was unable to reach anyone and left a message. *"No return"*[234] was written beside this entry and circled. Just below it, Mr. Harris penned:

Follow-up call
Any further problems between Eric + Brooks?
Eric hasn't broken promise to Mr. Place-the Dean-about leaving each other alone.

You told me of past problem c̄ another boy have you checked c̄ his parents?

At the bottom of the page, Wayne Harris again wrote: "*We feel victimized, too*" and "*Manipulative Con Artist.*"[234] The Jefferson County Sheriff's Department records indicate they did not follow up on these concerns because officers were unable to reach the Browns despite several attempted phone calls.[233] Interviews with the Browns in the years since the Columbine massacre dispute these claims.

On August 7, 1997, the police were contacted once more by the Brown family—this time for some disturbing content that the Browns' youngest son found on Eric Harris's website. The Browns provided police with seven pages of computer printouts from Harris's site. The pages included details of pipe bombs constructed by Eric and Dylan, the clan's "Mission Logs", as well as a series of "You Know What I Hate"/"You Know What I Love" blogs authored by Harris. The writings detailed his extreme reaction to pet peeves, such as "*YOU KNOW WHAT I HATE?–When there is a group of assholes standing in the middle of a hallway or walkway, and they are just STANDING there talking and blocking my fucking way! Get the fuck outa the way or Ill bring a friggin sawed-off shotgun to your house and blow your snotty ass head off!*"[235] And "*YOU KNOW WHAT I HATE?– People who say that wrestling is real! now, Im talking about the matches like hulk hogan or undertaker. If you think that these matches aren't faked and that these guys are REALLY punching and breaking arms, then please mail me. I would love to know where you live so i can BOMB your fucking house and ACTUALLY BREAK YOUR ARMS!*"[235] In these pages, Harris also referred to Brooks Brown as a liar and a narc and listed his home address and telephone number *"If any of you feel like pranking him."*[223]

The website content concerned the officer enough that he drafted a directed report for submission to an investigator in the Jeffco Sheriff's Department.[236] A directed report is *"an internal memorandum or intelligence report directed specifically from one person to another. A directed report is used to pass information, an opinion, or a theory from a patrol officer to an investigator."*[237] The investigator who received the report filed it in a binder for computer intelligence information but did not contact Eric Harris or Dylan Klebold, nor did he follow up on the claims of criminal mischief listed in the website pages. A supervising sergeant in the Investigations Division later told the Attorney General's Office that *"there are no guidelines on what an investigator does with a directed report, it is up to the investigators discretion."*[238] The directed report was not rediscovered until 2003, four years after the Columbine attack.[239]

Later in the fall of 1997, Klebold, Harris, and a friend hacked into a school computer to access student locker combinations.[240,241,242] They used this information to leave threatening notes in the locker of a male student. Harris and Klebold's friend was dating the student's former girlfriend, and the boys wanted to make sure the kid left her alone. According to one of the teacher's responsible for handling the incident, the note *"was something to the effect of: If you bother my girlfriend again, I'm going to kill you."*[243] The girl at the center of the matter was responsible for reporting the harassment to the school's vice-principal, resulting in the suspension of all three boys.[244,245] Eric was so angry with the teacher involved in meting out the suspension that Harris would not return to his position as an assistant in the teacher's tech lab.[243]

Eric's hatred for Brooks Brown only deepened over the next several months. When Brooks was allegedly tipped off by Dylan Klebold to death threats Eric Harris had made against him on his website, the Browns contacted police again in March 1998.[246] The Browns provided authorities with ten pages from Eric's site detailing his rage with society, the human race, Columbine, jocks, as well as his desire to kill people. He also described his growing expertise with pipe bombs. In his blog, Harris wrote of his life philosophy:

My belief is that if I say something, it goes. I am the law, if you don't like it, you die. If I don't like you or I don't like what you want me to do, you die. If I do something incorrect, oh fucking well, you die. Dead people cant do many things, like argue, whine, bitch, complain, narc, rat out, criticize, or even fucking talk. So thats the only way to solve arguments with all you fuckheads out there, I just kill! God I can't wait till I can kill you people. Ill just go to some downtown area in some big ass city and blow up and shoot everything I can. Feel no remorse, no sense of shame. Ich sage FICKT DU! [German for 'I say FUCK YOU!'] *I will rig up explosives all over a town and detonate each one of them at will after I mow down a whole fucking area full of you snotty ass rich mother fucking high strung godlike attitude having worthless pieces of shit whores. i don't care if I live or die in the shootout, all I want to do is kill and injure as many of you pricks as I can, especially a few people. Like Brooks Brown.*[247]

The deputy who met with the Browns "*classifies the report as a suspicious incident and refers it to JCSO investigations. Klebold is listed as acquaintance with knowledge of bomb-making activities.*"[248] Per the accepted reporting process, an Investigator Sergeant is responsible for reviewing a case and assigning it to an investigator. If the report is not so assigned, the case will be closed out by the JCSO Records Clerk. By the end of March 1998, the case had not been given to an investigator and was subsequently closed.[248]

A second meeting was held between the Browns and police on March 31, 1998. At that time, investigators discovered that the pipe bomb construction Harris detailed on his website was consistent with an unexploded pipe bomb that had been found on a bike path a month earlier. The bike path was located within two miles of Eric's home. Armed with this information and the website threats, Investigator Mike Guerra prepared paperwork to request a search warrant of the Harrises' home.[248] Prior to submission of the warrant to the DA's Office, Guerra was required to run the affidavit by his supervisor Lieutenant John Kiekbusch. Investigator Guerra later told the Attorney

General's Office that he did not remember showing the request to Kiekbusch. Detective Glenn Grove did recall the meeting and said he was also present when the two discussed the matter. Kiekbusch informed Guerra that there was insufficient evidence to tie the pipe bomb to Harris and that without a witness who had actually seen Harris with the pipe bomb, the warrant could not be approved.[248] It is unclear why, but the investigation stalled at that point, even though Eric and Dylan had been arrested only two months prior for criminal trespass, theft, and criminal mischief after breaking into a van. The boys had entered into a Juvenile Diversion Program on March 25, 1998—only six days before the search warrant request was drafted. No one in law enforcement ever made the connection between the two cases. During the Attorney General's review of the directed report in 2004, Investigator Guerra relayed that he worked on the case for a few weeks even though it was not assigned to him. When other assigned cases began coming in, the Harris matter fell to the wayside.[249]

Judy Brown placed a follow-up phone call to the Jefferson County Sheriff's Office on April 11, 1998 to report that Brooks had received a threatening e-mail that she believed was sent by Eric Harris. It stated, "*I know your an enemy of Erics. I know where you live and what cars you drive.*"[250] At that time, the Browns were under the impression that the police were actively dealing with Harris. Eric's website had been taken down by AOL and Brooks had told his parents that there were rumors around school that Eric and Dylan had gotten into some very big trouble.[251] In reality, AOL had removed Harris's site due to a complaint submitted by the Browns' youngest son [251] —not through any action of law enforcement. The "big trouble" was connected to the van break-in and property theft. Neither the Browns, nor those they dealt with at the Sheriff's Office, would become aware of the arrests for some time. Despite what she viewed as progress in the case, Judy Brown was taking no chances regarding her family's safety and took steps to ensure her neighbors were aware of Eric Harris as well. One neighbor later told investigators that while she had forgotten the boy's name, she remembered Judy giving her a Post-It note with a license plate number and physical description of a kid that was *"violent, dangerous, and apparently making bombs. She asked* [her] *to call the police immediately if she were to see that car out in front of the Browns' house."*[252]

The Browns' final contact with police regarding Eric Harris was on July 19, 1998. Late the previous evening Brooks, his younger brother, and a friend thought they heard glass breaking. According to the friend, Brooks's brother *"got outside in time to see the car and said it was HARRIS."*[253] The boys found nothing amiss, but the following day Brooks's father discovered that someone had shot a paintball through a garage door window. When an officer came to investigate, he discovered that several other homes in the neighborhood had also been targeted. There was no evidence to link Harris to the vandalism so the case languished.[254,255]

Brooks Brown was not the only object of Harris's derision. A classmate of Eric's relayed to investigators that he felt threatened by Harris because Eric would constantly stare at him in class.[256] Another boy, contacted by police because his name was found on a list in Eric's room, stated that he and Harris did not get along because the boy had once accused Eric of stealing his portable compact disc player.[257] One of the deans at Columbine told police that he had problems with Harris and other seniors picking on the freshmen at school.[32] Klebold confirmed their involvement in this activity with a note in Eric's yearbook: *"I can't wait to dub the new freshmen."*[258] He also reminisced about *"Sitting in the commons dubbing & laffing at fags"* and *"frisbee fags... orange mortars for them."*[259] A former friend of Harris's told investigators that Dylan began picking on him in a team sports class. The ridicule was so persistent that he and Klebold almost had a physical altercation as a result. The student told police that he had witnessed Klebold harassing other kids as well.[109]

In late December 1998, Dylan began bullying an underclassman with special needs. According to the boy, while other kids were with Klebold during these incidents, they did not participate in the harassment. He told police that Dylan would threaten to kill him if he went to class and that if he told anyone about Dylan's abuse he would be shot. The student reported the mistreatment to his parents who brought the matter to school authorities; the intimidation ended soon after.[260,261] A girl in Klebold's gym class informed police that she and Dylan had issues because he was always pushing others and cheated at the games during gym.[262]

When he began calling her a bitch, she got her football-playing boyfriend involved. After the boyfriend threatened to "*kick his ass,*" Klebold left her alone.[263] This incident was corroborated by a boy who appeared on a "Shit List" found in Dylan's home. He stated it was most likely because of something that had happened in gym towards the end of 1998. "*One day they were playing flag football with girls and Dylan called a girl a bitch. Not wanting a physical fight to start,* [name redacted by police] *intervened and told Dylan to back off from the girl.*"[264]

Harris and Klebold did not limit their contempt to Columbine students—teachers and administrators were fair game as well. While Harris tended to present an amiable façade and hide his true feelings from adults, Klebold often could not—or did not care to—mask his disdain. The boys' computer teacher told police he recalled either Eric or Dylan referring to a female teacher as a "*dumb bitch.*"[243] A keyboarding teacher reported that when she had reprimanded Klebold and Harris for playing their music too loudly in the video tech lab the boys would "*give her a 'dirty look,' but they did not give her a hard time or argue with her.*"[265] The teacher felt the two were "*cocky.*"[265] In early 1998, Klebold was caught vandalizing another student's locker because he was angry with him.[266] Dylan was sent to the dean's office and as they waited for his father to arrive, Klebold became increasingly agitated. He paced around the room and cursed "*although he did not personalize anything toward* [the Dean], giving the Dean the impression that Dylan was a "*pretty angry kid.*"[213] Klebold received a one-day suspension from school and was required to pay $70 to repair the locker he damaged.[266] Dylan referenced the incident in a January 1998 entry in his day planner: *"Talk to* [redacted] → *Buying locker front & moving fag away."*[267]

Classmates of Klebold's stated that Dylan was often disruptive in French class and that he *"would get very angry in class with the teacher* [redacted] *and the other students, and would start throwing things around."*[268,269] Dylan was often asked to leave the class and was eventually suspended from French class for a while as a result of his behavior. One of the boys Dylan shot in the library had partnered with him in French class the previous year. He reported that Klebold *"had a very bad temper and couldn't control it. He further stated that he had an extreme dislike for the French teacher and constantly made comments that were either derogatory or critical of her."*[270] The boy told police that Dylan would swear in class and was *"very openly 'disrespectful'"*[271] to the teacher. Klebold's chemistry and calculus teachers did not fare much better. His chemistry teacher described Dylan as angry and told investigators that his grades were poor. *"She stated after class was over Dylan would walk out of the class and slam her door against the wall,"*[272] only stopping after she confronted him about it. In calculus, Dylan often showed up late or not at all. When he did bother to attend, Klebold often slept in class so *"the teacher would yell at him and embarrass him."*[273] A Columbine English teacher discussed an incident in which she felt intimidated by a student who laughed inappropriately and defiantly at her in the hallway.

Following the shooting she realized that it was Dylan Klebold who had made her so uneasy.[274]

Dylan's temper created problems for him at work as well. While Harris was described as a model employee at both Blackjack Pizza[275] and his previous job at Tortilla Wraps,[276] Klebold could be a difficult co-worker. A former supervisor at Blackjack described Dylan as "*scary*"[212] and that he was "*a difficult person who was often rude. She said that he hit her once because she had counseled him on an infraction at work.*"[277]

In his journal, Eric Harris admitted that his own self-hatred was the cause of his abuse of other people.[190] Klebold made no such declaration in his writings, but the self-loathing expressed in his journal is abundantly clear. Did he lash out for the same reasons or was he seeking a sense of the control he lacked in his own life? While both boys write in one breath of their superiority over others, in the next they decry the lack of acceptance by their peers and a desire to belong. These contradictions seem to suggest that even Dylan and Eric did not fully comprehend what led to their actions.

Chapter Four

The Arrest and
Diversion Program

Dylan and Eric's arrest for breaking into a van seemed to be a traumatic experience for both boys. While the evidence suggests that neither Harris nor Klebold felt particularly apologetic for the incident, they were both sorry—and more than a little bit angry—that they were caught.

At about 9:20 pm on January 30, 1998, Deputy Tim Walsh noticed a car in Deer Creek Canyon Park after park hours. As he approached the car on foot, he could see two teenage boys inside the vehicle. The boys were listening to music and examining a pile of items stacked on the floor of the car behind the passenger seat. Klebold first held a yellow meter, which lit up when he pushed some buttons on it, causing both boys to exclaim that it was *"cool."*[278] Dylan then examined a flashlight, which Eric deemed as *"really bright."*[278] Harris popped the trunk of his car so that they could store all of the materials in there. When he stepped out of the car, Deputy Walsh identified himself and asked Eric where they had obtained all of the items. Harris told the officer that *"they were walking near the parking area when they found all the property stacked neatly in the grass."*[278] The officer had Eric and Dylan place all of the items on the trunk of the car and asked them a second time how the stuff had come into their possession. Klebold repeated the story about finding the property in the grass. At that point, Deputy Walsh told them their explanation did not sound plausible and that he would have to radio for another officer to look around the area and check for any vehicle break-ins. He asked the boys to level with him and tell him where they got the items. *"(S) Harris looked at (S) Klebold and there was a short silence. (S) Klebold then told me that there was a white van parked at Deer Creek Canyon Road and Wadsworth Blvd and they broke out the passenger window and stole all the property."*[278] Sergeant Phil Lebeda had arrived to assist Deputy Walsh, at which point Eric and Dylan were separated into two police cars and taken into custody. Their parents were contacted and advised to meet with the officers and boys at the South Sub Station.[278] At the same time, Deputy Mark Miller was directed by Walsh to locate the van the boys had robbed. Upon arrival at the van, Miller made note of a broken passenger side window and a rock inside the van between the front seats. *"Several items inside the vehicle appeared to be scattered around in disarray."*[279] The officer contacted the owner of the van who arrived on the scene and confirmed that someone had broken into the vehicle. The victim told the officer that he would need time to determine if items were missing from the van and that if there were, he intended to press charges for the theft.[279]

At the Sub Station, Harris was read his rights and both he and his parents signed a Miranda waiver. Eric then proceeded to tell Deputy Walsh that earlier in the evening he, Dylan, and another friend had met up in a church parking lot and hung out for a bit listening to music. Klebold and Harris parted ways with the boy at about 9:00 pm and then drove over to a parking area on Deer Park Canyon Road. The boys smashed some empty beer bottles and were just *"messing around"*[278] when Dylan began looking at items in a white van that was parked nearby.

According to Harris, Klebold asked, *"Should we break into it and steal it? It would be nice to steal some stuff in there. Should we do it? (S) Harris said his initial response was 'Hell no!'"*[278] As they were discussing it another car pulled up, so the boys returned to Harris's car and continued to debate whether they should break into the van. They soon decided they would. After the vehicle left, Dylan donned a ski glove and tried three times to punch through the glass on the passenger side window while Eric stood watch. When Dylan failed, Eric tried one time but was also unsuccessful. Klebold then found a rock and, after using it to hit the window several times, the window finally broke and the rock came to rest on the passenger's front seat. Harris knocked the rest of the glass out of the window and then returned to his car while Klebold took items from the van.[278] In addition to the broken window, the boys stole items worth approximately $1,719.00,[278] including:

A black metal briefcase, which contained a Hewlett Packard business calculator, a digital computer scaler, a Panasonic voice recorder, and miscellaneous proprietor paperwork

A cardboard box with miscellaneous tools, notebooks, and papers

A flashlight

A QTronix black control pad

A socket set

A black Sapco case containing a vacuum gauge

A Wagner control checker

A yellow meter with black and red probes

Black sunglasses

A checkbook

A daily planner

Miscellaneous tools and gauges.[280]

The robbery took several minutes and was interrupted once by a passing car. Harris reported that Dylan stood by his car until the other vehicle left. Then he returned a final time to the van to retrieve other items. The boys then drove to Deer Creek Canyon Park and were inventorying their take when they were contacted by Deputy Walsh.[278]

Dylan's parents allowed him to speak to Sergeant Phillip Lebeda after consulting with their attorney. At that point, a Miranda waiver was signed and Klebold was interviewed. In Dylan's version of events, the boys lit off fireworks and broke glass bottles for approximately twenty minutes after arriving at the parking area on Deer Creek Canyon Road. They then decided "*they could break into a vehicle, take stuff from it and not get caught.*"[281] Klebold told Sergeant Lebeda that both boys tried, and failed, to break the passenger side window by hitting it with their fists. "*After striking the window several times, (S) Klebold stated (S) Harris went and sat in his car in case they had to 'get away fast.'*"[281] Dylan said that he then found a rock and was able to break the window after hitting it with the rock "*at least 4 times.*"[281] Once he had achieved entry, he stole a number of items that he placed in the back seat of Eric's car. *"(S) Klebold stated he was wearing black ski gloves belonging to (S) Harris, so no fingerprints would be left"*[281] and admitted that "*he had no idea what they were going to do with the stolen property.*"[281] After the robbery, Eric and Dylan drove to Deer Creek Canyon Park where they were discovered by Deputy Walsh.

Both Klebold and Harris also provided officers with a written version of the events of that evening. Aside from the conflicting opinion over whose idea it was to commit the robbery, as well as Eric's omission of lighting off fireworks, the statements agree in their content. It is interesting, however, to note the vastly different writing styles of the boys. While Dylan's statement is conversational and typical of a sixteen-year-old kid, Eric's could easily be mistaken for that of an arresting officer. Aside from some grammar issues, the detail and language in Harris's account would be more characteristic of someone in law enforcement or the military than from a boy of his age.

Dylan's confession reads:

Eric & I were driving home (him driving his car), & we stopped at the parking lot thingy at Deer Creek Rd & Wadsworth. We got out, & he set off a few fireworks, & then we were going around smashing bottles. Then, almost at the same time, we both got the idea of breaking into this white van, which was something for an electrical (maybe) company. We hoped to get the stuff inside. I put on a snow glove, & then tried to punch thru the passenger window. I tried like 4 times & then Eric tried a couple times. We then found a rock, & I tried to break the window with that. After about 5 times, the rock broke thru, & I unlocked the door from the inside, & took electrical stuff (& other things)-(don't know exactly), & then sped off to Deer Creek Open Space Park. We parked, & turned on the dome light to see what we had. Then an officer saw us, got all that we had, & then went thru the process (arresting).[282]

While Eric wrote:

Me and Dylan Klebold were at a church off of Kendall and Ken Caryl with [redacted] *listening to music. We then left the church (Me and Dylan) and proceeded to the North west corner of Wadsworth and Deer Creek Canyon Road. We parked in the gravel and stayed there (in my car) for a few minutes listening to a new music CD. We noticed a white van to the West and a red truck to the East of our position. We got out of my car and looked around for something to do. We found some beer bottles and we broke those for about 15 minutes. We then went back up to my car and Dylan suggested that we should steal some of the objects in the white van. At first I was very uncomfortable and questioning with the thought. I became more interested within about 5 minutes and we then decided to break the passenger window with our fists. I looked for cars and I saw a white car come from the west and pull up beside the red truck. Dylan and I waited in our car for the white car to leave, after about 5 minutes a person got out of the car and into the red truck, then both the truck and the car left going westbound. We then got out of my car and I went out into the street and looked for cars as Dylan hit the window with his left fist 3 times. Then I came over and tried to hit it, one time. Then we decided to get a rock to use. We went North about 20 feet and Dylan found a rock big enough to have to hold in 2 hands. I went back to look for cars as Dylan broke the window on his 6th try. I then stood by my driver door and looked for cars while Dylan reached through the window and took items from the car and placed them in my back seat. After about 15 minutes (aprox) Dylan opened the door twice to get 2 more items and put them in my car. We then left the area and went to the Open Space area and parked up there. We then began to review the items and I suggested we put them (the items) into my trunk. That's when the officer confronted us.*[283]

After their police interviews at the Sub Station, Deputy Walsh transported both Harris and Klebold to the JCSD jail for fingerprinting and photographs. Eric and Dylan were released into the custody of their parents pending the filing of charges. The officer wrote, *"According to JCSD dispatch, neither (S) Harris or (S) Klebold have any prior contacts with JCSD or any criminal record."*[278] Somehow, despite having been brought to the attention of the Jefferson County Sheriff's Office by the Brown family four times in the previous year, Eric Harris went unnoticed.[233]

No documentation exists for how the Klebolds approached matters following Dylan's arrest for the van break-in. The journal kept by Wayne Harris, however, gives a glimpse into the actions taken by Eric's parents. Immediately after the arrest, Wayne Harris began making phone calls to figure out how to manage the fallout. By the following day, the Harrises were already hoping to get Eric enrolled in a Juvenile Diversion Program in order to avoid more serious consequences. In Wayne Harris's journal are the words: *"take any chances for reformation or diversion"* and *"talk to DA and Deputy."*[284] The word "diversion" was underlined four times for emphasis. On February 1, 1998, Mr. Harris contacted the father of Eric's former girlfriend who recommended that Eric see a psychologist. Eric's father immediately began reaching out to counselors to find someone to evaluate his son and to lawyers to help guide them through the upcoming legal process.[285] Eric's first appointment with a therapist was scheduled for Monday, February 16, 1998.[285]

The Harrises learned more about the Juvenile Diversion Program on February 13. The District Attorney's Office would be responsible for deciding the charges Eric would face; they could recommend he go to court, Diversion, or an assessment center. According to an entry in Wayne Harris's journal, a defendant would need to have a clean record for enrollment in the Diversion Program. Despite the four contacts the Browns had with police regarding Eric in 1997, at the time of his arrest in January of 1998 Harris still had no criminal record.[286] The Diversion Program would last from six to eighteen months and would consist of classes, counseling, and community service. Eric would be required to pay court costs and restitution to the victim. If he completed all the requirements of the program, he could petition for the charges to be expunged from his record one year after he was released.[286,287]

On February 24, 1998, Klebold and Harris were formally charged with *"First Degree Criminal Trespass to a Vehicle* (felony), *Felony Theft with a total aggregate value of $1719.00 and a Criminal Mischief* (misdemeanor) *with an aggregate value of $100 damaged"*[288] for the broken van window. The prior reports made about Eric Harris to the JCSO were again missed as the document delineating the charges indicated that Harris had no previous criminal history.[288] By March 3, the Harrises had managed to schedule an appointment for Eric's assessment for entry into the Juvenile Diversion Program for March 19. They were informed that during the assessment to determine his eligibility, Eric would be granted Limited Immunity and anything he said could not be used against him in court. In his journal, Wayne Harris wrote:

"Answer truthfully
Not usable in court (ex. Violence)
No weapons"[286]

Eric Harris underwent the needs assessment for eligibility into the Juvenile Diversion Program on March 19, 1998. Among the things discussed were his relationship with his family, drug and alcohol use, his school work and extracurricular activities, as well as his anger and mental health issues. Neither Eric nor his parents told the interviewer of the family's previous contacts with police regarding threats to the Brown family or damage to Brooks's car. No one mentioned that Eric had vandalized houses and property or had been building pipe bombs. Eric and his parents also failed to bring up his theft of computer parts from school.[57,289] According to a friend of both Harris and Klebold, the boys had *"acquired a key to this locked room full of computer parts, and had been taking parts out of there."*[289] The only infractions Harris and his parents listed were a speeding ticket, the suspension for computer hacking, and stealing locker combinations at school.[290] With regard to the latter offense, no mention was made of the threatening letter the boys placed into a student's locker. It is unknown whether Eric's parents were aware of the letter.

When asked about his attitude towards the Diversion Program, Harris wrote that he hoped it would set him straight and that he was looking forward to getting started.[291] He told his interviewer that in response to his arrest his parents grounded him for one month, forbade contact with Dylan, and revoked his computer privileges.[292] While Eric reported that he had friends, he indicated he considered himself to have only one close friend.[293] Under *"relationship (past and current) with co-defendants,"* he wrote that Dylan was his *"Best friend past and current."*[291] It is interesting to note that when Klebold was asked the same questions, he wrote of Harris as a *"very good friend"*[294] and reported having three close friends.[295] It was known that Dylan's best friend was not Eric, but rather the third member of the Rebel Clan. Klebold may have been the most introverted of the two boys, but he was able to develop more significant friendships than Harris. Eric may have been somewhat dependent on Dylan since Dylan was his only close friend.

In her report recommending Eric for the Diversion Program, the interviewer wrote: *"Eric was cooperative, open, and honest during his intake appointment. He feels Diversion is appropriate for his actions, but feels Dylan is more responsible since it was his idea. He said that he thought about the victim while he took the equipment, but said that it did not detour him. Eric is a 12 mo. CA, his contract includes: 45 hrs of community service, anger management, individual counseling, MADD victim panel, part time work, monthly progress reports, and the CJ class.*"[292] Harris was formally accepted into the Juvenile Diversion Program on March 25, 1998.[296]

Klebold's pre-Diversion assessment was also held on March 19, 1998. For his part in the crime, Dylan reported that his parents grounded him for one month and forbade contact with Eric Harris.[297] In addition to discussing his friendships, Dylan told the interviewer that he had never been sexually active and was not involved in a relationship.[298] The Klebolds were more forthcoming regarding Dylan's past transgressions, detailing his two traffic citations and explaining that he had been suspended from school twice. In her account of the school computer hacking incident, Sue Klebold wrote: *"He and two friends* ~~gained access~~ *who had access to the school's computer figured out how to find old locker combinations. Dylan downloaded this info to disk and opened a locker or two to test to see if list was current."*[299] Like the Harrises, she did not mention that a particular student was targeted or the threatening letter the boys put in the student's locker, so it is unclear if either set of parents knew this information. In addition, neither Dylan nor his parents cited his stealing the computer parts from the room at school. According to the boys' friend, in addition to taking the parts, *"Klebold had stolen an old laptop computer from this room, but that Klebold's father had found out about it and made him give the old laptop back."*[289] There is no evidence to suggest whether at the time of the JDP assessment if the Klebolds were aware of Dylan's involvement in the Rebel Clan missions or his experimentation with building pipe bombs. Sue Klebold was friendly with Judy Brown, but there is no documentation to show that the two women discussed Dylan's participation in these activities.

Under the mental health portion of the questionnaire, Klebold's parents indicated that he was having problems with anger, loneliness, authority figures, and jobs. They wrote, *"Dylan is introverted and has grown up ~~partly~~ isolated from those who are different in age, culture, or other factors. He is often angry or sullen and behaviors seem disrespectful to ~~others. He seems intolerant of those in authority~~ and intolerant of others."*[300] For his part, Dylan was far less forthcoming on this section of the assessment. Despite countless journal pages documenting his profound despair and thoughts of suicide dating back an entire year, Dylan chose not to reveal his true feelings or to seek help for himself. He simply wrote that, for him, mental health treatment was *"Not necessary, but I will do it if diversion deems it necessary or desirable"*[301] and that he felt in control of his life. When presented with a checklist of potential issues (e.g., anger, anxiety, depression, suicidal thoughts, etc.), Klebold indicated that he only had problems with finances and a job. He penned: *"Kind of difficult to find a technician job when I am only 16 years."*[301] Such an enormous opportunity bypassed with a single short sentence. Dylan gave up another chance for help a month later when he took a "Substance Use Survey" to determine if he needed drug and alcohol counseling. Despite indicating on the survey that he had a high degree of motivation for counseling or other help, Klebold's answers to key questions did not coincide with the feelings he revealed in his private writings. When asked to select either *No, Sometimes, Usually,* or *All the Time* in response to the following questions:

Have felt nervous or tense (uptight)?
Have felt down or depressed?
Have worried a lot about things?
Have felt upset?[302]

Klebold chose only "Sometimes" and answered "No" to the question *"Have felt mixed up or confused?"* Most notably, Dylan selected "No" to the question *"Have you had thoughts about not wanting to live (committing suicide)?"*[302] even though he had written of suicide at least seven times in his journal between March 1997 and February 1998.

When asked to describe the most traumatic experience of his life, Klebold wrote, *"The night I committed this crime."*[303] Its impact on him is evident in a letter he wrote to his crush sometime after February 2, 1998 and likely before he was accepted into the JDP. Dylan penned: *"Unfortunately... even if you did like me even the slightest bit, you would hate me if you knew who I was. I am a criminal, I have done things that almost nobody would even think about condoning. The reason that I'm writing you now is that I have been caught for the crimes I comitted & I want to go to a new existence. You know what I mean (Suicide) I have nothing to live for, & I won't be able to survive in this world after this legal conviction."*[304] Klebold seemed to feel that his future was utterly ruined by the arrest. A comment Dylan wrote in Eric's yearbook, *"My wrath for January's incident will be godlike,"*[204] may be a reference to their apprehension. Although, some believe it actually alluded to the time the boys were surrounded in the cafeteria, pelted with ketchup, and called "faggots." No definitive date for the latter event has been established. Klebold does go on to state: *"Not to mention our revenge in the commons,"*[204] which could arguably reflect the ketchup incident. Dylan's anger over the arrest was still evident in the "Basement Tapes" when he stated, *"Fuck you Walsh,"*[305] as he and Eric discussed the deputy who caught them. Klebold claimed the only reason they had gotten caught was *"because 'we didn't fucking plan it.' He also chided police for arresting the pair when 'they could've been busting niggers.'"*[306]

In her recommendation for Dylan's enrollment in the Diversion Program, Klebold's interviewer wrote: *"Dylan was cooperative and open during his intake. He said that Diversion is an appropriate consequence for his actions, and that his contract items are fair. His parents were surprised at his past usage of drugs and alcohol. It is my belief that even though Dylan knows what he did was wrong, he still lessens the seriousness of his offense. Dylan is a 12 mo CA, his contract includes: 45 hrs of community service, drug and alcohol evaluation, the CJ class, an ethics class, bimonthly progress reports, and an apology letter to his victim."*[307] The interviewer's impression of Dylan was correct and confirmed by both of his parents in the book *Far from the Tree: Parents, Children and the Search for*

Identity. Dylan's father told the author that the day after the arrest he was surprised by how angry Dylan was over the situation. *"He felt so above it all, totally justified in what he'd done,' Tom said. 'The morality of the whole thing escaped him.'"*[308] Dylan's mother agreed and indicated that Dylan reasoned that because it was a company van, and the company would have insurance to cover the theft, the crime was not that big of a deal. He also told her that he did not know why he had done it and that it scared him that he was capable of it.[308] Based upon his assessment, Dylan was also formally enrolled into the Juvenile Diversion Program on March 25, 1998.

According to notations made by his Diversion officers, Harris did well in the program. He was prompt with his payments to the court and his victim, passed every drug test, kept his grades up, and completed all of his assignments and classes in a timely manner. Eric performed 45 hours of community service at Link Recreation Center. Upon completion of his time, his Community Service Supervisor deemed him a *"Great Worker."*[309] Harris only experienced two minor bumps in the road during Diversion. The first came when he narrowly averted missing the deadline for completion of his community service. Eric was required to have all of his hours in by August 3, 1998. He had arranged to finish the last four hours on August 2. A flat tire delayed him, but since it was a Sunday the rink closed early, which meant he would be short two hours. Harris later wrote, *"The man there was nice enough to slide me the extra hours since I did such an outstanding job."*[310] Eric's parents found out about this and made him go back to the rec center to fulfill the hours he missed. The second problem arose when Harris received a speeding ticket on October 15, 1998. Eric's parents grounded him for three weeks for the infraction. The ticket was reduced through the court to a defective turn signal and Harris was required to—and did complete—a defensive driving course.[311]

One of Eric's first assignments in Diversion was to write a letter of apology to the owner of the van he and Dylan robbed. At his April 16, 1998 counseling appointment, Eric's Diversion counselor provided him with guidelines for the letter. Harris handed in his first draft at his next Diversion session. After making the improvements suggested by his counselor, he submitted the final version in mid-May.[312] The letter sounded sincere and gave the appearance that Eric was remorseful for his actions and sympathetic to how the man must have felt after being victimized:

Hello, my name is Eric Harris. On a Friday night in late-January my friend and I broke into your utility van and stole several items while it was parked at Deer Creek Canyon Road and Wadsworth. I am writing this letter partly because I have been ordered to from my diversion officer, but mostly because I strongly feel I owe you an apology and explanation.

I believe that you felt a great deal of anger and disappointment when you learned of our act. Anger because someone you did not know was in your car and rummaging through your personal belongings. Disappointment because you thought your car would have been safe at the parking lot where it was and it wasn't. If it was my car that was broken into, I would have felt extreme anger, frustration, and a sense of invasion. I would have felt uneasy driving in my car again knowing that someone else was in it without my permission. I am truly sorry for that. The reason why I chose to do such a stupid thing is that I did not think. I did not realize the consequences of such a crime, and I let the stupid side of me take over. Maybe I thought I wouldn't be caught, or that I could get away. I realized very soon afterwards what I had done and how utterly stupid it was. At home, my parents and everyone else that knew me was shocked that I did something like that. My parents lost almost all their trust in me and I was grounded for two months. Besides that, I have lost many of my privileges and freedom that I enjoyed before this happened. I am now enrolled in the diversion program for one full year. I have 45 hours of community service to complete and several courses and classes to attend over the course of my enrollment.

Once again, I would like to say that I am truly sorry for what I have done and for any inconvenience I have caused you, your family, or your company.[313]

Harris's ability to convince others of his sincerity was also evident in a paper he wrote for a class at school in the fall of 1998. When asked to write about a significant, life-changing event, Eric penned an essay about his arrest and its aftermath. He claimed that he was full of remorse and regret over his decision that night. Harris's words seemed so heartfelt that his teacher made the following comments when he returned the paper:

Wow, what a way to learn a lesson. I agree that night was enough punishment for you. Still, I am proud of you and the way you have reacted to this situation. We all make mistakes, how we respond to them is what makes us who we are. You have really learned from this and it has changed the way you think. This may be the best lesson you ever learn. I also think you should know that it's not one action that makes a person who they are. I would trust you in a heartbeat. Thanks for letting me read this and for being in my class.[314]

Privately, Eric was far less empathetic. Even before he met with his Diversion officer to discuss writing the apology, Harris expressed his anger at being punished for the theft. On April 12, 1998, Eric wrote in his journal: "*Isnt America supposed to be the land of the free? how come, If i'm free, I cant deprive a stupid fucking dumbshit from his possessions If he leaves them sitting in the front seat of his fucking van out in plain sight and in the middle of fucking nowhere on a Frifuckingday night. NATURAL SELECTION. fucker should be shot.*"[315] Harris was genuinely upset about the arrest, but not for the reasons he indicated in his apology letter or essay. Eric was furious that he had gotten caught and for all the things he was required to do to atone for his crime. He was not appreciative of other people—police, school officials, or his parents—telling him what to do or how to behave.[315] Harris's rage was evident in an exchange he had with a friend in German class. While discussing how someone on his "Shit List" could get off if he allowed Eric a retaliatory punch in the face, Harris wrote: "*I just don't want the little fuck going to admin. or the cops and start whining that we are threatening him or intimidating him. because if I get in ANY more trouble w/ cops I will fucking lose it.*"[177]

Eric's façade of repentance impressed his Diversion counselor. He received a glowing review upon early termination of his JDP contract. The counselor stated that Harris had impressed him "*as being very articulate and intelligent*"[296] and gave him a good long-term prognosis. He wrote: "*Eric is a very bright young man who is likely to succeed in life. He is intelligent enough to achieve lofty goals as long as he stays on task and remains motivated.*"[296]

Klebold's diversion did not go quite as smoothly as Harris's. Whereas Eric kept to his due dates, maintained his grades, and paid all of his fines on time, Dylan muddled through. He was instructed to complete ten of his 45 hours of community service by June 1, 1998, but by June 3 he had only put in seven hours. As punishment, his Diversion counselor required him to type a two-page paper on time management.[316] Klebold then vowed to make a concerted effort to get his hours in. By working at the Link Recreation Center, St. Philip Lutheran Church, and Eldorado Canyon State Park,[317] he was able to knock off 39 hours of his community service requirement by the end of June— which was well before the scheduled August completion date.[317]

Dylan had trouble maintaining his grades and progress reports from his teachers were not always favorable. In the first month of school, his calculus teacher indicated that Dylan was sleeping in class. When Klebold told his Diversion counselor that this happened because he had stayed up late finishing an assignment he had procrastinated on, the counselor told him that he needed to straighten up or he would be required to come to the Diversion office every day after school to work on his homework.[318] A few months later, the counselor discovered that Dylan had a D in gym class, which he claimed was due to tardiness. By his next session, his gym grade had dropped to an F and his math teacher had written that Dylan was not using his class time appropriately. Klebold told his counselor that a policy change for tardy make ups was the reason for the F and that the math teacher's comment arose because he was reading a book in class.[318] The Diversion counselor took Dylan to task telling him, *"the tardies never should have happened so the change of policy would not have mattered."*[318] He also said *"that his effort needs to improve or he will face consequences here including possible termination. I also confronted him on his minimizing and excuse giving. I told him to listen to himself and think about what he is saying. It all sounds like he feels like the victim although he denies this."*[318] Klebold buckled down a bit. He made up some gym absences, improved all but his math grade (which remained a D), completed the remainder of his assigned classes, and paid all of his fines by January 19, 1999.[318]

Among Dylan's requirements for the JDP was attendance at an I.S.A.E. Discovery class. The class was designed to teach youth offenders to value themselves and learn life skills that would enable them to make more appropriate, positive choices. In the paper Klebold wrote summarizing his experience, he made it clear he was above it all. Dylan explained:

"The class, truthfully, was not worth my time. If I wasn't me, I would be voicing a different opinion. The teacher was informative, and the information was valuable, but I already knew almost all of what the teacher had to say."[319] Dylan relayed that the teacher spoke of different coping mechanisms and stated, *"I, unfortunately for my boredom, knew these things too, and use them and have used them on a regular basis for quite some time."*[319] He ended his paper with a no-holds barred opinion of the class by stating, *"All in all, the class was a waste of time for me, and even though it went over important skills that would be greatly beneficial to someone else hearing them for the first time, it was an eight hour day of pointless review and cramped conditions. I feel that I shouldn't have had to take that class, but I'm just trying to get out of the diversion program, as evidenced by my reluctant attendance to this fit-for-an-uneducated person's class."*[319]

Despite some bumps in the road, Dylan finished all of his Diversion requirements and received early termination from JDP on January 20, 1999.[320] Klebold's Diversion counselor gave him a good prognosis for the future and wrote: *"Dylan is a bright young man who has a great deal of potential. If he is able to tap his potential and become self motivated he should do well in life."*[320] The counselor added, *"He is*

*intelligent enough to make any dream a reality, but
he needs to understand hard work is part of it.*"[320]

Chapter Five

Luvox

Eric Harris's psychiatric records have not been made available to the public, so a definitive clinical diagnosis of his mental state is not known. The only semi-official diagnosis proffered was a notation made by Harris's first Diversion counselor. In early July 1998, as his case was being transferred to another Diversion officer, Harris's previous counselor prepared a brief summary of Eric's progress by way of introduction. In part, it read: *"He suffers from Depression, he changed meds and feels better, he has difficuties handleing stress, but says he has a good handle on it now."*[321] The Harrises granted access to Eric's therapy records upon his acceptance into the Juvenile Diversion Program (JDP).[322] As such, Eric's counselor may have been in a position to give some details regarding his diagnosis and treatment.

During his assessment for entry into the JDP, Eric himself revealed that he *"began taking Zoloft for depression about 6 weeks ago. He said that he is feeling better now that he is on Medication Eric said that he has problems with anxiety and allows his anger to build up until he explodes. Eric says when he gets really mad he punches walls. He is seeing a therapist once or twice a month, the family also meets with him on occasion. Eric said that he has thought about suicide a couple of times, but never seriously, mostly out of anger."*[323] Harris's JDP Intake and Assessment Checklist, filled out by the interviewer on March 3, 1998, indicated that he had been taking Zoloft for only three to four weeks—not six—[324] and handwritten notes by the intake counselor state that Eric started the drug at the end of February.[325] Since Eric's first meeting with the therapist was February 16, 1998,[285] late February would appear to be the most accurate time frame for when he began to take Zoloft. Many media reports surrounding this case indicated that Zoloft is a drug used in the treatment of Obsessive-Compulsive Disorder, thereby implying that Harris suffered from this condition. No evidence supports that implication, and it should be known that Zoloft is also used to treat Depression, Anxiety (panic attacks, Social Anxiety Disorder), and Post Traumatic Stress.[326]

Documents in the case indicate that Harris was switched from Zoloft to Luvox in early May 1998. During a biweekly meeting with his Diversion counselor on April 16, 1998, Harris relayed that he had *"been having difficutly with his medication for depression. A few nights ago, he was unable to concentrate and felt restless. He went to the doctor and the Dr. is changing his medication. He can't start the new medication for 2 weeks b/c the Zoloft needs to get out of his system first."*[312] The shift from Zoloft began in mid-April and, according to the records, he was medication-free two weeks later at his April 30 Diversion counseling visit. By his May 14 session Harris had begun using Luvox, but Eric told his counselor that despite starting the new medication he *"[didn't] feel a difference yet, his Dr. said it would take a few weeks."*[312] Over the next couple of appointments, Harris reported that he was feeling better and was managing stress easier. At his July 10 appointment, Eric told his new Diversion counselor that his Luvox dose had been changed to 100 mg. Presumably, this was an increase in dosage.[312]

Much has been made of Harris's use of Zoloft and, later, Luvox: two antidepressant medications in the selective serotonin reuptake inhibitors (SSRIs) class of drugs. There are claims that the drugs either caused, or exacerbated, Eric's tendency towards violence. Some have reported that Harris admitted to suicidal and homicidal ideation—a potential side effect of SSRI medications—[326,327,328] shortly after starting Zoloft. Ann Blake-Tracy, Executive Director of the International Coalition for Drug Awareness, claimed that *"Harris became obsessed with homicidal and suicidal thoughts 'within weeks' after he began taking Zoloft. Due to his obsession with killing, Harris was switched to Luvox."*[329] It is not known how she acquired this information. Blake-Tracy has admitted that she did not have direct access to Eric's medical records even though she worked with Columbine victim Mark Taylor in his lawsuit against Solvay Pharmaceuticals. Blake-Tracy claimed a PhD in Health Sciences from George Wythe University, however, GWU revoked this degree after an investigation revealed it was obtained under questionable circumstances with the absence of any coursework or graduate-level research.[330,331] Blake-Tracy was not a physician, psychologist, or psychiatrist. This would have legally prevented her from reviewing the notes of Harris's psychologist.[332] All evidence was kept in a locked room and access was severely limited.

It should be mentioned that Blake-Tracy has alleged that Dylan Klebold was also taking antidepressants. In a 2006 interview, she told journalist Christopher Bollyn that both Eric and Dylan were diagnosed with "*some kind of 'Defiant Disorder*'"[333] after the van break-in and that both were started on medication.[333] Klebold's medical records have not been made public, but his autopsy showed no drugs in his system at his time of death.[334] Dylan made no mention of being in therapy or on antidepressants in his journals, and his closest friends were unaware of any such treatment. Furthermore, subsequent statements from his parents also refute this assertion. According to Susan Klebold, she consulted with those in charge of the JDP to find out if Dylan required any counseling. She said, "*they administered standardized psychological tests and found no indication that he was suicidal, homicidal, or depressed.*"[335] Unlike Blake-Tracy, Dr. Peter Breggin—a psychiatrist hired as an expert witness for the *Taylor v. Solvay* case—did have access to Harris's medical records. The report Breggin prepared for the court is not available. While he has been vocal in his belief that Luvox caused Eric's violence,[336] he makes no mention publicly of Harris experiencing the Zoloft side effects attributed to him by Blake-Tracy. Dr. Breggin also makes no assertions about Dylan having used antidepressants.

Since Harris's psychiatric records have not been released, it cannot be determined whether he did report suicidal and homicidal ideations to his psychologist after starting Zoloft, or if those making the claims based them solely on interpretation of Eric's replies during the mental health portion of the JDP assessment. Harris filled out this questionnaire three to four weeks after he was prescribed Zoloft. Under the question *"Have you had (or are you having) problems or difficulty with any of the following?"* Eric placed a check mark beside: *Anger, Anxiety, Authority Figures, Depression, Disorganized thoughts, Homicidal thoughts, Jealousy, Loneliness, Mood swings, Obsessive thoughts, Racing thoughts, Stress, Suspiciousness, and Temper.*[337] When asked to explain the items he had checked, Harris wrote: *"Short temper. Often get angry at almost anything I don't like, like people I have no respect for trying to tell me what to do. People telling me what to think. I have too many inside jokes or thoughts to have very many friends, or I hate to many things."*[337] These statements were consistent with views Eric had expressed before he began seeing the psychologist, so it seems likely that he had many, if not all, of these thoughts and emotions prior to starting Zoloft. According to Eric's parents, the reason the doctor prescribed the first antidepressant to Harris in February 1998 was because Eric relayed that he was already having these feelings.[338] They did not mention, perhaps because they were unaware of, Eric's thoughts of homicide.

It is important to acknowledge that Harris was expressing extreme anger, vengefulness, violence, and even homicidal tendencies long before he began antidepressant therapy. In the web pages that the Brown family provided to police in August 1997, a full seven months before Eric was initially prescribed Zoloft, his contempt and rage were already evident. In Harris's *You Know What I Hate?*" rants, he wrote of shooting people with a sawed off shotgun, ripping out a person's ribs and shoving them into their eyeballs, bombing people's houses, and stabbing someone with a broken baseball bat.[235] In addition, the web pages the Browns gave to police on March 18, 1998—less than a month after Eric started therapy and the day before his Diversion assessment—were filled with Harris's plans to go on a shooting spree and kill as many people as he could, including Brooks Brown.[339] The exact dates on which this second series of pages were written have not been made available. It seems unlikely that all of the content would have been written in the three to four weeks after Eric began taking Zoloft, especially considering that the nature of the writings were so similar to statements that he had made online long before beginning the medication. In addition, Harris's parents revoked his computer privileges following his arrest on January 31, 1998.[292] Provided that he abided by these restrictions, he would have had limited ability to update his web pages in the first few weeks he was on Zoloft. Finally, the only evidence we have indicating that Eric did experience side effects from Zoloft was his Diversion counselor's notation on April 16, 1998. There is no mention in this entry of suicidal or homicidal ideation. Instead, Harris described a feeling of restlessness and difficulty concentrating. These are also known side effects of the drug.[328] Eric discussed the matter with his doctor in mid-April when the signs began to occur. Since the Browns had discovered his second series of web pages a month earlier, we know that writing was done well before Harris began reporting that he was having problems with his medication.[312]

While Harris was assuring his Diversion counselor that all was well with his mental and emotional states on the drug, Eric's personal journal demonstrated no appreciable change in his rage or attitude towards others. In the "Basement Tapes," Harris referred to his journal as the *"Writings of God,"*[340] and in an entry dated April 10, 1998— just before he was taken off of Zoloft— Eric wrote: *"I hate this fucking world. So many god damn fuckers in it."*[341] Harris asserted that only he and Dylan possessed *"self awareness"*[341] and that they knew what everyone meant to the world. He penned, *"we have been watching you people. we know what you think and how you act, all talk and no actions."*[341] Eric wrote about this being "HOE" (Hell on Earth) because the world was corrupt and everyone was caught up in their own opinions, schedules, and agendas. He mentioned that he knew he and everyone else would die soon: *"maybe we will be lucky and a comet will smash us back to day 1."*[341] Eric also wrote in support of natural selection and his view that we should *"KiLL all retards, people w/ brain fuck ups, drug adics, people who cant figure out how to use a fucking lighter."*[341] This belief echoed what he had written several months earlier prior to taking Zoloft in his *"You Know What I Hate?"* rants. At that time, Harris said he hoped the government would remove all warning labels so that *"the dumbasses would either severely hurt themselves or DIE!"*[235]

Harris's April 21, 1998 journal entry is likely his first written reference to "NBK". The entry on this date is interesting because it is the only time that Eric discussed his therapist or his antidepressant medication. *"my doctor wants to put me on medication to stop thinking about so many things and to stop getting angry. well, I think that anyone who doesnt think like me is just bullshitting themselves."*[342]

According to the notes made by Harris's Diversion counselor on April 16, Eric's doctor had decided to change his medication a few days before. It is recommended that when stopping Zoloft, the drug should be tapered. Weaning is necessary because abrupt discontinuation of Zoloft may result in dysphoric mood, irritability, agitation, anxiety, headache, and lethargy.[326] Pfizer, the makers of Zoloft, recommend tapering the dose *"as rapidly as is feasible,*"[326] but most mental health professionals prefer a slow withdrawal. The weaning schedule is generally dependent upon the current dosage, how long the patient has been on the medication, and the patient's response to weaning. Recommendations vary, but most commonly the patient's dose is decreased by twelve and a half to 25 mg every one to two weeks. By the time of his April 30 Diversion visit, Harris was off all medication and *"feeling ok."*[312] Given knowledge of these factors, it is likely that at the time of the April 21 journal entry and his first reference to "NBK", Eric would have been nearly weaned off of Zoloft, bringing into question whether the drug would have had much of an influence over his actions or thoughts at that time. If there was, in fact, a link between the medication and Harris's behavior, was it because the drug was in his body or because he was experiencing side effects from being weaned from the medication too rapidly?

There have been several reports about Eric's manipulation of the side effects of Luvox. Mark Taylor, in his testimony before the FDA, reported that Harris would misuse his medications in order to *"fuel the rage."*[343] Brooks Brown stated, *"Eric was on Luvox and wrote about how he would go on and off his drug often to gain 'greater self awareness'"*[344] The claim can also be found in a *TIME* magazine article about the "Basement Tapes." The context of the statement, however, does not specify whether this knowledge was gained from the tapes or if it came from another source. It reads: *"It's easy now to see the signs: how a video-game joystick turned Harris into a better marksman, like a golfer who watches Tiger Woods videos; how he decided to stop taking his Luvox, to let his anger flare, undiluted by medication.*"[107] However, the police transcripts of the "Basement Tapes" indicate no such reference to misuse of the drug by Harris[345] and his autopsy report shows that he had a therapeutic level of Luvox in his system at the time of his death. Moreover, none of the videos or documents— including Eric's personal journals that have been released to the public—contains mention of Harris abusing his medication. John DeCamp, a lawyer and former Nebraska State Senator, handled the Solvay lawsuit for Mark Taylor until he was let go from the case. DeCamp told an interviewer that he was the only person involved in the lawsuit to take depositions from the Harris family and from Eric's doctor. He has seen many pieces of evidence that are now sealed from the public until 2027.[346] In speaking about Eric's use of Luvox, DeCamp asserted that Harris would "*double up and triple up, and then go off them for a few days and get the exciting effects of this and that. Feel like King Kong, you can kill anybody. He learned the whole mechanism.*"[347] Unfortunately, DeCamp does not indicate whether this information was contained within the materials only he had access to or if he made an assumption based on other things he had learned about the medication since. In the same interview, DeCamp did make statements regarding Klebold's death—which can be disproven upon evaluation of Dylan's writings and forensic evidence at the crime scene—[348] suggesting that not all of his beliefs are supported by the facts of the case.

Psychiatrist Peter Breggin, Taylor's expert witness, was able to review Harris's mental health records for the Solvay lawsuit. Publicly, Breggin did not indicate that he came across information showing Harris misused the medication to enhance the side effects from taking—or abruptly stopping—the drug, nor to purposely alter his mental state. Breggin wrote an article for *Natural News* in January 2013, discussing details he claimed were found in Harris's health records. In the article, Breggin mistakenly used 2009 instead of 1999 as the year in which the events occurred. Breggin revealed that Eric's Luvox dose *"was increased 200 mg per day on February 9, 2009 [sic], two and one-half months prior to the April 20th assaults. He saw his doctor and his prescription was renewed on March 13, 2009 [sic]. At that time, the medical record described him as suffering from medication-induced tremors, indicating a degree of toxicity."*[349] Breggin does not mention whether the presence of this side effect resulted in Eric's doctor recommending a dosage decrease at that time. In the report Breggin submitted to the court, he wrote: *"On April 20, 1999, at the time he committed multiple homicides and suicide, Eric Harris was suffering from a substance induced (Luvox-induced) mood disorder with depressive and manic features that had reached a psychotic level of violence and suicide."*[336] Breggin also stated, *"Absent persistent exposure to Luvox, Eric Harris probably would not have committed violence and suicide."*[336] He reached this conclusion without reviewing the vast majority of evidence in the case, including: journal writings, as well as audio and video recordings made by Harris and Klebold. Breggin's failure to evaluate that evidence prompted a Solvay attorney to request that Breggin and another expert not be allowed to testify at trial because they had not gone *"to the highly secured evidence room at the federal courthouse in Denver to look at hundreds of documents and other evidence connected to the Columbine case, although they've had months to do so."*[350] The lawyer maintained that they could not possibly render a meaningful opinion without seeing the materials relevant to the case. He told the judge that *"Breggin's final report lacks any discussion or analysis of the evidence. Breggin's final report doesn't mention the facts, circumstances, or evidence concerning the conception, planning, execution, or investigation of the Columbine incident."*[350] The judge was infuriated at Breggin's lack of preparation and ruled that *"Solvay lawyers will be free to attack them on the basis of the evidence they haven't seen and haven't factored into their opinions."*[350] He also forbade Breggin and the other expert from being allowed to go back and look at the vaulted evidence because they failed to do so before formulating their reports.

The tone of Harris's writings seemed to be consistent both pre- and post-antidepressants. He continued to share his nihilistic beliefs, as well as his anger and hatred towards other people. The evidence seems to indicate that most, if not all, of Eric's anger and violent tendencies were present before the antidepressant medication and that Zoloft and Luvox did not cause Harris to experience those emotions. The Taylor lawsuit claimed Luvox made

Eric kill, but he had mentioned "NBK" before he ever started the drug. Eric was being weaned off Zoloft when those ideas were initially written. Those claiming that Zoloft caused Harris's homicidal thoughts do not acknowledge the similar tone of his writings before medication. Many of these "experts" never reviewed Eric's psychiatric records, nor any other materials pertinent to his state of mind prior to beginning therapy. Without evaluation of these materials, no credible opinion could be formed regarding the effect the medication had on him. As such, it would seem to be nearly impossible to prove a causal link between the antidepressants and Harris's behavior in the planning and execution of the attack on Columbine.

Given all of the evidence, it seems unlikely that the antidepressants were a factor in what happened at Columbine. If they contributed at all, they were likely not a direct cause of his behavior, but rather served to exacerbate Eric's already volatile thought processes. If Harris's psychiatric records indicate that the medications played even a minor role in the course of events, however, it is disturbing to think that the information will be inaccessible for almost two decades.

Chapter Six

Girlfriends

Dating was difficult for both Eric Harris and Dylan Klebold because they were considered among the lower echelons of Columbine High School. Reports in recent years portray Harris as something of a ladies' man, however, this is not at all supported by available evidence. Each boy had some experience with the opposite sex but, by all accounts, it seemed to have been rather limited.

Examination of police reports and Dylan Klebold's journal indicate that Dylan did, briefly, date a Littleton High School student in October 1997. The relationship consisted of only a few dates. The girl broke up with him because she felt *"there was something strange about Klebold and she felt uncomfortable with him."*[351] A few weeks later, the same girl began a four- month courtship with Eric Harris. Klebold referenced his relationship in his journal on October 14, 1997 after the pair had broken up. In a rambling entry, Dylan despaired that he did not find the happiness that he was seeking in this "phony" relationship and wished that his real crush, whom he believed was his one true love, would feel the same way about him. Despite his protestations that their love was not *"true"*, the breakup with this girl seemed to affect Klebold deeply. His writings on this day reveal his profound sadness and desire to end his life:

Me. sorry I didnt write. A SHITLOAD in my existence mist. Ok... hell & back... ive been to the zombie bliss side... & I hate it as much if not more than the awareness part. Im back now... a taste of what I thought i want... <u>*wrong*</u>*. Possible girlfriends are coming then* [redacted]*... i'll give the phony shit up in a second. want* <u>*TRUE*</u> *love... I just want something i can never have... true true I hate everything. why cant I die... not fair. I want pure bliss... to be cuddling w.* [redacted]*, who i think i love deeper than ever... I was hollow, thought I was right. Another form of the Downward Spiral... deeper & deeper it goes. to cuddle w. her, to be one w. her, to love; just laying there. I need a gun. This is a wierd entry... I should feel happy, but shit brought me down. I feel terrible. The Lost Highway apparently repeats itself. I want drink. NOW.* [Redacted] *lucky bastard gets a perfect soulmate, who he can admit FUCKIN SUICIDE to & I get rejected for being honest about fuckin hate for jocks.*[352] Later in the entry Dylan penned, "*No emotions. not caring. yet* *another stage in this shit life. suicide… Dylan Klebold.*"[352]

It is the only dating relationship that Klebold is known to have had. Dylan did ask a few other girls out but was turned down. A few years before the shooting, he had a crush on a girl that he communicated with online. Klebold asked this girl on a date but she declined, so he did not continue to pursue her.[353] In one instance, a girl Dylan was interested in worked at Southwest Plaza Mall. After she declined his date request, Dylan *"stated words to the effect of, 'Maybe I'll ask you out again.'*"[354] A friend of Klebold's also tried to set him up once, but that girl said no as well.[355]

After the shootings, several students told investigators they felt that Robyn Anderson had romantic feelings for Dylan, but that these feelings were not reciprocated.[356,357,358] Klebold's parents told police that while Anderson and Dylan were friends and often studied calculus together, they did not feel that Dylan considered her to be his girlfriend.[359] It is likely that Robyn also viewed the relationship platonically. In a letter penned to a friend of hers before the massacre, Anderson explained how she had convinced Klebold to attend the Prom with her, even though he had no real interest in going:

I couldn't decide who, if anyone, I wanted to go with, so finally I convinced my friend Dylan, who hates dances, jocks, and has never had a date let alone a girlfriend to go with me! I am either really cute or just really persuasive! I think we will have a good time though because we always have fun when we hang out. He's a blast as a friend, but I guess it will be kinda wierd to be out with him all dressed up because mostly when we do stuph we just go bowling, watch movies, or I help him catch up on the calculus assignments he waits until the last night to do all of. So, point being, I figured it would be better to go with someone that I know I will have a good time with, but won't expect anything than someone that I half like that half likes me where who knows what the night could bring. See my point? Of course if you were in town I would take you, but I didn't figure you would be.[360]

After the shootings, Anderson re-emphasized to her friend that she and Dylan were not an item in an e-mail in which she wrote: "*oh, and I wanted to let you know to only believe half of what the press says… cuz I was never Dylan's girlfriend-I asked him to go to prom with me as a friend and he did it as a favor-I didn't want to go with someone that might ditch me or would end up being a jerk all night-I knew that we would have fun cuz I always had fun with him.*"[361]

The majority of Dylan Klebold's romantic life revolved around an unrequited love. Dylan filled pages in his journal with hearts containing her name and his. He lamented that she did not even know he existed and pined for the chance to hold her and to have her love him. Klebold discovered his "true love" sometime between July 23 and September 5, 1997; the first journal entry in which he mentioned her is not dated. According to Dylan, she was perfect in both looks and personality—particularly because she was not popular. In his euphoria he wrote: *"I just hope she likes me as much as I LOVE her. I think of her every second of every day, I want to be with her. I imagine me & her doing things together, the sound of her laugh, I picture her face, I love her. If soulmates exist, than I think I've found mine. I hope she likes Techno… :)* [Redacted], *I love you-Dylan"*[362] Klebold's bliss was short-lived as it became obvious to him that the girl of his dreams was not aware of him or his feelings for her. His journal entries fluctuated from despondency to hope and back again.

Sometime between February and June 1998, Dylan wrote a love letter in his journal to the girl. It may have been a draft because it contained several corrected mistakes. It is not known if this was the only copy or if Dylan ever gave her the letter or another one like it. Given its content, it is likely that if the girl had read the missive, Klebold's inner turmoil would have been brought to light and he might have gotten the help that he needed. The note is deeply personal because Klebold not only expressed his affection for the girl, but also revealed his self-loathing and desire to end his own life. Dylan told her that her love could save him, but that if she did not share his feelings it was not his intent to make her feel guilty if he committed suicide. Did Klebold really believe that she, or anyone, could read such a letter and not stop him? Was the letter a form of emotional blackmail—the only way Dylan knew to get the girl's attention? Was he seeking help? Or was Klebold's judgment so clouded by his misery that he did not consider the impact the note could have?

(Please don't skip to the back: read the note as it was written)

[Redacted],

You don't consciously know who I am, & doubtedly unconsciously too. I, who write this, love you beyond infinice. I think about you all the time, how this world would be a better place If you loved me as I do you. I know what you're thinking: "(some psycho wrote me this harrassing letter)." I hoped we could have been together… you seem a lot like me. Pensive, quiet, an observer, not wanting what is offered here (school, life, etc.). You almost seem lonely, like me. You probably have a boyfriend though, & might not have given this note another thought. I have thought you my true love for a long time now, but… well… there was hesitation. You see I can't tell if you think of anyone as I do you, & if you did who that would be. Fate put me in need of you, yet this earth blocked that with uncertainties. I will go away soon, but I just had to write this to you, the one I truly loved. Please, for my sake, don't tell anybody about this, as it was only meant for you. Also, please don't feel any guilt about my soon-to-be "absense" of this world. It is solely my decision: nobody elses. Oh… the thoughts of us… doing everything together, not necessarily anything, just to be together would have been pure heaven. I guess it's time to tell you who I am. I was in a class with you 1st semester, & was blessed w. being with you in a report. I still remember your laugh. Innocent, beautiful, pure.

This semester I still see you rarely. I am entranced during 5th period, as we both have it off. To most people, I appear... well... almost scary, but that's who I appear to be as people are afraid of what they don't understand. I denied who I was for a long time, until high school... Anyway, you have noticed me a few times, I catch every one of these gazes w. an open heart. I think you know who I am by now. Unfortunately... even if you did like me even the slightest bit, you would hate me if you knew who I was. I am a criminal, I have done things that almost nobody would even think about condoning. The reason that I'm writing you now is that I have been caught for the crimes I comitted, & I want to go to a new existence. You know what I mean (Suicide). I have nothing to live for, & I won't be able to survive in this world after this legal conviction. However, if it was true that you loved me as I do you... I would find a way to survive. Anything to be with you. I would enjoy life knowing that you loved me. 99/100 chances you prob. think I'm crazy, & want to stay as far away as possible. If that's the case, then I'm very sorry for involving an innocent person in my problems, & please don't think twice. However, if you are like I hoped for in my dreams & realities, then do me a favor: leave a piece of paper in my locker, saying anything that comes to you. Well, I guess this is it- goodbye, & I love(d) you. Dylan Klebold

Locker #837 near the library. Combo-19-37-9
304

Klebold repeatedly chastised himself in his writings for being unable to pick up the phone and call his "soulmate". As the weeks and months passed, his perceptions about his relationship with this girl changed; Dylan came to believe that it was not meant to be in this life, but that once he could break free of the bonds of his humanity he would have her in eternity. In another undated entry that appears to have been written within weeks—if not days—of the massacre, Klebold again addressed a girl (presumably the same one) directly. He repeated his request for her to leave him a note in his locker expressing her feelings whether good or bad. The letter does not contain the same desperate tones as the first, and is decidedly more matter-of-fact, as though he had by that time accepted what he believed was his fate. Amongst the drawings on this page is a symbol that Dylan referred to as the "Downward Spiral", a nod to a concept album by Nine Inch Nails about a man questioning the reality of everything outside his own mind and his descent into despair and suicide.

If you don't know who I am still, then I apparently havent been noticeable enough... please don't take offense or worry about this note... if you do know who I am, or if you want to anyway, please leave a note in my locker saying whatever you want- whether that be telling me to fuck off or else youll call the cops, or if you want to say whatever, just please do me that favor... if you tell me to leave you alone, I will. I like you [redacted]*, but I won't force that ever. #837 19-37-9 P.S (I* <u>*DID*</u> *try to call you but you must have been asleep*).[363]

Five days before his death, Dylan wrote his final thoughts to the girl he loved: *"The zombies were a test to see if our love was genuine. we are in wait of our reward, each other. the zombies will never cause us pain anymore… the humanity was a test. I love you, love. Time to die, time to be free, time to love."*[364]

Eric Harris had decidedly more success with girls than Klebold, but his experiences do not appear to have been any more fulfilling. Eric did date a few girls, albeit briefly. Harris possessed enough confidence to at least ask out several people, unlike the very shy Dylan. Unfortunately for him, he was turned down far more often than he actually managed to secure a date.

Eric had a short relationship with a girl in his freshman year of high school. The two went on one date to Columbine's Homecoming dance; then the girl broke up with him. In response, Harris enlisted a friend to bring the girl over to his home. When they arrived, she found Eric lying on the ground with a large rock in his hand and fake blood all over his head. He had staged his suicide for her benefit, either to convince her to take him back or to get revenge for her dumping him.[365] Harris was also asked to a dance by another girl in eighth or ninth grade. The relationship did not develop, but the two remained on friendly terms with one another.[366]

In his sophomore year, Eric dated a girl he met at a mall near the high school. The relationship lasted a total of two weeks and consisted of three dates. The couple split up because the girl lived too far away and it was difficult to travel to see one another. Although the breakup was mutual, Harris persisted in calling her in the week following the demise of the relationship professing his love for her. When she told him it was over and to quit calling, he did.[367]

Eric's most significant relationship appeared to have been with the girl who had also briefly dated Dylan Klebold. The two got together a few weeks after her relationship with Dylan ended in October 1997 and continued until she broke up with Harris in January 1998. The girl told police that in July 1998 *"she began receiving threatening phone calls with the caller claiming, 'I'm going to kill you' or 'a bomb is coming.' She believed HARRIS was responsible for these calls."*[351] The girl also revealed that, at one point, Harris had sent her an e-mail stating that he was trying to tie up all of his loose ends and that she was one of them. The e-mails stopped after the girl changed her online screen name.[351] Eric's bitterness towards this girl can also be found in a yearbook dedication he wrote to a fellow student: *"[She] is a fat trendy whiney annoying terd and I went out w/ her cause I felt sorry for her I guess. Oh well. I bet you'll show her this."*[368]

Around the summer of 1998, Eric began another relationship with a girl that he met at a soccer game. They saw each other two more times: at a second soccer game and at an amusement park. After only three dates, the girl determined that she was not interested in Eric. In her initial meeting with police, she told investigators that she broke up with Harris because he was not personable or talkative. She described him as *"nice, but sort of weird."*[369] In her second meeting, however, she reported that she was not sure what she did not like about him, "*but [that] he just seemed a little evil.*"[370] Rather than tell Eric that she did not want to see him anymore, the girl just stopped answering his calls and pages hoping he would get the message. When she saw him at another soccer game and he questioned her lack of response, the girl only told him that it was because her pager was broken. Eventually, Harris stopped calling.[369] Apparently, having his calls ignored was commonplace for Eric as he expressed his anger about it in one of the "Basement Tapes." Harris listed the names of five girls "*who never even called me back. You know who you are. Thanks. You made me feel good. Think about that for a while, fucking bitches.*"[371,372]

In February 1999, Eric took a freshman girl that he liked on a Saturday night date at Chili's.[373,374] The two talked on the phone several times, but when the girl's parents found out that Harris was a senior they put a stop to the relationship because they felt that he was too old for their daughter.[373,374] When the girl told Eric of her parents' wishes, he said he understood and the two remained friends.[373] Although, Harris may not have been as accepting of this decision as he let on. A good deal of information was redacted from the police statement given by the girl's mother, but the context suggests that the mother may have been on Eric's "Hit List".[374] In the same statement, the woman told investigators that her daughter's friend had expressed to her that the girl was actually scared of Harris. During her police interview, one of the girl's friends told investigators that the girl turned down

Eric's prom invitation because she thought he was "*weird.*"[375] There are, however, several statements that conflict with this view. Another friend told police that the girl and Harris got along very well and that she could not be his prom date "*because her mother wouldn't allow it.*"[376] Eric took the freshman girl and two other friends to lunch approximately two weeks before the attack.[377] After the shootings, in a class exercise designed to help students deal with what had happened, the girl wrote fondly of Harris. Her teacher told investigators that she felt the girl had a "freshman crush" on Eric, the senior.[378]

Harris reportedly asked many girls out but was repeatedly shot down. One young woman caught his attention because she had a window sticker of one of his favorite bands, Rammstein, on her car. Eric left a note on the car with his name, phone number, and a request for her to call him. The next several times he saw her, he asked her if she intended to get in touch with him, but she never did.[379] Harris met many girls through his jobs and developed many crushes that never seemed to pan out. During his time at Tortilla Wraps, he was interested in his immediate supervisor. The girl was aware that he was attracted to her, but she already had a boyfriend and felt it was inappropriate to have a relationship with a subordinate, so she did not reciprocate his feelings. She and Harris were on friendly terms and often hung out after work with other co-workers. Later, when she went away to college, the girl and Eric would occasionally communicate via AIM.[276] While at Blackjack Pizza, Harris asked out a fellow employee several times, but she always turned him down.[380] He also tried to secure dates with at least three of the girls that worked at the Great Clips hair salon next door to Blackjack's. One of those girls was in a relationship, but it did not stop Eric from asking her out. The girl described his attempts to police as *"very nice and courteous"* but that he *"didn't take no for an answer."*[381]

Harris had an equal amount of difficulty finding someone to take to the Senior Prom. In addition to the freshman girl, Eric was turned down by two other prospective dates as well. Roughly two weeks before the Prom, Eric had a friend ask a girl if she would attend with him. Harris looked on from across the room as this took place. The girl being asked *"looked at Eric Harris, then shook her head no, indicating to* [his friend] *that she would not go to the Prom with Eric Harris.* [His friend] *said Eric Harris saw* [the girl] *shake her head no, and was very upset about being turned down.* [His friend] *said that Eric Harris would not talk to* [the girl] *after this and in fact would not look at her.* [His friend] *also said that Eric Harris later told her he could not believe that* [the girl] *would not go to the Prom with him."*[382] The girl later told reporters that she had nothing against Harris and that, in fact, he had always been very nice to her. She just felt that it was very short notice and she had not planned on going.[383] Following this rejection, Eric asked another girl but she also declined. According to her statement to police, her refusal *"embarrassed him"*[384] in front of the class. Several of Harris's friends tried to help him find a date, but they were also unsuccessful.[385] As a result, Eric had to skip the Prom but did attend the party afterward.

Despite his inability to find someone to take to the Prom, Harris did end up spending time with a girl on prom night. Eric had been interested in the Great Clips's receptionist, a fellow Columbine student, since January 1999. He had asked several mutual friends about her and if they thought she liked him, too. The night before the Prom, both of them were working their respective jobs when they crossed paths again. When the girl went into Blackjack to pick up a pizza, he asked for her number and she complied. Harris called her house later that night, but the girl was not at home. Her mother told investigators that when she told Eric the girl was not available, he seemed to become a little angry.[386] Many researchers have highlighted this event as a rare moment in which Harris lost control and let his true personality slip. Perhaps that is the case. It might also be possible that Eric— fully expecting to be dead in four days— was more than a little anxious to have one last date. Finally having sex was prominent on his to-do list of things left to accomplish before "NBK".[387,388] Harris's quick temper may have been frustration over what he viewed as his final lost opportunity.

Eric and the girl did connect by phone that night and arranged to talk again the following day. Harris called her on Saturday night and invited her over to his house to watch a movie. They viewed his favorite film— *Event Horizon*—talked, and listened to music. Eric told her about a former friend who had been making fun of him and called the kid a "*jerk.*"[389] The girl told police that he did not seem angry about it—just hurt. She spent a good deal of time in Harris's room that night and never noticed anything out of the ordinary—

a testament to how well Eric had managed to hide his cache of weapons and ammunition when it suited him. Despite Harris's private writings about wanting sex, he did not make any real advances on the girl. She told investigators that at one point he put his arm around her and that at the end of the evening he kissed her on the cheek as she was leaving.[389] Eric appeared to care for the girl, as she was one of the few people he mentioned fondly in the "Basement Tapes." In the tape the boys made 30 minutes before their attack on Columbine, they "willed" some of their possessions to two close friends. Harris then said, *"[redacted], sorry. Under different circumstances it would've been a lot different. I want you to have that Fly CD."*[390]

Being one of the last people to have spent any significant amount of time with Eric weighed heavily on the girl. It was very difficult for her to reconcile the boy that she knew with the horrific carnage that Harris had caused. In the days after the attack, Columbine High School received a grant from the National Endowment for the Arts targeted for use in support of helping the school heal from the tragedies of April 20, 1999. With the grant, a memory book was created to allow students and faculty the opportunity to express their feelings and how they were affected by the shootings. For her part, the girl penned a letter addressed to Eric Harris:

Eric David Harris,
I didn't know the person hiding under your smile. I didn't know about the pain you carried in

your heart. I didn't know the torture you endured for so long. And I didn't want to believe you were capable of such destruction. I didn't know I could feel such pain for someone I really didn't know. If I knew what your eyes hid, and what your mind was screaming, maybe I could have helped you. I could have loved you. All I know is the pain I am feeling inside. All I know is the person I talked to every day, the person who seemed happy, the person who always helped me and made sure I had everything I needed. I see your picture on the pages, they say what a monster you are, they say how you were mean and cruel. But you see, I can't believe what they say. I knew the smiling person, the person who helped me. I don't want to hear it anymore. I want it to go away, the angry cries well up in me and I hate you for making me so scared and sad. Leaving me without any explanation. Leaving me with wandering thoughts and hollow cries. Did you try and reach me? Did you try to tell me? I will live with the memories and the unanswered questions I hold in my heart. Not a day will go by that I will not wonder why. As time goes by, I am getting stronger, but then the moment comes when I break down and cry. I am so sorry I didn't see the rage you had inside. I am sorry I was so blind and couldn't see all the things you tried to show me. No matter how wrong you were, I will love the person who smiled and said 'Hi' to me every day. I promise to never forget the person I knew, and forget the person they say you were.

Love Always and Forever,
[redacted][391]

There does not seem to be any evidence that Eric Harris had a romantic relationship with any other girls. A few websites mention the names of individuals he was supposed to have been involved with, but no documentation exists to verify those assertions. Written claims that Eric had sex with an older woman are also unequivocally false. The woman, a 23-year-old with her own Internet business, claimed that she had dated Harris the previous year. She told police that she had met Eric and Dylan at an area mall in January 1998 when she was there with a friend. When questioned, the woman could not tell investigators which mall it was, nor could she provide them with the last name of the friend who accompanied her there.[392] She told police that, in addition to Klebold, she had met two of Harris's other friends: Chris Morris and Brooks Brown.[392,393] In reality, Morris had no knowledge of this woman and Brooks and Eric did not reconcile until a year later in January 1999.[394,395] It would be highly unusual for Harris to introduce the woman to a boy he despised and wanted to kill. Brown did eventually meet her, but only when she initiated contact after the massacre claiming to be a friend of Eric's.[396] In fact, of the people she asserted she met while in a relationship with Harris: two are dead (Eric and Dylan), two deny being introduced to her (Morris and Brown), and one will never speak to anyone about Eric (Harris's brother).

The woman reported to investigators that she and Harris had been intimate on two occasions. During Eric's Intake Assessment for the Diversion Program on March 19, 1998— two months after the woman and Harris allegedly met— Eric told the interviewer he "[did] *not currently have a girlfriend, and he* [had] *never been sexually active.*"[292] Police questioned the woman about identifying characteristics on Eric's body that might help to confirm they had been intimate, but she told them that she had not seen anything because it was dark.[397] The residual indentation of his chest, as well as the surgical scar related to the correction of his pectus excavatum, would likely have been noticeable to someone being physically intimate with Harris.[398,399] At the time of his 1998 arrest, it was described as a *"5" inverted V surgery scar on his chest.*"[400] It is also likely that Eric, as a 17-year-old boy, would have been quite vocal about having bedded an older woman. He never wrote of it in his journal, however, nor did he speak of it to any of his friends. In fact, Harris made ten journal entries during the time that he was supposed to have carried on a relationship with the woman (January 1998-Fall 1998), but never mentioned her. Harris referred to wanting to "get laid" three times in his personal writings, but never mentioned having already done so.[387,388,401] Moreover, Brooks Brown—one of the people the woman claimed to have met while she was dating Eric—has stated that he believes Eric died a virgin.[402]

The woman provided police with a photograph of a boy she asserted was Eric Harris. The authorities determined that it was not Harris in the picture and that the *"photo could not be identified as anyone related to the case.*"[393] She also gave them a voice recording of a male that she claimed was Eric. Again, the police concluded that the *"voice on the tape did not sound like other known HARRIS recordings.*"[393] Both the picture and recorded message were returned to the woman because they were found to be of no evidentiary value. The woman told police that she and Harris would communicate daily by phone, but no phone records substantiated this claim.[392] Phone records for Eric, Dylan, and three of their friends were included in a search warrant. Two dozen or more of the numbers obtained were listed in a follow up warrant; the 23-year-old woman's number was not among them.[392,403]

There is no evidence that this woman even knew Eric Harris. All of the information she provided to police about Harris—including his friends, his family, his place of employment, and the kind of car he drove—was readily available through the avalanche of news coverage that surrounded the case. Moreover, some of her actions in the aftermath of the attack led many to believe that she may have been a "fangirl" enamored by Harris and was trying to insert herself into his story. The first incident arose when Brooks Brown and his family contacted police on August 31, 1999 with concerns that this woman intended to "*finish what Harris and Dylan Klebold started.*"[396] The woman, using the e-mail address "VoDkAREB@aol.com"—a combination of Klebold and Harris's nicknames—and username "VoDkAREB" had been contacting gun dealers inquiring about the purchase of a TEC-DC9, one of the guns that Dylan used in the rampage:

Hello,

*I am really curious on where I can get a TEC-DC9.
If you know, please e-mail me back
at…*
VoDkAREB@aol.com
Thank you,
[Redacted]

The dealer replied with the following e-mail:

Hello [redacted],
*I have no more Tec-DC9's. I can obtain only the
AB-10's, the postban version.*
*The stainless AB-10 will cost $300 + shipping. The
AB-10 stainless includes a stainless
32 round magazine. The firearm must be shipped to
your local dealer.*
Regards,
[Redacted][396]

The Browns also provided investigators with an
AIM conversation the woman had with the webmaster
of a site devoted to Columbine victims. In it, the two
make reference to a possible conspiracy by the
government to cover up the truth about Columbine.
When she is asked what she wants to do about it, the
woman replied: *"start killing government people until
someone tells us THE TRUTH."*[404] She also said that
she wanted to go to the school one night and sneak into
the library *"just to be in there to see."*[405] Her friend
inquired as to how she would accomplish this and the
woman told her that having been on many "missions"
with Eric and Dylan, she had lots of experience
sneaking around at night.[405] The claim is untrue, as

Harris's journals clearly indicate that there were only three individuals involved in the Rebel Clan missions: Eric Harris, Dylan Klebold, and a male friend. In addition, the boys had largely finished with the missions by January 1998— which is the same month the woman asserted she met Eric because Harris and Klebold were arrested for the van break-in later that month.

In a disturbing form of tribute, she told her friend: "*lets go to the mountains and detonate a pipe bomb in rememberance of them. go to the school have a b-day cake for Dylan and a 13 gun shot salute.*"[405] The number thirteen most likely represented the number of victims who died on that terrible day. She goes on to say that she was supposed to be with Harris and Klebold during their rampage[406] and that she had felt guilty and suicidal because she had missed the bus and did not meet Eric at the bus stop like they had arranged.[406,407] From the bus stop, they were to rendezvous with Dylan at Clement Park. She told her friend that the boys carried four guns that day because there were supposed to be four people involved: Eric, Dylan, herself, and another boy.[407] The third boy had backed out some time the week before. According to this woman, the plan was for her and the third boy to stand watch outside while Eric ran into the school and began shooting, flushing people outside where the four of them would then start killing. She also wrote that they would then escape to her house up in the mountains.[407] In addition to this claim to her friend, the woman referred to her "involvement" on an online bulletin board called "trenchcoaticp".[408]

All available evidence completely discounts this version of Harris and Klebold's plan. Eric's journals clearly indicated that each boy intended to carry two guns during the attack. Klebold and Harris purchased three guns at the gun show: a double barrel twelve-gauge shotgun, a pump action twelve-gauge shotgun, and a nine-millimeter carbine. Eric wrote that the carbine and one of the shotguns were his[409] and in a later journal entry, before the boys bought Dylan's TEC-DC9, he penned: "*now I just need to get Vodka another gun.*"[388] Harris and Klebold also practiced with both of their guns in the now infamous "Rampart" videos, so it is clear that they intended to carry two guns a piece during the attack. The boys' writings, as well as the "Basement Tapes," also plainly show that they had arranged for two bombs to detonate in the cafeteria, resulting in large numbers of causalities. Dylan and Eric planned to start their attack outside the school and shoot survivors that tried to escape the building. There was no intention for Eric to flush people outside by shooting at them from inside the building. Both Harris and Klebold fully intended to die on April 20, 1999— an escape to a secluded mountain hideaway was never on their minds. In the "Basement Tapes," Harris— alone in his car— commented that "*It is a weird feeling knowing you are going to be dead in 2 ½ weeks,*"[410] and 30 minutes before the attack both boys "willed" their possessions to friends.[390] Klebold referenced his impending death a few times in his journal, including starting— but not completing— a written will.[411] In an entry just over a day before the attack, he wrote, "*In 26.4 hours i'll be dead, & in happiness.*"[411] Moreover, Dylan wrote two separate event timelines for that day and neither included Eric picking someone up at the bus stop or meeting Harris and others at Clement Park. While he does reference the park in one of these entries, Dylan's writing indicated that he and Eric had already met up and would proceed to the park together. Here is what Klebold wrote in Harris's day planner some time before the attack:

> *5:00 Get up*
> *6:00 meet at KS* [indicates King Soopers]
> *7:00 go to Reb's house*
> *7:15 he leaves to fill propane*
> *I leave to fill gas*
> *8:30 meet back at his house*
> *9:00 make d. bag*
> *set up car.*
> *9:30 practice gear ups*
> *Chill*
> *10:30 set up 4 things*
> *11:00 go to school*
> *11:10 set up duffel bags*
> *11:12 wait near cars, gear up*
> *11:16 HAHAHA*[412]

The second timeline found in Klebold's journal was less detailed, but showed that they would go to Clement Park after bringing the bombs into the cafeteria. Neither timeline mentioned Eric flushing people out while Dylan waited outside, nor that they were to meet with others at the park. This timeline clearly indicated that the bombs were a vital component of their plans.

Walk in, set bombs at 11:09, for 11:17
Leave, ~~set car bombs~~
Drive to Clemete Park. Gear up.
Get back by 11:15
Park cars, set car bombs for 11:18
get out. go to outside hill, wait.
when first bombs go off, attack.
have fun! [413]

Unlike the more general information made available about Eric immediately following the shootings, the extent of Klebold and Harris's planning and their desire to perish during the massacre were not known to the public right away. Authorities did not begin releasing such evidence until a year and a half after the attacks. Unlike her ability to provide information to suggest she could have known Eric Harris, the woman could only formulate this story based on what she believed could have happened.

The AIM chat session ended with the woman telling her friend that she was in the presence of Dylan Klebold's ghost. She insisted that Dylan was with her telling her things and that she could feel, in her own head, the bullet that had ended Dylan's life.[414]

Given the information regarding her interest in purchasing a TEC-DC9 and her claim of involvement in the events at Columbine, the woman was interviewed by police on September 7, 1999. Initially, she denied writing that she had prior knowledge of the attacks, stating that someone else had added that information into the chat. She then changed her story and told investigators that she did say those things, but that she was only relaying a dream she had. Finally, after *"a lengthy discussion,"*[408] the woman admitted that those were her words and that she had made it all up. She had no desire to hurt herself or anyone else. *"She stated she has no life and spends way too much time on the Internet."*[408] Despite admitting this, the woman continued to deny that she had issued any threats, particularly the section of the chat that read: *"Oh GAWD why didn't I just go along with the plan? I could be with them right now BUT NO I WAS CHICKEN SHIT and now I have to be stuck here all by myself with pathetic little STUPIDHEADS! Well not nt more! I guess I will do what I should've done on 4-20 Boom! No more pain!"*[408]

The woman's name reappeared in the Columbine investigation when it was associated with death threats that had been mailed to Columbine High School and the Jefferson County Sheriff's Office. A disturbed individual thought it would be "fun" to pretend to be Eric Harris and send threatening notes and computer disks in the mail to authorities. The man called this pursuit "The Game."[415] He also sent a menacing e-mail directly to the woman, whom he had met online at an AOL site discussing the Columbine shootings.[416] When asked why he had involved this woman in his "game", he told police it *"was because she kept saying how cute Eric was, etcetera, etcetera."*[415] During the investigation into these threats, officers also contacted the woman's cousin and aunt because the cousin was mentioned in the e-mail. Both women were very upset that they had gotten dragged into the matter. The woman's aunt told police that her daughter *"has enough problems without getting involved with* [redacted] *'s fantasies,"*[417] adding that the young woman *"is obsessed with the Columbine High School shootings."*[417]

Taken in total, the police reports, journal writings, and other documentation seem to disprove any claim that Eric Harris ever even met the 23-year-old woman, much less went out with or had a sexual relationship with her. The police were aware, from initial interviews with her in 1999, that her entire story was fabricated. Inclusion of this woman's claims in later narratives of the Columbine shooting are, therefore, highly suspect.

Harris's documented dating history appears to have consisted of seven girls. Of those seven, there were three or fewer dates with six of them. Eric often enlisted the help of friends to determine whether or not a girl might be interested in him before he would ask her out. This "testing of the waters" could have been a reflection of a lack of confidence, a desire to avoid embarrassment, or the inability to put himself out there if he was unsure of the outcome. By the same token, there were many other instances in which he would forgo this help and ask a girl for her number or ask her out directly. Harris's seemingly contradictory courtship techniques were likely not related to any significant behavioral traits and were probably typical of many teenage boys.

Chapter Seven

Dylan: The Follower?

It has been almost universally accepted that Eric Harris was the driving force behind the Columbine school shootings. Dylan Klebold has been portrayed, by some, as almost a victim of the single-minded Harris. Manipulated and pushed into doing things that he did not really want to do; coaxed along until he became so deeply involved that he was unable to back out. A thorough review of Klebold's journal entries, school and criminal records, and interviews with those who knew or met him does not seem to support this depiction of Dylan's character. Klebold was a deeply troubled young man who struggled with thoughts of suicide for at least two years before he brutally attacked others and then took his own life. In the midst of his private expressions of self-loathing, however, he displayed a tremendous amount of anger and resentment for authority figures and for those who possessed the kind of life he desired but felt unable to create for himself.

Klebold has been described by several who knew him as a shy person.[289,418] A female friend told investigators that Dylan was very quiet and shy around people he did not know.[419] His father, in a statement to police, said his son was *"extraordinarily shy in high school."*[359] It was not new behavior for Klebold. Judy and Randy Brown recalled Dylan being painfully shy as a child. Although he often visited their home and the Browns adored him, Klebold always needed time to warm up to being there, as though he had never visited before.[420] A neighbor, who had known Dylan since elementary school, described him as someone who was very quiet and never spoke.[421] A family friend relayed that Klebold was so shy that even though they played on the same baseball team and their families sat near each other at Colorado Rockies games, Dylan rarely did more than say "hi" or talk a little about baseball.[422] His introverted nature was also noted by the students at school. Classmates told authorities that Klebold usually kept to himself, rarely participated in class, said very little to the other kids, and did not make friends with the other students.[100,164,423,424,425,426,427]

A boy who shared an economics class with Dylan the previous semester remarked that he could never get Klebold to talk,[428] and Klebold's ninth grade government teacher described Dylan as being an intelligent boy who was introverted and *"lacking in social skills.*"[429] Dylan himself felt that his shyness was one of the greatest obstacles to his ability to attain the type of social life he desired. In his journal, amongst a list of all the things wrong in his life, Klebold wrote: "*nobody accepting me even though i want to be accepted,*" "*me looking weird & acting shy-BIG problem,*" and "*i never know what to say or do.*"[196] Dylan expressed his fears about school, writing that he was "*scared & nervous*"[195] about people accepting him and being able to accept people in return. Social interactions were very difficult for him and made him feel inadequate and radically different from everyone else. "*... as i see the people at school-some good, some bad-i see how different i am (arent we all you'll say) yet i'm on such a greater scale of difference (as far as I kno, or guess).*"[195]

Many who were familiar with Dylan, even tangentially, also described him as a follower.[164,430,431,432,433,434,435] Of the students at Columbine they could envision participating in such horrors, Eric Harris came near the top of the list. Dylan Klebold was not even on it.[435,436,437,438,439] Only a school dean claimed "*he was not totally shocked that Dylan and Eric did this because in his dealings with them he saw the potential for an 'evil side'.*"[213] Robyn Anderson told police that Dylan was "*quiet a lot of the time and will go along with the rest if the activity sounds like fun.*"[440] She also reported that although she did not know Eric Harris well, she felt he could "*convince Dylan to do certain things.*"[440]

This sentiment was shared by another friend of Klebold's—a girl who was dating one of his closest friends. In speaking with investigators about Dylan she said, *"he was a follower and Eric was the leader."*[441] A boy whose relationship with Dylan had cooled in the ninth grade when Klebold grew closer with Harris described Dylan as *"very gentle,"* claimed that he *"would not do this on his own,"* and that he was *"always sort of a follower."*[442] Another acquaintance said, *"he could not believe that Dylan had been involved in such a thing and from what he knew about Dylan, Dylan did not have that sort of thing inside of him.* [He] *thought that Dylan had come under the influence of some outside person."*[436] Klebold's father told investigators that although he did not feel like there was a leader in Dylan's association with Harris, sometimes *"Eric would get mad at Dylan if he 'screwed something up.'"*[443] Beyond their circle of family and friends, other kids at Columbine had their own opinions of the relationship between Harris and Klebold. A male student stated to police that Dylan followed along with what everyone else was doing and he believed that *"if Chris Morris and Eric Harris told Dylan to go jump off a cliff, Dylan would do it."*[444] A boy in Harris and Klebold's creative writing class echoed this thought, telling investigators that *"if Eric Harris would say something, a short time later Dylan Klebold would be saying the same thing."*[98] Dylan's mother, when speaking to author Andrew Solomon about his childhood, said something very similar: *"He was very malleable; you'd reason with him and say, 'This is why I think you should do something,' and you could almost always persuade him to change his mind.*

Which I used to see as a strength, from the perspective of a parent. But I see now that it might have been a terrible detriment."[445]

Review of these testimonies indicate that portrayals of Dylan as a shy follower have some basis in fact. There are, however, other descriptions of a more assertive, aggressive Klebold that demonstrate he was capable of imposing his will when he chose to do so. Klebold's conflicts with teachers, school officials, co-workers, fellow students, and his involvement in the van break-in shows this, as outlined in chapters three and four. It is also important to note that based on the evidence, the idea for the attack on Columbine could have originated from Dylan—not Eric. In July 1997, almost two years before the massacre, Klebold wrote that he would like to kill his best friend's girlfriend because she had taken his friend away from him.[446] Dylan's despair deepened when Eric also began dating someone a few months later. At this point on November 3, 1997, Dylan noted his worry that Eric would also abandon him and, being completely alone, he would get a gun and "*go on my killing spree against anyone I want.*"[447] Klebold's journals even suggest that he had another partner, someone other than Eric Harris, in mind for the crime. On February 2, 1998, just days after his arrest for the van break-in, Klebold lamented that society was trying to destroy him because he was different. Dylan wrote, "*Soon... either ill commit suicide or ill get w.* [redacted by police] *& it will be NBK for us.*"[202] He followed this sentence with, "*My hapiness. her hapiness. NOTHING else* *matters.*"[202] Investigators have censored the writing to protect the individual's identity so that his original partner is unknown, but the context suggests Klebold was fantasizing that his secret crush would accompany him on his spree, much like the characters Mickey and Mallory in *Natural Born Killers*. Eric Harris's journal entries do not show his first mention of "NBK" until more than two months later on April 21, 1998.[342] The date is almost one year to the day of the massacre.

Klebold may have presented other ideas to Harris as well. According to a friend Eric met on an Internet bulletin board system, an early version of an online message board, Harris seemed to be the leader in his relationship with Klebold. The boy did tell police, however, that the Rebel Clan's "missions" may have been Dylan's idea. When the investigator asked what suggestions Dylan had come up with that Eric followed along on, the kid replied: "*Uh, like going out at night and lighting off fireworks. I remember he said that was a good idea, that he, that Vodka had and he said that he was gonna go do it and stuff.*"[448] In addition, according to Klebold's friend, it was Dylan who provided Harris with the *Anarchist's Cookbook*. The boy recalled that in the summer or fall of 1997 he had seen the cookbook on Klebold's computer and "*Klebold mentioned that he sent it to Harris.*"[449] Both boys had already been experimenting with bomb-making by this time but utilized the cookbook to improve their designs. Klebold and his best friend also got Eric Harris involved in the computer hacking that earned the three of them suspensions. While Harris's parents felt his involvement was minor, Eric seemed to be a willing participant.[213] Finally, according to Harris, the van break-in was Dylan's idea and that both boys told police that Klebold was the one who actually broke the van window and removed the items from the vehicle while Eric stood watch.[282,283]

Klebold not only instigated some of the trouble the boys got into, but also did not seem to have qualms about putting Harris back in line if needed. A female student told investigators that her friend accidentally ran into Dylan's car in the parking lot at school. Klebold assessed the damage and told the girl it was no big deal. *"Harris then got out of the passenger side of Klebold's car and was angry. Klebold ordered Harris to get back in the car, which he did."*[450] While it appears to be a rare opinion, a friend and student who participated in various video projects with Eric and Dylan felt that— of the two— Dylan was more dominant.[56]

It has also been suggested that Harris did the vast majority of the planning for the attack on Columbine and that Klebold only began participating a short time before the massacre. This idea comes, in part, from a comment that Dylan made in his private journal on January 20, 1999. At that time he wrote, *"I hate this non-thinking stasis. Im stuck in humanity. Maybe going 'NBK' (gawd) w. eric is the way to break free. i hate this."*[451] If a point is to be made of Klebold's uncertainty in the months leading up to the assault, however, then the doubts expressed by Harris should be given similar weight. On November 17, 1998, Eric wrote: *"If people would give me more compliments all of this might still be avoidable... but probably not"* and *"you know what maybe I just need to get laid. maybe thatll just change some shit around."*[401]

There is ample evidence to illustrate Eric's extensive preparation, which he outlined in his personal journals and day planner. Dylan's actions, however, show he also spent a large amount of time and monetary resources in planning for "NBK". A search warrant of the Klebold residence executed on the day of the attack yielded six pipe bombs, a box of shotgun shells, a metal hollow tube that police believed was intended to be a silencer, *"a blue suitcase which had numerous items attached inside, and appeared as if it was being prepared to be used as an explosive device of some sort,"*[452] a piece of paper with hand signals the two boys would use to communicate with one another,[452,453] a glass jar containing a black-colored powder, and a metal pipe.[452] Police also seized a hit list,[454,455] plans for the creation of nicotine poison,[456] and a list of supplies he still needed to acquire (*finger armor, leather duster, Uzi 9 m, DB, 2 calicos, new sunglasses, flask*),[457] all of which were written months before the assault. Klebold also gave a friend $80 to purchase fireworks for him in the summer of 1998.[458] Eric and Dylan used the powder from the fireworks to make their bombs. Several of the Harrises' neighbors told investigators that Dylan spent a great deal of his time at Eric's house[459] where similar items were found.[460] Dylan's parents reported that Eric spent the night at their home in the week before the attack, but prior to that had not visited the house in about six months.[443] It is possible, and even likely, that at least some of the bomb-making and assault plans were devised by both boys at the Harrises' home over the previous year, particularly since they filmed the majority of the "Basement Tapes" at that location.[345]

Other evidence of Klebold's active participation throughout the preparation stage include his purchase of a shotgun and shells at the gun show he attended with Harris and Robyn Anderson in late November 1998,[409,461] as well as his arrangement of the meeting with Mark Manes on January 23, 1999 to buy the TEC-DC9 he would use during the rampage.[462,463,464] The abundance of evidence indicates that Dylan did not just "get on board" with the attack in the weeks immediately preceding it. He made a conscious effort to save the money he earned to purchase weapons and ammunition, actively participated in the design and construction of explosive devices, was involved in planning the details of the assault, and practiced target shooting to learn how to handle his guns and perfect his aim. In some ways it would appear that for both boys, despite a year of detailed planning, "NBK" was more of a fantasy than reality during a good portion of that time.

It has been hypothesized that Eric Harris, concerned that Dylan was not fully on board with the attack, devised the idea for the diversionary bombs—not only to keep the police occupied and away from the school, but also to rope Klebold further into the plan. According to the theory, Dylan would view the decoy bombs as harmless, but once the boys had planted them Klebold would be fully committed to the crime and unable to back out. The evidence in no way supports this presumption, however. Prior to the attack on Columbine, Eric and Dylan placed two backpacks containing pipe bombs, fireworks, aerosol cans, propane cylinders, and ignitable liquid[465] by the greenbelt at the northwest corner of a property on W. Elmhurst Drive against a privacy fence.[466] Two surveyors working in that area on the morning of April 20, 1999 came upon the packs and had to move them from the spot in order to access the corner of the fence to locate the survey pin. The surveyor who physically moved the packs a few feet from their original position just minutes before they exploded noted that the smaller of the two had *"what appeared to be a Walkman in an open pocket."*[466] His co-worker also noted the open pocket but could not see inside the backpack from his vantage point.[467] According to police and the property owner, the location where the backpacks were placed saw heavy foot traffic.[468,469] Harris and Klebold likely would have known that this area was well-traveled by pedestrians because it was just two minutes from Eric's current home and three minutes from his previous one. As such, both boys would have realized the strong possibility that a passerby might be injured by the blasts. In fact, they discussed this very issue on March 18, 1999 on one of the "Basement Tapes." It was Dylan Klebold who suggested the *"trail by Wadsworth, 'by your old house.' According to the in-house computer Eric Harris previously lived at* [redacted] *South Teller Court. They then begin discussing that they should 'rig something up with a trip bomb between two trees, so when someone goes down the path it will go off.' Klebold and Harris then discuss the possibility of placing 'time bombs down there.' They then discuss it would be 'harder and take more resources.' Harris and Klebold then say 'This will add a few frags to the list,' and that the 'fucking fire department is going to be busy for a month.'"*[470] The term "frag" is used in video gaming and refers to killing someone with a grenade or other explosive device. With these statements then, it might even be argued that the open pocket and readily visible Walkman observed by the surveyor were intended as a lure to attract the attention of someone looking to steal from the packs, thereby increasing the likelihood of at least one casualty from the ensuing explosion. Classmates from Columbine told investigators that they had seen Eric Harris and a taller individual, possibly Dylan Klebold, on the walkway coming from the greenbelt area the day before the attack. One of the boys jokingly asked Harris if they had just come from killing someone, to which Eric replied: *"'Yeah, so don't go back there for a couple of days.'"*[471] It is not known whether the bombs were planted at that time or not. The police believe they were actually placed there the following day because the concrete pathway was so heavily traveled that backpacks would have been discovered rather quickly.[468] Dylan and Eric may have been evaluating the area the day before the attack in order to determine the optimal place to put the bombs. Klebold was actively involved in the planning and placement of these diversionary bombs. His statements on the "Basement Tapes" indicate that not only was he aware that someone could potentially be injured by the explosions, but that he was hoping that would be the case. As such, the theory that these bombs were used by Eric to make sure a reticent Dylan went along with the massacre does not hold up to scrutiny.

It is now common knowledge that the attack on Columbine was not intended to be a shooting. Harris and Klebold had built large bombs that they placed inside the cafeteria/Commons area that were timed to go off at the busiest hour of the day in order to maximize casualties. The boys planned to lie in wait outside of the school during the initial part of the assault and shoot individuals outside or exiting the building. It has been speculated that, based on where Eric and Dylan parked their cars, they intended to flank the school. With Klebold in the west side seniors' parking lot and Eric in the east side juniors' lot, it was thought that one boy was supposed to cover the west entrance doors and the other would cover the east. We know that when the shooting began, both Harris and Klebold were standing outside the west entrance at the top of the stairs. This has led some to hypothesize that Eric—realizing the bombs were not going to detonate and trying to salvage the plan and his panicking partner—gathered up his gear, ran over from the juniors' lot to collect Dylan from his position, and brought him to the upper west entrance in yet another demonstration of Harris's cold and calculating demeanor. Eyewitness accounts and a to-do list left by Klebold, however, suggest that the upper west entrance was likely where they both intended to wait out the explosions. Dylan penned two itineraries for the day of the attack: one in Eric's planner and a second in his own journal. The latter read, in part:

Park cars, set car bombs for 11:18
Get out, go to outside hill, wait.
When first bombs go off, attack.[413]

The list indicates that the boys planned to be at the upper west entrance at the start of the slaughter. Moreover, had they stayed by their cars, Harris and Klebold would have been blown up when the car bombs detonated at 11:18. Even if the car bombs failed, they would have quickly been completely surrounded and captured or killed once law enforcement arrived on scene. In addition, several students saw Eric at the top of the hill, alone outside the west entrance before Dylan joined him. One boy told police that when he exited the upper level west doors, he saw *"Harris was standing near a tree perhaps 20 to 30 feet from the west doors* [he] *had exited from. He stated that Harris was standing in front of the tree looking over the senior parking lot. Harris was wearing a black trench coat and sunglasses. He may have been wearing a black baseball cap."*[472] The boy also relayed that *"Harris was putting on a pair of black bicycle gloves which did not have fingertips.* [He] *saw Harris put a small grayish-colored duffle bag on the grass. He stated that the bag appeared heavy and when it hit the ground it had a metal sound. Harris placed the grayish bag by his feet and slightly behind him.* [He] *stated there was no one around when he walked out of the school except for Harris. He never saw Klebold."*[472] Eric was, indeed, wearing *"a black glove on the right hand with the fingers cut away"*[186] as evidenced by his autopsy report and the death photos of Harris and Klebold available online. Dylan wore the corresponding glove on his left hand.[206] A female student saw Harris alone in the same location shortly before the shooting began. She told police that *"she saw Eric Harris standing at the top of the stairs to the right side of the sidewalk. She stated he was standing on the grass, not on the sidewalk.* [She] *stated Harris was looking down the stairs and was standing by himself."*[473] The girl also described *"a backpack, possibly black, sitting on the ground near his feet."*[473] One of the girls who did not respond to Harris's hints for a date confirmed he was alone outside the upper west entrance before the attack. She explained to investigators that she saw Eric *"at the top of the stairs, near the library"*[379] and that he was *"looking over the parking lot at everyone in the area."*[379] The girl *"did not see anyone even near Eric at this time."*[379] Yet another student advised that as she left the school after class, *"she observed Eric Harris and Dylan Klebold standing next to the fence and grass at the top of the stairway which leads down from the upper level to the cafeteria and seniors' parking lot."*[474] The citing was confirmed by a friend who accompanied her.[142] Shortly thereafter, dozens of witnesses (see Chapter Nine and Appendix A) would identify both Harris and Klebold in that spot. Since Eric was seen alone in this location with his duffel bag, it seems likely that the boys did not arrive in this area through Harris's quick re-strategizing when the cafeteria bombs failed to detonate. Instead, the upper west entrance was probably the intended starting location for the attack.

Those theorizing that Dylan was not as enthusiastic about the massacre as Eric also point to the number of times each of the boys fired their weapons. When the attack began, two students told police that Harris was shooting at kids and Klebold appeared to be running over to assess the damage. The male student told investigators *"the first male in the white shirt would fire the rifle, and then the male in the trench coat would take three to four steps down the stairs, look at the victims, and then run back up to the person with the rifle. He stated at that time he would see the person with the rifle fire two to three more shots, and then the male in the trench coat would go back down, look at the victim, and then come back up."*[475] Both a male and female student confirmed these actions and the female told police that at that point she did not see Dylan firing his weapon.[476] During their investigation, the Jefferson County Sheriff's Department found evidence that Klebold fired only two times with his shotgun and three times with his TEC-DC9 while the boys were outside the school. Both Eric and Dylan were observed firing at people on the soccer field,[477,478,479,480,481] so it is unknown why more ballistics evidence was not found from Klebold's guns. The dearth of casings found is also contradictory to the testimony of several witnesses who saw Klebold shooting his TEC-DC9 repeatedly outside the school. For instance, a male student observed Dylan shooting and reloading his TEC-DC9, which suggests that he fired it more than the reported three times. The boy *"stated he observed suspect #2 unzip and take out a gun, described as a short gun, believed to be a fully automatic gun because of how fast the gun was firing. [He] stated he observed suspect #2 shooting towards the west doors and reloading a large magazine approximately 12 inches in length.*"[482] A teacher watching from the library window described Klebold shooting a 9 mm. He stated that "*Dylan began to fire rounds out of a 9 mm assault type of rifle. It was silver/brown in color and approximately 12 inches long. Dylan ejected a clip and put in another one. He fired in the area. Dylan was outside on the corner of the building, firing north west. (Please refer to diagrams 1, 2 & 3 drawn by* [name redacted]*). As the clip was ejected with Dylan's right hand, he reached down and inserted another clip. The gun was being held in Dylan's left hand.*"[483] The teacher mistakenly used the term "clip" instead of "detachable magazine", the latter of which is used with a TEC-DC9. The minimum number of rounds held in a TEC-DC9 detachable magazine is ten,[484] which suggests that Dylan fired at least this number of times while outside. Two other outside witnesses who also saw a gunman fitting Dylan's description, although could not identify him by name, said that he was "*spraying bullets everywhere*"[485] and that he not only shot at the double doors and the cafeteria windows, but that he also fired upon two different groups of students with a gun holding a "*banana clip,*"[486]—which is another misnomer for the detachable magazine. One of these witnesses also saw this suspect reloading his gun. These observations were reiterated by a female student who saw "*the taller of the two suspects fire several rapid rounds in an easterly direction (towards the building)*"[487] and by one of the wounded who saw both gunmen firing their weapons towards the doors.[488] Another girl told police that she saw Dylan with what she described as a rifle, which may have been his shotgun. She stated that she saw him load it *"three or four times."*[489] She also saw both boys shooting at the glass doors of the school. It is not unusual for eyewitness accounts, particularly in traumatic situations, to be incomplete or inaccurate. However, with multiple people reporting the same actions by Klebold, it is difficult to reconcile the lack of forensic evidence with these testimonies.

Klebold severely injured two boys outside, leaving one partially paralyzed[16] while shooting the other at point blank range in the face after the boy asked him for help.[490,491,492,493] Such brutality would seem to negate any belief that Dylan had doubts about his involvement. In addition to Harris's victims, two other students were seriously injured during the attack outside. The absence of bullets or fragments, however, made it impossible to determine which of the two shooters were responsible for their injuries. At least one witness, including a boy who was with the victims, reported that both gunmen were firing in their direction.[494] One of the injured boys gave conflicting accounts regarding his assailant. In his statements to investigators on April 28 and May 11, 1999, the young man told police that he did not know who shot him.[495] When recalling the event, he relayed *"seeing an unknown male wearing a 'black trench coat and red beret' firing an unknown weapon at his direction."*[495] The description is more consistent with Klebold, because by this time in the incident Eric Harris had removed his trench coat. In addition, Dylan was wearing a baseball hat backwards with the Boston Red Sox symbol of the letter "B" in red with a white outline appearing on the back side of the cap. According to the Governor's Columbine Review Commission report, however, this same boy informed an officer at the scene that he was shot by *"Ned Harris."*[496] The Jeffco deputy who reported this conversation stated that the boy *"said he thought the kid's name was Eric Harris, but he wasn't sure."*[497] The injured student relayed that he thought that he might have passed out at some point and that he had difficulty remembering much of what happened after he was able to hide himself behind a storage shed. The boy did state that while hiding, two other male students found him behind the shed and helped him until police arrived. Both of those assisting had survived their own turmoil in the school's library. One of the boys, in particular, was injured by debris after Harris shot at him and had a confrontation with Klebold right before the two gunmen left the library.[119] It is unknown whether these students told the injured boy that Eric and Dylan were the shooters while they were providing him aid. To further complicate matters, other witnesses—including two students who were with the victims—told police that it was Klebold who fired upon the group, which included the two gravely injured students.[486,492,498,499,500] The two friends closest to the injured boys also made statements implicating Dylan as responsible for two casualties that the police have attributed to Harris. With the number of conflicting testimonies and without ballistics evidence, it is difficult to determine what took place when the two students were hurt with any high degree of certainty.

Once inside, investigators found that Klebold's firing rate was nearly equal to that of Harris. Despite shell casings and bullet fragments indicating that Dylan fired his gun half as often as Eric during the rampage, he caused an enormous amount of destruction. Of the nineteen survivors who sustained penetrating gunshot wounds, Klebold was proven to be responsible for injuring ten. Witness testimonies suggest that he may have wounded three additional students for which no ballistics evidence was found.[486,498,499,500,501,502] Dylan murdered three students alone[503,504] and, with Harris, inflicted fatal injuries upon two others.[503] A girl lying beside one of the latter two victims reported that she watched the murdered boy pass away immediately after Dylan shot him in the head.[505]

Klebold's lack of participation in Harris's gunfight with the School Resource Officer (SRO) has also been used to suggest that Dylan had reservations about the attack. The evidence, however, indicates that Klebold was inside the school at the time that the SRO initially engaged Harris, so it is possible Dylan might not have been aware of law enforcement's presence at that time. According to the SRO, prior to exiting his vehicle he radioed for assistance from his dispatch and *"pointed out at the time he made the above radio transmission, he heard another explosion coming from inside the school. Deputy* [name redacted] *stated he believed the explosion was coming from a 'deeper' location inside the school. At almost the same time, Deputy* [name redacted] *stated he then observed a suspect come to the double doors located at the southwest entrance/exit of the high school. According to Deputy* [name redacted], *the suspect then stepped outside the doors approximately two feet.*"[506] At no time during this exchange did the SRO observe Dylan Klebold outside the school building. Dylan's absence was confirmed by one of Columbine's Campus Supervisors (CS) who was near the SRO's vehicle at the time of the gun battle. They only saw Eric Harris *"come out of the west doors upper level."*[507] The CS was familiar with Dylan prior to the assault and told authorities that he did not see Klebold outside at that time.[507,508] The SRO heard an explosion deeper within the building as Harris was stepping outside the doors,[506,509] which would seem to indicate that Klebold may have been responsible for the blast and was not in the immediate vicinity when Eric exchanged fire with the SRO. Furthermore, a 39 minute 7 second recording between a Jefferson County dispatcher and Officer John Lietz of the Denver Police Department suggests that Dylan was in the cafeteria/Commons area at the time Eric engaged the deputy. A student, whose father was a DPD officer, tried to reach his dad to apprise him of the situation at the school. He had to leave a message on his father's pager; the time stamp on the message was 11:23 am.[510] The boy then quickly gathered some other students to hide in the food prep area with him and he *"stated as he was closing the door he saw an object being thrown into the cafeteria area, near where table S sits. A few seconds later there was an explosion in the same area. He stated there was a flash then a loud bang. He stated the door was not quite closed at that point and he saw a gunman come into the*

141

cafeteria. He described the gunman as wearing a long black coat and he had long shoulder length hair. The gunman was carrying a twelve-gauge shotgun at his side."[510] He identified the suspect as Dylan Klebold.[510] After failing to get through to his father and 911, the student called DPD again and was connected to Officer Lietz. Lietz set up a relay between himself, the boy, and Jefferson County Dispatch. Forty-one seconds into the conversation, Officer Lietz reported that a gunman was in the southwest corner of the Commons area.[511] Upon hearing the suspect's location, the dispatcher surmised that this gunman was the one currently firing upon the School Resource Officer.[511] The gun battle between Harris and the SRO began at approximately 11:24 am.[512] The SRO's gunman, however, had exited out of the upper level of the school near the library entrance. The library is located directly above the Commons area. Lietz's suspect could be heard in the lower level inside the cafeteria at the same moment Eric was exchanging fire with the SRO. As such, the explosion that the SRO heard as Eric stepped outside was likely the device that the policeman's son observed Dylan throw as he entered the cafeteria. Dylan did not participate in the gun battle with the SRO because he was downstairs in the Commons area when it occurred.

In the School Resource Officer's testimony, he relayed that after several minutes the same suspect re-appeared just inside the doorway and, using the lower metal half of the door for cover, began firing out the broken window upon him and Jeffco's

Deputy Smoker who had arrived on the scene.[506] The officers were afforded only a brief glimpse of Harris at that point because he remained inside the school, hunkered down behind a door. It is unclear where Klebold was during this second altercation, but the deputies who exchanged gunfire with Harris did not observe Dylan during that time either.[506,513]

Eyewitness accounts of Dylan's behavior during the assault also belie the assertion that Klebold was an unwilling or reluctant participant in the slaughter. No one who saw Dylan Klebold on April 20, 1999 felt that he was just going along with Harris's plan to destroy the school and its occupants. By all accounts, Dylan appeared to be enjoying the carnage he and Eric were creating. Several witnesses reported to police that both Klebold and Harris were laughing throughout the attack and exclaiming about how much fun they were having.[514,515,516,517,518] Dylan showed no signs of remorse and was described by various people as having a smirk on his face,[519,520] smiling,[516] laughing,[517,518,521] and that he seemed "*nonchalant about what he was doing.*"[522] His indifference was evident in the exchange observed between himself and the friend he allowed to escape from the library. When the friend, who was hiding under a library table, asked Dylan what he was doing, Klebold "*responded by shrugging his shoulders and replying, 'Oh, just killing people.'*"[523,524] A boy who was shot by Dylan told police that "*Klebold looked directly at him and smiled. Klebold then lifted up the sawed off shotgun he had in his hand and shot directly at [the boy's] table.*"[525] The victim, a member of the wrestling team, was wearing a white ball cap that day. According to witness statements, Dylan seemed to relish his role of selecting who would live and who would die. When he encountered another student athlete behind the library's circulation desk, Klebold first asked the boy if he was a jock. After the teen wisely replied in the negative, Dylan said: *"Well, that's good, we don't like jocks."*[526] The student told police that *"Dylan Klebold looked him straight in the eyes and stated, 'Give me one good reason why I shouldn't kill you.'"*[526] After a brief altercation, during which Dylan held a shotgun to the boy's head,[119,526] Klebold looked away and told Harris: *"I'm gonna' let this fat fuck live, you can have at him if you want to."*[526]

There are several witness accounts that suggest that while Klebold seemed to participate willingly, he did take direction from Harris during the attack. Prior to their entry into the library, one of the wounded victims *"remembers hearing one of the gunmen say to the other one, 'Are you still with me?' and 'We're still gonna do this, right?'"*[527] She did not specify, and may not have known, which of the two shooters asked these questions. The boys entered the library shortly after Harris fired upon the deputy. It is unknown whether Klebold made the inquiry because he did not know why Harris had been delayed in following him into the school, or if Eric sensed hesitation in Dylan and asked the question of him. According to eyewitnesses, Klebold entered the library a few steps ahead of Harris.[122,125,128] A female student stated that while in the library, Eric seemed to be doing most of the talking and that *"Klebold would follow Harris as*

Harris would move."[520] A male student who was shot by Klebold reiterated this statement. He told investigators that it appeared to him that Harris "*was in charge of what was going on*"[525] and that "*the shorter suspect took the lead, and the taller suspect would follow him.*"[525] A girl who witnessed interactions between the two in the cafeteria said that not only was Eric ordering Dylan what to do, but that she also "*felt Klebold was doing things to try and impress Harris.*"[528] Another cafeteria witness "*advised that she heard Eric tell Dylan, 'Shoot over there.'*"[529] This observation was echoed by a third girl who heard Harris direct Klebold to shoot from one corner of the cafeteria, then cross over and shoot from the other corner.[530] There were a few witnesses to the attack who felt that the boys' actions were coordinated, with one student telling police that "*the two gunmen stuck very close together as if protecting each other's back*"[119] and another boy relaying that he heard Dylan and Eric shouting orders to each other "*such as 'go to that side' and 'check the kitchen.'*"[531] A girl in the library remembered that at least twice she heard the gunmen say "*cover me*" to one another.[532]

While it is likely impossible for us to understand the reasons for the horrific attack on Columbine High School, it is vital that we comb through all the available facts in order to obtain the clearest picture we can of Harris and Klebold. Considering some of the evidence while ignoring other parts of it or, worse, assuming we know about events that did not actually transpire, will bring us no closer to the answers we all seek. Dylan was depressed, he was shy, and he tended to follow along with what Eric and his other friends wanted him to do. But his writings and his actions over the last year and a half of his life indicate that he could envision himself perpetrating this terrible crime. Both boys expressed doubts about whether they would actually go through with it, but despite their doubts they both continued to painstakingly work on the details of their deadly rampage. In some ways it may have seemed surreal, even to them, as both Dylan and Eric commented in their private journals and on the "Basement Tapes." Harris may have been more fully committed, and he may have committed earlier. Once they obtained their guns in late November he viewed it as "*the point of no return.*"[409] Thoughts, feelings, and actions have been attributed to Klebold on that day that no one can reasonably assume based on evidence and eyewitness testimony. Dylan did not appear nervous, ambivalent, or conflicted. To those who witnessed the carnage, Dylan seemed at various times angry, nonchalant, and—worst of all—happy. It does not benefit the understanding of this tragedy to create a scenario of events that is not supported by the wealth of information collected during the investigation of the crime. It does not help parents, teachers, or school administrators to identify potentially at-risk students by comparing them to this simplified version of Dylan Klebold as the hapless, depressed follower when it does not represent the true complexities of his thoughts and feelings in the time leading up to and during the attack. We have to examine all that we have learned about Dylan from his family, his friends, his personal writings, and his behavior in the eighteen months before the shootings. Only then can we hope to recognize signs of trouble in other young men and women.

Chapter Eight

Foreshadowing

The attack on Columbine High School not only shocked the community of Littleton, Colorado, but the country as a whole. School shootings were, sadly, on the rise in America. Few could have imagined, however, the wholesale destruction Eric Harris and Dylan Klebold brought upon Columbine. Not many could conceive of kids that age quietly harboring such deep-seated hatred and rage. Looking back now, we all know that there were warning signs. In addition to Harris's conflicts with the Brown family and the boys' arrest for the van break-in, they both dropped other hints in the year before the massacre. Some were big, some more subtle, but none raised enough of an alarm to alter the course of events.

After the assault, many came forward to tell police that they had heard both Harris and Klebold make reference to killing people and bombing the school. In fact, the sheer number of individuals who had heard such comments from the killers is nothing short of disturbing. Eric and Dylan did not try to hide their hatred and had no shame in speaking frankly about it. Since they couched their vitriol in casual conversation and jokes, however, no one really took them seriously. In essence, it was an open secret. Close friends, acquaintances, and people they barely knew all told police variations of the same theme. Eighteen individuals reported similar threats by Harris and Klebold:

"Eric always said that he was going to 'blow his school up and make kid's sorry. "[533]

"she had overheard Harris and Klebold, and other members of the individuals known to be Trench Coat Mafia, talking about blowing up the school after they graduated. She never took these statements seriously, and thought it was just talk to try and impress each other."[534]

Harris wrote in someone's yearbook: *"natural selection needs a boost, like me with a shotgun."*[535]

"stated he did remember Eric Harris asking him at one time to buy him a .44 mag pistol sometime in 1998."[536]

Harris had *"talked about blowing up the King Sooper's store and had a thing about talking about guns."*[441]

Harris *"had joked about blowing up the school, but [the boy] stated that he did not take him serious."*[537] The same boy also said that Harris and Klebold *"talked about how it would be fun as a senior prank to ride through the school on a dirt bikes with guns and shoot it up."*[537]

A friend told police that he had knowledge of Harris and Klebold making pipe bombs, was aware that Klebold had bought a shotgun, and *"that Eric Harris had come to him and expressed an interest in making napalm."*[538]

"sometimes they would get together with the group and talk about tactically how to blow up a room. She stated they did it more in a jokingly manner. They even talked about how you would go about killing someone if you wanted. Again, she stated that it was all in a jokingly manner."[539]

"both Eric and Dylan were talking about the 'Jocks' and said they wished that they (Jocks) were all dead. That he thought that Eric and Dylan were joking and he just blew it off and did not take them seriously."[540]

"they would say something like, 'I'm going to get back at that guy,' or 'I'm going to kill him,' but that this was always said in a joking manner. The

subject further stated that they would also say things such as they were going to burn the school to the ground or blow it up but according to the subject, half the students said something like this, with it also being said in a joking manner."[541]

"She stated that around October of 1998, they had made what she deemed to be an idle threat that they should 'blow up' Columbine High School."[212] The same girl stated that *"both Harris and Klebold often talked about wanting to blow up Columbine High School and kill the jocks. She said that they talked about it for about a year prior to her leaving the store, but she never took them seriously."*[277]

A friend told police that both boys had been making bombs for a while and had read the *Anarchist's Cookbook* and things about Hitler. He also relayed that *"Harris was saying, 'Wouldn't it be fun to kill all the jocks?'* [He] *did not think Harris was serious, but Harris continued with comments about blowing up the school. Harris said they could put bombs on the school's generators and that should blow up the school."*[542]

"stated that he knew about Eric and Dylan talking about blowing up the school, because it was the big rumor for two years. I asked [him] *if any school officials knew about the threats and he stated he had heard they did, but no one took it seriously."*[99]

"they talked a lot about guns and bombs and killing people. She stated they weren't specific about what

their targets would be, but that they were 'obsessed' with it."[543]

Eric Harris talked about bombs and *"Harris asked him if he was 18. When he said yes, Harris replied, 'Then you can buy me a gun.'"*[544]

About a year before the attack, Harris asked a co-worker at Blackjack Pizza *"if he could buy 'us a gun.' [He] took 'us' to mean Harris, Klebold, and [name redacted]."*[545] Both Eric and Dylan told this boy repeatedly about their hate for jocks.

"had last seen them about 3 months ago and that during that visit Eric had spoken about bombing a school but she didn't believe he was serious."[546]

"while Eric Harris and Dylan Klebold were in his philosophy class, Eric Harris and Dylan Klebold would tell the class how they had dreams about killing people and about shooting people."[170]

Unfortunately, no one took the boys seriously, believing it was just a way for them to act tough or blow off steam. Perhaps it is a testament to their charm that Eric and Dylan could tell so many people and yet have no one suspect them of actually going through with it. Perhaps, and just as alarming, this kind of talk was so common amongst their peer group that it did not rouse any suspicions.

In addition to alluding to their plans in conversation with others, both Eric and Dylan revealed some of their thoughts through their class assignments. The most glaring examples of this were Harris's "Trench Coat Mafia Hit-Men For Hire" video, which depicted them hunting down, threatening, and murdering jocks,[65,66,67,68] as well as Klebold's violent essay of a killer targeting a group of preps.

The town, even at 1:00 AM, was still bustling with activity as the man dressed in black walked down the empty streets. The moon was barely visible, hiding under a shield of clouds, adding a chill to the atmosphere. What was most recognized about the man was the sound of his footsteps. Behind the conversations & noises of the town, not a sound was to be heard from him, except the dark, monotonous footsteps, combined with the jingling of his belt chains striking not only the two visible guns, in their holsters, but the large bowie knife, slung in anticipation of use. The wide-brimmed hat cast a pitch-black shadow of his already dimly lit face. He wore black gloves, with a type of metal spiked-band across the knuckles. A black overcoat covered most of his body, small lines of metal & half-inch spokes layering upper portions of the shoulders, arms, and back. His boots were newly polished, and didn't look like they had been used much. He carried a black duffel bag in his right hand. He apparently had parked a car nearby, & looked ready for a small war with whoever came across his way. I have never seen anyone take this mad-max approach in the city, especially since the piggies had been called to this part of town for a series of crimes lately. Yet, in the midst of the nightlife in the center of the average-sized town, this man walked, fueled by some untold purpose, what Christians would call evil. The guns slung on his belt & belly appeared to be automatic hand guns, which were draped above rows of magazines & clips. He smoked a thin cigar, and a sweet clovesque scent eminated from his aura. He stood about six feet and four inches and was strongly built. His face was entirely in shadow, yet even though I was unable to see his expressions, I could feel his anger, cutting thru the air like a razor. He seemed to know where he was walking, and he noticed my presence, but paid no attention as he kept walking toward a popular bar: The Watering Hole. He stopped about 30 feet from the door, and waited. 'For whom?' I wondered, as I saw them step out. He must have known their habits well, as they appeared less than a minute after he stopped walking. A group of college-preps, about nine of them, stopped in their tracks. A couple of them were mildly drunk, the rest sober. They stopped, and stared. The streetlights illuminating the bar & the sidewalk showed me a clear view of their stare, full of paralysis & fear. They knew who he was, & why he was there. The second-largest spoke up, 'What're you doin man... why are you here...?' The man in black said nothing, but even at my distance, I could feel his anger growing. 'You still wanted a fight, huh? I meant not with weapons, I just meant a fist fight... c'mon put the guns away, fuckin pussy!' said the largest prep, his voice quavering as he spoke these words of attempted courage. Other preps could be heard muttering in the background: 'Nice trench coat dude, that's pretty cool there...' ... 'Dude we were jus messin around the other day chill out man...' ... 'I didn't do anything, it was all them!'... 'c'mon man you wouldn't shoot us, were in the middle of a public place...' Yet, the comment I remember the most was uttered from the smallest of the group, obviously a cocky, power hungry prick. 'Go ahead man! Shoot me! I want you to shoot me! Heheh you wont!! Goddam pussy...' It was faint at first, but grew in intensity and power as I heard the man laugh. This laugh would have made Satan cringe in Hell for almost half a minute this laugh, spawned from the most powerful place conceivable, filled the air, and thru the entire town, the entire world. The town activity came to a stop, and all attention was now drawn to this man. One of the preps began to slowly move back. Before I could see a reaction from the preps, the man had dropped his duffel bag, and pulled out one of the pistols with his left hand. Three shots were fired. Three shots hit the largest prep in the head. The shining of the streetlights caused a visible reflection off of the droplets of blood as they flew away from the skull. The blood splatters showered the preps buddies, as they were to paralyzed to run. The next four preps were not executed so systematically, but with more rage from the man's hand cannon than a controlled duty for a soldier. The man unloaded one of the pistols across the front of these four innocents, their instantly lifeless bodies dropping with remarkable speed. The shots from that gun were felt just as much as they were heard. He pulled out his other pistol, and without changing a glance, without moving his death-stare from the four other victims to go, aimed the weapon out to the side, and shot about 8 rounds. These bullets mowed down what, after he was dead, I made out to be an undercover cop with his gun slung. He then emptied the clip into two more of the preps. Then, instead of reloading & finishing the task, he set down the guns, and pulled out the knife. The blade loomed huge, even in his large grip. I now noticed that one of two still alive was the smallest of the band, who had now wet his pants, and was hyperventilating in fear. The other one tried to lunge at the man, hoping that his football tackling skills would save his life. The man sidestepped, and made two lunging slashes at him. I saw a small trickle of blood cascade out of his belly and splashing onto the concrete. His head wound was almost as bad, as the shadow formed by the bar's lighting showed blood dripping off his face. The last one, the smallest one, tried to run. The man quickly reloaded, and shot him thru the lower leg. He instantly fell, and cried in pain. The man then pulled out of the duffel bag what looked to be some type of electronic device. I saw him tweak the dials, and press a button. I heard a faint, yet powerful explosion, I would have to guess about 6 miles away. Then another one occurred closer. After recalling the night many times, I finally understood that these were diversions, to attract the cops. The last prep was bawling & trying to crawl away. The man walked up behind him. I remember the sound of the impact well. The man came down with his left hand, right on the prep's head. The metal piece did its work, as I saw his hand get buried about 2 inches into the guy's skull. The man pulled his arm out, and stood, unmoving, for about a minute. The town was utterly still, except for the faint wail of police sirens. The man picked up the bag and his clips, and proceeded to walk back the way he came. I was still, as he came my way again. He stopped, and gave me a look I will never forget. If I could face an emotion of god, it would have looked like the man. I not only saw in his face, but also felt eminating from him: power, complacence, closure, and godliness. The man smiled, and in that instant, thru no endeavor of my own, I understood his actions.[547]

With the benefit of hindsight, it is painfully clear that there are strong similarities between Dylan's story and the destruction he and Eric wrought upon Columbine. The diversionary bomb, the weaponry, the black duffel bag, the prep targets, and the killer's dress were all borrowed from their plan. Some have suggested that Dylan modeled the gunman after the "psychopath" Eric, due to the main character's apparent detachment from his victims. However, Klebold's description of a left-handed killer who *"stood about six feet and four inches and was strongly built"*[547] could just as easily have been a reflection of the way Dylan would have liked to envision himself: powerful, strong, and "godlike". His journal entries were those of a young man who felt he had no control over his life or the things that happened to him. Perhaps in his stories he could give the characters the power he wanted for himself.

The essay unnerved Dylan's teacher so much that she wrote: *"I'd like to talk to you about your story before I give you a grade. You are an excellent writer/storyteller, but I have some problems with this one."*[547] In a statement to police, the teacher explained: *"Dylan wrote the most viscious story I have ever read.*

It concerned a man walking into a town and 'blowing away' all the popular kids. I told Dylan the story was violent and unacceptable-viscious. Indeed, I made a copy for his counselor [name redacted]. *I also talked it over with his parents. Dylan simply remarked, 'It's just a story.'*"[548] According to the teacher, "*she spoke to Klebold's parents at length about him handing in a disturbing story.* [She] *stated that they did not seem worried and made a comment about trying to understand kids today.*"[549] In an article written for *O Magazine*, Klebold's mother relayed that neither she nor her husband actually saw the essay until six months after the attack. "*Although it had alarmed his English teacher enough to bring it to our attention, when we asked to see the paper at a parent-teacher conference, she didn't have it with her. Nor did she describe the contents beyond calling them 'disturbing'.*"[550] The teacher told the Klebolds that she would pass the essay along to Dylan's guidance counselor and "*if he thought it was a problem, one of them would contact me. I never heard from them.*"[550] The police statement from Klebold's counselor makes no mention of the paper, so his accounting of the event or of his conversation, if any, with Dylan is unknown.[551]

In a journal from Dylan's creative writing class, another unsettling piece of prose was found. Penned from the point of view of a gun, Dylan identified the weapon as a god designed for killing people. "*I was never made for hunting, just to kill humans. When someone needs to die, I kill them. There was this bald guy once. He was gay & arrogant &*

superficial & had a false sense of power. I blew off half his head with 1 shot. I am god. he died."[552] It is unclear if he ever submitted this piece for a grade.

Harris's class journal often held dark themes as well. He, too, wrote from the gun's perspective, but his composition consisted of only one sentence: *"Im gonna spit a hell of a lot of buckshot out my barrel into this pansy's face."*[553] Harris's work also made subtle references to his hatred and attack plans, but nothing that would have raised any alarms. In an assignment in the fall of 1998, Eric had to list 25 things that made him different. Included in his list were: the bullet hanging from his rear-view mirror, his personal views of other people and his first impressions of them, his knowledge of fireworks and of *"conventional/amateur explosives,"*[554] his anger management problems, his bullet shell collection, and his black box and its contents.[554] Harris does not elaborate that the black box held his bomb-making materials.

A few other incidents may have also been the work of Eric and Dylan, however, there is no definitive proof that they were involved. One of these concerned the defacement of several prom posters. The Columbine High School Junior/Senior Prom and After Prom Party were scheduled for April 17, 1999. In promotion of the event, the Student Senate put up yellow flyers around the school reading simply: *"It's coming… 4/17/99."* At some point, in the weeks before the attack, someone changed the date on these flyers to read "4/20/99".[555,556,557,558,559,560] It is unknown whether this was done by Harris and Klebold as a prelude to "NBK", or if another student wrote in the new date—

April 20—in reference to the informal National Pot Smoking Day.

Equally prophetic was a message etched into a park picnic table. The day before the attack, a woman noticed two individuals carving something into the table. Following the shootings, she returned to the area and observed the words: Doom, Revenge + Terrorism, Wrath, V, as well as the date April 19, 1999 scratched into the table surface.[561,562] During the assault, Dylan wore a T-shirt with the word "Wrath" printed in red across his chest.[206] His nickname was Vodka and he often signed his notes and writings with the letter "V". After seeing their pictures on television, the woman believed that Harris and Klebold were the boys she observed carving the table.

Eric and Dylan left behind several clues to their plans. Unfortunately, none would be recognized until after the attack. Given their keen interest in video production and their belief that they should be the subject of movies and books, it is possible—even likely—that the boys left these clues intentionally. In his journal, Harris wrote: "*I wonder if anyone will wright a book on me. sure is a ton of symbolism, double meanings, themes, appearance vs reality shit going on here.*"[563] Though skilled at harboring their true feelings and murderous intent, Harris and Klebold did provide hints to what they were planning. Tragically, despite those hints, few felt there was any real cause for concern.

Chapter Nine

Rumors

In the aftermath of the Columbine shootings, when students got together with their friends to discuss what they had seen and heard about that day, many unfounded rumors were born. It is not unusual that following a traumatic event those involved would want to share their experiences with others. In doing so, however, some information was misunderstood, misinterpreted, and—in some cases—made up. The massacre occurred during the infancy of the Internet but enough people were online that the gossip quickly made it around Colorado, and then the world. Several unsubstantiated rumors were spawned in the weeks after Columbine, many of which have not been debunked until now.

Columbine High School hosts the Rebel News Network (RNN), an in-house "TV station" that allows students in video production classes to practice their hand at developing and producing videos for the school community. Klebold and Harris were heavily involved in video production and had contributed material to the RNN in the past. Each morning during the second hour, daily announcements and a "Thought of the Day" were broadcast on the RNN. The morning of April 20, 1999 was no exception. Based on the events that transpired, however, the perception of that day's "Thought" would be drastically altered in the minds of those present at the school during the attack. Although no one could quote it verbatim in interviews with police, a large number of people claimed that the gist of the "Thought of the Day" was *"you're going to wish you weren't here today"* or *"it's going to be a bad day."*[18,27,100,111,158,159,564,565,566,567,568,569,570] This led many to believe that Eric, Dylan, or one of their friends with foreknowledge of the massacre had intentionally broadcast the message.

In reality, the "Thought" had nothing to do with the attack and was actually much more benign than had been reported to investigators. The student who wrote the message was a friend of Klebold and Harris, and he had worked on video productions with both boys in the past. The phrase he aired that day, however, was a last-minute substitution for one he felt was unsuitable. *"He stated the phrase of the day that had been planned for, he did not feel was appropriate, so he changed it. He wrote the phrase, which was aired that morning. The phrase was 'how could you expect us to stay in school on a day like this?'*"[571] The boy was referring to the unseasonably warm temperature, which was in the low 70's, and indicated that the kids would rather be outside enjoying the nice weather.[572] He went on to say that the "Thought" that was originally supposed to air was *"quit your bitching."*[571] The boy spoke to the student who authored the latter comment, a senior identified by name in the police statement. He said *"he didn't care if it was inappropriate because he was going to be graduating in 16 days."*[571] This explanation of the "Thought of the Day" was substantiated by another classmate who took care of the audio for the RNN broadcasts.[573] A female student told investigators that she thought *"it said something to the effect of 'You shouldn't be inside here today. It is nice outside'"*[574] and another girl remembered the phrase as *"It's a nice day outside, I bet you wish you weren't here today."*[575] A teacher recalled it best, telling police he heard something like, *"how can you expect us to be in school today."*[576] In a sad twist of irony, after brutally shooting a female student in the library, Eric Harris told the moaning girl to *"stop her bitching."*[577]

Another prevalent misconception was that Dylan Klebold did not commit suicide but was actually murdered by Eric Harris before Harris killed himself. The rumor likely began in the days immediately following the assault before the public was given a glimpse into Dylan's personal demons and inner rage through his journal writings and the "Basement

Tapes." No one could believe that the "gentle" Klebold could have committed such horrific acts, and no one knew that he had been longing for death for more than two years. Eric was the angry, violent one—surely he must have masterminded the entire thing and slaughtered Dylan before he was through. Although none of this was true, the idea took hold. Even after crime scene photos and police reports were made public, it continued to persist in some circles. The main point of contention for those who refused to consider any other scenario is the manner in which Klebold was killed. According to his autopsy report, Dylan died of a self-inflicted gunshot wound to the left temple. *"The wound of entrance is designated wound 'A' in the region of the left temple. The projectile penetrated the cranium through the left temporal bone, extended across the undersurface of both cerebral hemispheres, exiting the head through the right temporal bone. The perforated area on the left side is beveled inward; the perforated area on the right side is beveled outward. Powder is associated with the wound on the left side of the head. The projectile traveled left to right slightly front to back and slightly downward. The characteristics of the wound are consistent with a large calibre weapon with a close contact range of fire consistent with self-infliction. The wound is consistent with 9 mm ammunition."*[578]

Klebold was left-handed and could be seen holding his TEC-DC9 in his left hand in still photos from the cafeteria surveillance tape. It would then make sense that he would have placed the gun to the left side of his head. The conspiracy arises, however, because when Dylan's body was discovered, his TEC-DC9 *"with a live round in the chamber was in the right hand and under the right leg of Klebold. It was also attached with a strap to Klebold's body."*[579] Many do not think that it is possible for Dylan to have shot himself in the left temple while holding the gun in his right hand and have concluded that Eric must have murdered his friend. Even John DeCamp, the lawyer involved in the lawsuit against Luvox maker Solvay Pharmaceuticals had been vocal in his belief that Harris killed Klebold.[348]

The major problem with this theory is that the positioning of the boys' bodies at the crime scene makes murder appear to be a physical impossibility. As the death scene photos—which are readily available online—and the police report indicate, Eric's body was found with his lower back against a bookshelf and his legs fully extended. *"The stains on the ceiling and shelves were consistent with HARRIS receiving the gunshot wound to his head while he was in a seated position." "The left knee area of his pants was blood-soaked and a piece of skull was found to the north of his left calf."*[580] The blood and skull fragment belonged to Klebold. In the photos, Dylan was lying on his back with his head in line with—and to the south of—Eric's left knee. *"His legs were bent at the hip with his knees towards the north and his lower legs pointing west."*[581] The picture was taken after the coroner rolled Dylan onto his back *"exposing right pants cargo pocket, which had not been searched due to the position of his body."*[582] A member of the bomb squad found an additional eight explosive devices after the body was moved. Once on his back, Klebold's right arm was extended along his right side and his left arm lay across his stomach. Description of the blood patterns noted on Dylan indicated that his body had initially been in another position before he came to rest on his back.

"A pool of blood on the carpet was to the north, east and south of Klebold's (#11) head, as well as to the west under his left shoulder. There was a bloodstain area on the back of his left arm above the elbow that was not consistent with being formed with the arm in the position found. In addition, some of the blood flows on the face were also formed with the head in a position other than as found. These flows were consistent with KLEBOLD's head resting on the right side of the face to allow the blood flow on the left side out of the wound. There were bloodstains on his right bicep and left center portion of his neck. The underside of the bill of the ball cap to the north of KLEBOLD appeared to be blood-soaked. This cap was in close proximity to the bloodstained area of the left knee of the pants worn by HARRIS."[580]

These details indicate that after the shot to his head, Dylan fell onto his right side. His head landed on Eric's left knee and the impact of the fall knocked off his hat and jarred loose a piece of his skull. The hat came to rest just south of Harris's knee—the skull fragment just to the north. Dylan's autopsy revealed that he aspirated blood into his lungs, signifying that he was still breathing for at least a short time after the bullet penetrated his skull.[583] According to the coroner, Dylan *"could have been capable of involuntary movement,"*[584] just prior to his death.

In order for him to shoot Klebold and have Dylan fall on his right side with his head landing on Eric's left knee, Harris would have had to have been seated during the murder with his legs fully extended. He then would have had to lean forward, stretch his arm past his own feet, and reach around to the opposite side of a squatting or kneeling Klebold. This would have, effectively, aimed the gun back towards Eric in order for him to be able to shoot Dylan from left to right. An alternate scenario would have Dylan looking towards Harris, with the rest of Klebold's body facing to the north when he was shot. In addition, the evidence indicates that Eric's gun did not deliver the fatal bullet to shoot Klebold. Dylan was killed by a 9 mm bullet. Eric's Hi-Point 9 mm carbine rifle measured 31 inches in length[585] and was far too long to be able to maneuver around Dylan's head from Eric's seated position. Furthermore, no blood was found in the barrel of this weapon[586] and the only DNA on the gun belonged to Eric Harris.[587] Klebold was killed by his TEC-DC9; blood was found *"extending inside the barrel muzzle about 1 to ½ inches."*[586] Therefore, even if the mechanics of such an awkward physical maneuver by Harris could be rationalized, it would indicate that Klebold willingly submitted to being executed as there would have been no way for Harris, in such an ungainly position, to forcibly hold Dylan down to accomplish the task. Moreover, Klebold would have had to have given Eric his own gun to do the job.

The conspiracy is fueled by the question of why, if Dylan's entrance wound was to the left temple, the gun would have been found in his right hand. This discrepancy is difficult to see in the available crime scene photos in which the TEC-DC9 is not readily visible, but the strap connecting the gun to Klebold's chest holster lays atop his right forearm and alongside his right hand. The position of Dylan's fingers does not suggest that he was actively holding the gun at the moment of death, but it is assumed that the TEC-DC9 lays beneath his hand as described in the police report. Several possible scenarios for the outcome of this positioning may be postulated. While none can be proven, any of them are more physically plausible than the one in which Harris shoots Klebold. It is speculated that Dylan shot himself in the left side of the head while holding the gun in his left hand. After the shot, Klebold fell onto his right side. It would then make sense that the gun, which was attached to his chest via a strap, was dropped from his left hand and fell to Klebold's right when he went to the floor. The weapon, which measured 12.5 inches and when carrying a loaded magazine weighed about 4.5 pounds,[588] ended up beneath Dylan when he went down. In this way, Dylan came to rest with both his right hand and his right leg over the top of the gun.[579] Only a cadaveric spasm at the moment of death would have enabled Klebold to retain his grip on the weapon after a shot to the head and a fall to the floor. No such spasm was indicated on autopsy.

While this is the most reasonable theory, another may be advanced. Klebold's TEC-DC9 was both bulky and heavy, which would have made holding the gun in his right hand while shooting himself in the opposite side of the head difficult. In spite of this, there is an explanation for how this could have been accomplished. Dylan was rather tall, measuring six feet, two and a half inches (74.5 inches) at autopsy.[206] It has been shown that there is a good correlation between a person's arm span and their height. When measured fingertip to opposite fingertip, the span between an individual's outstretched arms closely matches that person's height measured from head to toe.[589,590,591] As such, Klebold's long arms may have made the length of his weapon a less significant factor than it would have been for a shorter person. In addition, contrary to some reasoning, it would not be necessary for Dylan to reach completely around or over the top of his head to make contact with his left temple. Merely turning his face to the right would bring the left temple in close proximity with his right hand. In this position he would then be holding the gun, wrist bent inward, in front of his body. Given the weight of the TEC-DC9, it may have been pointing somewhat downward, regardless of which hand he used. The autopsy indicated "*the projectile traveled left to right slightly front to back and slightly downward.*"[578] In order to land as he did after shooting himself, Klebold likely fired his weapon while in a kneeling or squatting position a few feet or so beyond the end of Harris's outstretched legs. The subsequent fall resulted in Dylan's head landing on Eric's left knee, his right arm coming to rest beside Harris's left leg with his right elbow almost in line with the toe of Harris's left boot.

The final rumor is the biggest and has caused the most controversy since April 20, 1999. It has also spawned a series of conspiracy theories, some of which reach all the way up to the federal government and involve clandestine secret societies and covert operations. It is the belief, in some circles, that there were more people involved in the planning and execution of the Columbine attack than just Eric Harris and Dylan Klebold. Initially, it seemed as though this must be the case. With the sheer number and variety of the bombs, weaponry, and ammunition; the intended scale of the attack; the areas inside and outside the school where shooters were seen, as well as the painstaking attention to detail involved in the plot, it was too unbelievable to accept that two teenage boys could be the sole perpetrators. There had to have been others involved; they could not have accomplished all of this by themselves. But they did. Extensive investigation and witness testimony revealed that Eric and Dylan were the only individuals committing violence on that day. It also revealed that both boys had discussed bombing the school or killing this or that person with several people. Despite what some have written, however, there is no evidence to show that they tried to enlist others to participate in the weeks leading up to the attack. In fact, it seems rather implausible that they would risk exposure of their year-long plan by trying to recruit an additional participant at the last minute. In addition, there is no indication in any of the written material or video they left behind that Eric and Dylan were taking orders from, or sharing specific information with, anyone else. Moreover, a statement made by a lead police investigator shows that by 12:06 pm, less than 50 minutes after the start of the attack, *"preliminary interviews obtained from students coming from the school indicated that Eric Harris, dob/04-09-81, and Dylan Klebold, dob/09-11-81, had been tentatively identified as two suspects that were shooting students inside of Columbine High School."*[592]

In the chaos that surrounded the massacre, several eyewitnesses named other individuals they believed took part in or had firsthand knowledge of the attack. Most of those named were involved in the Trench Coat Mafia or were friends or acquaintances of Eric and Dylan. Despite testimony that exonerates each of those young men, many people today still harbor suspicion and the belief that they were somehow co-conspirators in this tragedy. Their vindication is long overdue.

Robert Perry = Innocent

Perry was one of the original members of the Trench Coat Mafia. After an altercation with Chris Morris in August 1998 in which Perry alleged that Morris threatened to kill him, Perry did not hang around with the members of the group as much as he had previously.[593] Robert was on good terms with Eric and Dylan, but the two were not close friends of his. Perry told police that he had last spoken to them in January 1999 in passing.[593] Police interviewed hundreds of people, including friends and family of Harris and Klebold. Of those questioned, very few knew of any association between the boys and Perry, with most of them only assuming one because they all wore trench coats.[594,595] Robert's best friend told police that Harris and Klebold did not like Perry: "*in talking to KLEBOLD and Brooks BROWN in English class last year, they said Perry was 'stupid' and described him as 'goofy'.*"[596] Perry dropped out of Columbine High School a few months before the attack and had begun working nights at a local Safeway.[593]

On the morning of the massacre, Robert spent some time talking with his grandmother. Although he did not have to work that evening, he kept to his regular sleep schedule and headed downstairs to bed at 11:00 am. Approximately 40 minutes later, his mother stomped on the kitchen floor to wake him and told him about the trouble at the school. Perry's younger sister was a freshman at Columbine. Robert quickly got dressed and, after examining her schedule and figuring out that she would be in the cafeteria at that hour, began walking the 2.18 miles[597] to the school to find his sister.[598,599] Most of those who still believe in Perry's involvement cite, as one reason, the fact that only his immediate family members can provide him with an alibi. This is true during, roughly, the first 40 minutes of the attack from 11:19 am to noon. However, if Perry's family members had conspired to make sure his whereabouts were accounted for, then one would expect that his grandmother—whom he claimed to have talked with that morning— would have been in on the collusion and all of their stories would have been identical. But his grandmother's story differs somewhat from the others because, according to her, Robert did not leave the house after learning about the shooting at the school. Instead, he remained home until his father got there.[600] This was disproven by students who saw Perry heading to Columbine High School. On the way to the school, Robert spotted his father, who had been alerted to the trouble by his wife. The elder Perry had left work around noon and drove a route he thought his daughter might take on her way home from the school, hoping to find her.[598,599] On the way, he spotted his son. Robert got into his dad's car, a Toyota,[601] and they returned home.[599] A witness saw Perry flag down a Toyota near the school, telling police he was "*in the vicinity of S. Pierce and Roxbury when he saw a person known by him to be a member of the Trench Coat Mafia. He said this person was on foot by the Pizza Hut and had waved down a Toyota Tercel, blue in color. He described the male as being very tall, approximately, 6'5", with very long hair, wearing jeans and a tie-dyed shirt, black and red in color and a black and red cap, worn backwards.*"[602] The intersection of S. Pierce and Roxbury is approximately a quarter mile from Columbine and three-quarters of a mile from the Perry residence. Walking at a brisk pace, Robert may have been able to cover the distance from his house to this location in roughly ten to fifteen minutes. The student who observed Perry had been in the cafeteria when the attack began and was able to get out of the building quickly and run to Clement Park. He estimated that he waited there for approximately fifteen minutes before he was able to get a ride home with a friend's father. He saw Robert while being brought home. The boy's timeline is consistent with Perry meeting up with his father a little after noon that day and with Perry leaving his house at about noon.[598] Another student also saw Perry getting into a Toyota and was able to provide police with a partial license plate number. He described a *"subject 6'- 6'2", ear-length brown hair, tie-dye shirt and jeans"* and a *"blue Toyota Tercel, HDB-510 or HDO-510."*[603] The license plate number for the elder Perry's Toyota was H8P510.[601] No time frame was given for when this boy made his observation of Perry.

Once home, Robert received a call from a friend, who informed him that his sister was at the public library with other students from the school.[598] Prior to leaving to retrieve her, Perry had a brief conversation with another friend who stopped by his house.[598,604] Robert and his father then went to the library to pick up his sister and her friend. Several witnesses noted Perry's presence at the public library. Some found it odd because he was known to have dropped out of school; they did not realize that he had a sibling who still attended Columbine.[605] A teacher's aide told police that while at the library, a female student saw Perry there and *"became noticeably alarmed,"*[606] indicating that she had seen Perry with the two suspects.[606] The implication was that Perry had been with Harris and Klebold the day of the shooting. Further investigation revealed this was not the case. The female student did not see any gunman on April 20. In fact, she had gone out for lunch the day of the attack. She was only referring to having seen Robert with Eric and Dylan in the past.[607] Witness testimony as to the time Robert made his appearance at the library varies. One girl told police that she had been at the library for ten to fifteen minutes with her friend when they saw Perry *"walking towards the library wearing a tie-dyed T-shirt."*[608] The time of her arrival at the library is unknown. She was able to escape the school fairly early during the incident, first retreating to Clement Park and then to the library. A second girl, who had gone on a friends-only date with Perry in December 1998, stated that she saw him at the library *"shortly before noon"*[594] as he came to pick up his little sister. According to her, *"he was wearing a tie dye shirt with the primary colors being hot pink and yellow."*[594] Yet another girl said she saw Perry at the library around 2:00 pm. She described him as wearing a *"tie dye T-shirt, blue jeans, black boots, and a turned around baseball style cap"*[595] and told investigators that he was *"with a group of students, four or five all together,"*[595] including the girl who had called him earlier to tell him where his sister was. The most accurate estimate indicates Robert probably got to the public library around 1:00 pm. One girl who saw him there told police that she saw Perry wearing *"black pants, a tie dye shirt, and a black baseball cap turned backwards."*[609] The student was unsure of the exact time Perry arrived but felt that is was *"within two hours after the incident began."*[609] Placing Robert at the public library around 1:00 pm is consistent with the testimony of Perry's mother,[599] as well as a Denver dispatch communication at 1:09 pm that described a possible suspect: *"unknown what he's wanted for"* as a "*w/m in a tie-dyed T-shirt*"[610] that had just left the public library.

Perry's height, slim build, longer hairstyle, as well as his usual manner of dress that included dark clothing, a trench coat, boots, and backwards baseball caps were very similar to that of Dylan Klebold at the time of his death.[611,612] The confusion about Perry's guilt or innocence was further fueled by false rumors that Robert had turned himself in for the crime. Many who did not know Klebold, or who had not seen Dylan in recent months, were not aware that Klebold had grown his hair longer. When witnesses pulled out their 1998 yearbooks at home in the initial days after the attack, Dylan's clean-cut photo did not stand out. Perry's, however, did. One boy, who stated that he "*did not know Dylan Klebold at all*" [613] told police that sometime before the attack he "*saw a tall kid standing by Klebold's car. He stated he did not know this kid, but he identified him, by looking through the yearbook, as Robert Perry. He was not sure what day he saw Robert Perry by the BMW.*"[613] There is no way to know for certain who stood near the BMW, but odds are in favor of it being Dylan beside his own car. The same mistake was made by four individuals who believed that Robert Perry was the gunman they had seen going up and down the stairs outside the cafeteria and library, and that he was throwing pipe bombs into the parking lot.[614,615, 616,617] Two other witnesses initially thought Perry was responsible, but after viewing more recent photos of Dylan they were uncertain if the person they saw was Klebold or Perry.[618,619] Of these six individuals, five of them were with friends at the time they saw the suspect and most of those friends obtained a good enough look that they were able to identify this same shooter as Dylan Klebold.[476,620,621,622,623] In fact, more than 50 eyewitnesses were able to place Dylan Klebold above, below, or on the staircase outside the west entrances of the school (see Appendix A). The majority of those witnesses could identify Dylan with certainty, or reasonable certainty, based on more than passing familiarity with Klebold. Eleven had seen Dylan in school but did not know his name until they saw the media reports, and thirteen had never seen Dylan before but were able to identify him based on photos released in the press. There were several students who initially believed the person they saw was Robert Perry because they were more familiar with him than with Klebold. These witnesses, upon review of cafeteria surveillance video stills or more recent photos of Dylan released in the media, were able to determine that the suspect they observed was, in fact, Klebold. Many of these students, upon realizing their error, explained why they thought they had made a mistake in identification. One girl told police "*that the person she saw and Robert Perry have similar physical characteristics*"[620] and "*that she was familiar with Robert Perry because she used to see him during her off period. She had never seen Dylan Klebold, which may have caused her to believe the person she saw was Robert Perry.*"[620]

Another female student relayed that prior to the attack she had never seen Dylan and so when "*she looked at his school photo in her school yearbook. [She] noted that in the photo Klebold had short hair;*

the gunman she saw had long hair. Based on Klebold's yearbook photo, [she] *concluded that Perry was the shooter she saw."*[476] A male witness told investigators that after looking through the 1998 yearbook photos with other students, he *"thought the person he saw with the gun outside the window might have been Perry. Then when the senior class photo appeared in the newspaper, he recognized Dylan Klebold, seated at the top left of the student body, as the individual he saw outside the cafeteria. That photo was a more recent photo of Klebold."*[491]

A female student, and one of the six witnesses who believed it could have been Perry outside the west entrance, described the gunman's clothing in great detail to police. In addition to mentioning the *"machine gun"*[617] on a strap around his neck, she described the length of his black trench coat, and that he wore a *"black baseball hat in the backward position,"*[617] a black T- shirt, *"black tighter fitting jeans,"*[617] black high-top tennis shoes, and *"had a red colored cloth* (sic) *type item attached to the left side of his waist."*[617] The online death photos of Klebold show that her recollection of his dress is quite accurate. The photo with Dylan's feet in the foreground of the frame even reveals the red-colored material at his waist, visible just beyond the pink evidence flag.

Two witnesses told police that they had seen Robert Perry in the cafeteria just prior to the start of the shooting, however, further investigation showed this was not the case. Cafeteria surveillance video does not show Perry in the cafeteria at any time that day. The female student who believed she saw Perry in the Commons area making a sweeping motion back and forth at the same time that she heard gunfire, later informed investigators that *"she has a vivid imagination and is unclear on exactly what she saw occur in the cafeteria on April 20, 1999."*[624] The vivid imagination statement was corroborated by a friend of hers, who stated that the girl told her that she had seen Perry and he *"came up to her and said 'Hi* [name redacted]*' then stepped around her and began firing into the cafeteria."*[625] This did not occur. The second witness was a male student who claimed to have seen Perry in the cafeteria talking with friends and then again, just minutes later, in the hallway near the tech lab putting ammunition into his gun. The boy was familiar with Perry from seeing him at school and the Safeway where he worked. *"This male party was putting a clip into a pistol-like weapon and* [the witness] *then turned around and heard a shot."*[626] *"*[He] *was then shown a picture of Dylan Klebold in the cafeteria and* [he] *stated that this was the person he saw in the hallway loading the weapon and he also remarked that Klebold and Perry look alike."*[626] Several other eyewitnesses, four of whom knew Klebold personally, also identified Dylan as the gunman they saw in the cafeteria that day (see Appendix A).

A female student saw a gunman in the main hallway. She told police that she thought it was Perry but that she *"did not clearly see that individual's face and could not positively identify the person as Robert Perry."*[627] Three additional witnesses also observed the gunman at this time and indicated to police that this person was actually Dylan Klebold.[137,628,629] A girl who knew both Perry and Klebold told investigators that she saw a suspect all in black, wearing a trench coat, and holding a gun near her math classroom. She thought it was Perry but told police that other students had informed her it was Dylan. The girl commented, *"they look alike."*[52] The only other alleged sighting of Perry was by a girl who was dating a former TCM member. She was unable to identify the gunman she saw in the science hall, but after describing him to her boyfriend they concluded that the shooter was Robert Perry.[630] The girl's boyfriend was not present for the attack and based his opinion solely on the clothing the gunman wore and his familiarity with Perry. Seven other witnesses told police the gunman they saw in the science hall was Dylan Klebold (see Appendix A). These witnesses included a teacher who called 911 during the attack and identified Dylan by name to the 911 operator.[631] All other statements regarding observations of Perry at the school during the attack were found to be hearsay and inaccurate. Students and staff that were interviewed would tell investigators that they "had heard" second or third-hand that "so and so" saw Perry at the school with a gun. Follow-up interviews with the alleged witness, if that individual could be identified, invariably proved that no such observation or claim was made by that person.

A final rumor regarding Perry involved a statement made by a male student. The boy told investigators that at approximately 2:30 pm on the day of the shooting, he saw two individuals wearing trench coats speeding down South Yukon Street near the high school in a red Geo Metro. The boy said that he was certain that the vehicle's passenger was hanging out of the window holding a gun. Concerned that the two individuals were heading towards the school, the student contacted a nearby police officer. The boy stated that he believed the driver of the car to be Robert Perry, however, when asked to rate his belief on a scale of one to ten with ten being positive that Perry was driving, "*he stated number three.*"[632] He could not assign a name to the passenger but told police he believed it was a former Columbine student with whom he had a class the previous year. It is very unlikely that Perry was the driver of the vehicle because Robert did not own a car at that time. His parents had a blue Toyota Tercel and a Plymouth Grand Voyager SE.[601,633] When he did not have access to a family vehicle, Perry was known to take the bus.[596] Moreover, by 2:30 pm on that day, the Perrys had retrieved Robert's younger sister from the public library and remained together for the rest of the afternoon.[599] It is also important to note that the young man who claimed he saw Perry was accompanied by his girlfriend when they saw the Geo Metro pass their car. The girlfriend asked him, at that time, "*Was that guy holding a camera?*"[632] She told police that "*she was almost positive that the object being held by the suspect was a video camera until her boyfriend* [name redacted] *told her that it was a hand gun.*"[634] The girl described it as "*a black thing, approximately two feet long and was positive that the individual was holding it with two hands.*"[634] She also said that the Geo was only traveling at about 25 miles per hour and that she *"observed the suspects in this incident for approximately two to three seconds total time."*[634]

In fact, her boyfriend did not take note of the object until after she mentioned it to him. The two cars had already passed one another at that point, so he had to turn around to view it. The boy *"stated he slowed down his car and looked behind him to watch the Geo Metro."*[632] He also told investigators that the gun was small, *"black in color, with a small hollow circle on the tip of the gun"*[632] and that *"the individual had the gun in his hand next to his face and shoulder with the barrel of the gun pointing upward."*[632] Arguably, the same position one would hold a 1990's era video camera.

Despite some confusion based on their physical similarities, there is overwhelming evidence in the form of roughly 70 eyewitnesses to indicate that the gunman a handful of people thought was Robert Perry was actually Dylan Klebold. Perry has alibi witnesses, including non-family members, accounting for his whereabouts during the first hour of the assault. A police executed search warrant of his home and computers revealed no indication of his involvement.[635] Furthermore, Perry's own sister was in the cafeteria when the massacre began and would certainly have perished had the bombs served their intended purpose. Friends who spoke with Robert in the hours after the attack relayed that he was furious that she had been put in harm's way.[594,596] Robert Perry was not present at Columbine High School on April 20, 1999 during the shooting and was in no way responsible for the events that took place on that tragic day.

Chris Morris = Innocent

Chris Morris was a friend to both Dylan Klebold and Eric Harris and worked with both boys at Blackjack Pizza. It was this association that made him a prime suspect in the eyes of many. Morris was photographed in handcuffs the day of the attack, which only further fueled the gossip. In reality, Chris had contacted police on his own to offer whatever information he could to help stop the carnage. An officer picked Morris up at his friend's house and transported him to the Jeffco Command Center near the high school. Unfortunately, the image of him with his hands shackled behind his back left the public with an entirely different impression of Chris's role in the shooting.

On the day of the attack, Morris was waiting at home for Eric Harris to pick him up for their early-morning bowling class. Harris never arrived, so Morris took his own car and showed up at the bowling alley a bit late. He missed the taking of attendance and was marked absent, but several students have verified his presence in class that morning.[636,637,638,639,640] After bowling, Morris went to McDonald's for breakfast and then attended his second and third hour classes. Chris left school around 10:20 am, skipping his fourth period acting class.[641] His absence from the class led many to believe that he had foreknowledge of the events that would transpire that day, but Morris had actually been ditching fourth hour for most of the month of April.[183,642] A female student confirmed that fact, telling investigators that Morris "*hadn't been in the class for approximately the past two weeks.*"[643] A boy observed Chris leaving school after third hour around 10:20 am. He told investigators that he saw Morris walking toward Pierce Street from the main doors.[644] Morris's car was parked in the teachers' parking lot that day. It kept overheating so he wanted to park closer to the school.[641] The teachers' lot is located between the Columbine main entrance and Pierce Street. Two witnesses mentioned seeing Morris driving out of this lot, but their stories conflict with regard to when this occurred. The two girls were together and, according to them, a third female student was also present. One of the girls told police that she saw Morris leaving the teachers' parking lot at 10:20 am in *"a small red compact car."*[645] Chris owned a red Dodge Lancer.[641] According to this witness, he was dressed in black and wearing his green beret and sunglasses. She further explained that she and her friends went to the Southwest Plaza area to eat and did not find out about the shooting until they tried to return to school around 11:36 am.[645] The second girl gave a similar account but said they did not see Morris leaving school until they returned from lunch and were pulling into the teachers' lot around 11:40 am.[646] She told police it was shortly after this that a teacher told them what was going on and that they needed to leave. To add to the confusion, the third girl— interviewed by police four weeks after the massacre— stated that she had lunch at home that day and was turned away by other students when she tried to go back to school. She made no mention of having seen Chris Morris.[647]

Since police arrived at Columbine within minutes of the start of the shooting and began blocking all public access to the school by 11:27 am,[512,648] it is highly unlikely that these three students would have been able to make it all the way into the teachers' parking lot, located right beside the school, a full twenty minutes into the attack. In the police report, the girl who claimed to have seen Morris at 11:40 am mentioned the name of the teacher who directed them to leave. No police statement exists from any individuals whose surname is spelled as listed in the report. However, there was a special education teacher whose name is spelled differently but pronounced in the same way. That teacher told police that after fleeing the building he was helping to direct traffic away from the school. He *"indicated that he was still in the area of Pierce and Polk, directing traffic south onto Pierce and back west on Polk for those vehicles that were in the area."*[649] The intersection of Pierce and Polk Streets is located approximately an eighth of a mile south of the entrance to the Columbine teachers' parking lot. If the girls spoke with this teacher, it would mean they never made it back to the teachers' lot after lunch. As such, it seems most plausible—given the two eyewitness accounts and Morris's statements—that Morris was sighted as the girls were leaving for lunch rather than when they returned.

After leaving the school, Chris stopped at a store and then proceeded to a friend's house to talk and play video games.[641] The father of that friend was a science teacher at Columbine. Approximately 30 minutes to an hour later, the friend's mother called to tell him of the trouble at the high school. Morris and his friend tried to get to Columbine to check on Chris's girlfriend and his friend's father.[540,641] A female student confirmed that around 12:15 pm she saw *"Chris Morris and another unknown individual drive up in a rusty red, older model, hatchback. He was wearing the green beret that he usually wears. Morris seemed in a hurry to get to the school and was angry that the police would not let him drive through to the school."*[28]

Having been turned away, Chris and his friend returned to the house. Along the way, Morris received some pages and found out his girlfriend was at a local restaurant. The boys went back out to find her and after discovering she had already left, made their way to her house.[641] A girl told police that Morris and the other boy arrived at the girlfriend's house around 12:20 pm and that she observed Chris in the yard hugging his girlfriend.[650] Worried about his father, Morris and his friend soon returned to the friend's house to await any news on his whereabouts. While there, the two watched events unfold on television and quickly realized that Eric Harris and Dylan Klebold were likely responsible. Chris attempted to call the police to offer his help, but had trouble getting through to someone. He then called his mother who was an employee of the Cherry Hills Police Department. She connected him with a Cherry Hills detective who indicated that he would pass along Morris's information to the Jeffco Sheriff's Department. Chris attempted to call the Sheriff's office again and was put in contact with Investigator Tom Acierno.[641] Acierno sent an officer to pick up

Morris at his friend's house. He was handcuffed and transported to the temporary Jeffco Command Center near the school, where he tested negative for gunshot residue and was questioned by police.[642]

Morris consented to a search of his bedroom, which was carried out the day of the shooting. According to police, *"Nothing of evidentiary value was immediately observed. Paperwork, photograph negatives, fireworks, computer CPU and miscellaneous items taken into custody."*[651] Investigators also collected the clothing that Chris was wearing to submit for forensic testing. Authorities found nothing to implicate Morris in the crime.

Two male students initially identified Chris Morris as the gunman they saw outside by the staircase on the day of the shooting. Both boys based their identification on the height, build, and manner of dress of the shooter. After viewing the cafeteria surveillance video stills, however, these two individuals recognized Dylan Klebold as the gunman they saw.[652,653,654] More than 50 other witnesses confirmed that Dylan was the trench coat-wearing shooter by the stairs outside (see Appendix A). A third male student thought he saw Morris with a gun in the hall by the library. He told investigators that he *"was basing his identification of the individual being Morris based solely on how tall he was and his clothing."*[655] When describing the gunmen, the student also reported that he did not see *"either the individuals' faces very well as they were being backlit by the doors on the west end of the hallway.*[655] A teacher, who is also the father of the friend Morris was with that day, identified Dylan Klebold as the shooter in the library hall. The man was very familiar with Dylan, who had been to his house to play pool with his son.[656] A second witness also believed she saw Klebold in the library hall and identified him on November 3, 1999 in the cafeteria video stills. She could not be definitive in her identification at that time, however, because she recalled the shooter as having long, black hair.[657] Prior statements given six and 23 days after the attack show that the girl initially described the color as *"brown,"* and *"dark brown."* [657]

For those who claim that Chris Morris was involved in the shooting, the most often cited witness is a ninth-grade girl who said she saw Morris and a second gunman *"coming around the corner of the library hall into the north hall."*[658] The student told investigators that she was uncertain of Morris's identity until her sister *"showed her a Columbine yearbook and she saw his picture in the book."*[658] The girl said she *"is sure the two shooters she observed were Eric Harris and Chris Morris."*[658] Further examination of the girl's identification, however, seems to rule out Morris as a possible suspect. She described the individual she believed to be Chris as a *"White male, about 5'8" tall (described as the 'same size as me* [the girl]*'), with a 'scrawny body' and glasses."*[659] The girl told investigators that he had dark brown hair and was wearing a white shirt, trench coat, black boots, and dark pants. She also informed police that Chris Morris was *"shorter and scrawnier"*[659] than Dylan Klebold. In reality, Chris Morris was six foot two inches and 175 pounds, only half an inch shorter than Dylan and more than 30 pounds heavier.[206,660]

Based on this description, the shooter the girl saw could not possibly have been Morris. It is actually a much better fit for Eric Harris, whom she described as the taller of the two gunmen. Harris was a full six inches shorter than both Klebold and Morris.[186] Finally, this student was accompanied by another girl when they encountered the gunmen. The other girl positively identified Dylan as the tall shooter she observed in the north hallway at that time.[661]

None of the available evidence places Chris Morris at Columbine High School during the assault launched by Dylan Klebold and Eric Harris. Morris's whereabouts have been verified by a number of individuals, including members of law enforcement. Of those witnesses who believed they saw Morris at the school, two later realized that it was actually Dylan Klebold after viewing the cafeteria surveillance video stills, and one told police that he was basing his identification solely on the gunman's height and clothing and did not really see the shooter's face. The only individual who was able to give a detailed account of the suspect she thought was Chris Morris described someone who was far smaller in height and build than he was. Furthermore, a second witness who was with this girl definitively named Dylan Klebold as the shooter present at that time. Gunshot residue testing on his hands and a search warrant executed at Morris's home failed to yield any evidence of his involvement. Chris Morris did not participate in the planning or execution of this terrible crime.

Brian Sargent = Innocent

Brian Sargent was one of the original members of the Trench Coat Mafia and is pictured in the 1998 yearbook photo of the group along with Chris Morris. As a TCM member, suspicion quickly arose regarding any possible involvement Brian may have had in the attack on Columbine. In his interviews with police, Sargent indicated that he was mostly an acquaintance of Eric Harris and Dylan Klebold. Brian stated that while he was not *"direct friends"*[51] with Eric, he would sit with Harris and others in the cafeteria in the mornings before class. Sargent also said he did not know Dylan *"personally,"*[51] but a friend of his told investigators that the previous year Sargent was in a video class with Dylan and that the three of them *"would often go to breakfast at a local McDonald's."*[31] Brian did report that since the fall of 1998 he *"did not talk to Eric Harris or Dylan Klebold, only to greet each other while passing in the hall,"*[94] which seems to indicate that his previous statement was meant to imply that he and Dylan were not close, and not that they were unfamiliar with one another.

On the day of the shooting, between 11:10 and 11:15 am, Brian left the school grounds for lunch with a male and female friend. Sargent often ate off campus during fifth hour. The trio drove to Burger King in Brian's car. Some circulating rumors refute this alibi by stating that other Columbine students eating at Burger King that day did not report seeing Sargent there. In reality, these students were never asked by investigators to verify his presence at the fast food restaurant. Implying otherwise is misleading and appears to be designed to throw suspicion on Sargent without any corroborating evidence. Only one boy mentioned seeing TCM members, Brian Sargent specifically, at Burger King on April 20. According to this student, however, Sargent was with five or six other TCM students in a *"full size red Chevrolet Blazer."*[662] The sighting was not mentioned by the friend who accompanied the boy to lunch[663] and it is contradictory to statements made by others who rode in Brian's compact car only a short time after the attack began.[664,665] The student was not interviewed until seven weeks after the massacre, so it is possible he was mistaken regarding which day he saw Sargent and other Trench Coat Mafia students in the Burger King parking lot.

After leaving Burger King,[31,666] Brian and his friends drove to a movie theater parking lot across from Clement Park to smoke.[667] They only learned of the shooting at Columbine when trying to make their way back to the school. While driving, the trio spotted three students—two girls and one boy—near the Mormon House on Pierce Street. The three were acquaintances of his female passenger but were unknown to Sargent. Brian picked the kids up and gave them a ride to a friend's house.[664,665,667] One of these acquaintances told police that Sargent had delivered them to the other house between 11:30 and 11:40 am, noting she was able to call her mother at that time.[665] The time frame is consistent with that reported by others in the party. Sargent's friend indicated that they had headed back to the school at approximately 11:45 am.[31] The male student who caught a ride from Brian estimated he picked them up roughly fifteen minutes after the start of the attack, which began at 11:19 am.[664]

The third student who got a lift from Sargent was not interviewed regarding what she did after she escaped the school building. As such, she did not mention Brian to investigators. However, she did indicate that she had been sitting with the other girl Sargent picked up before they fled the cafeteria.[668] Moreover, the latter girl identified this third student as one of the passengers in Brian's car.[665]

Sargent's name was directly brought into the investigation when a female student told police that she saw a gunman at the top of the stairs outside the west doors. *"She described the gunman as a white male with a very full face, 'pudgy, overweight.' The gunman had dark hair, possibly 1 ½" long. He had dark eyes and dark thick bushy eyebrows. He was wearing a long black trench coat that appeared to be closed."*[669] Police asked the girl to look through the Columbine yearbook to see if she could identify the shooter in the trench coat and, after doing so, she indicated that Brian Sargent looked like the person she had seen. The girl further described witnessing this particular gunman shoot a female student in the chest, as well as seeing two girls and a boy run to assist the injured girl.

In addition to Sargent's four alibi witnesses, dozens of other people recognized Dylan Klebold and Eric Harris as the shooters on and near the outside stairs that day (see Appendices A and C). Among those was a friend of the young lady that identified Brian Sargent as one of the gunmen. The two girls were walking together toward the parking lot when the attack began. This student also felt the shooter appeared heavyset and she, too, initially believed him to be Sargent. After viewing cafeteria surveillance video stills, however, the girl told police she was "*certain*" the trench coated assailant was actually Dylan Klebold.[670] Both of the girls witnessed the injured female student being assisted by three classmates. Two of the students who came to the wounded girl's aid definitively identified Dylan Klebold, not Brian Sargent, as the nearby suspect in the trench coat.[482,671]

A handful of other witnesses described the trench-coated shooter outside as being heavy in stature, which has led some to implicate Brian Sargent. One boy, who could not identify the assailant but claimed it was not Eric or Dylan, said the gunman had "*a very round face.*"[672] The student described this individual as having walked up and down the staircase, and shooting a victim in the face. These actions have been linked by more than a dozen people to Dylan Klebold (see Appendix A). During the attack, this boy was accompanied by several of his friends. Of these, one thought the gunman in question was Klebold,[673] a second believed he resembled either Dylan or Robert Perry,[674] a third felt it was probably Klebold but was unsure,[623] and a fourth "*reported that he was too far away to recognize the subjects.*"[675] Another female witness told investigators that shortly before the shooting, she saw Eric Harris and a second individual "*out in the field area between the equipment building and the soccer fields.*"[676] Both were wearing trench coats and she described the boy with Harris as big and fat with "*chin length black hair.*"[676] No other witnesses reported seeing suspects in this area at this time, so it is difficult to corroborate or refute this testimony.

Brian Sargent's hair was considerably shorter than that described, however, and he was known to wear it in a bowl cut, as shown in the TCM photo available online. Moreover, in one of the "Basement Tapes," Dylan demonstrated what he would be wearing on the day of the attack and how he intended to carry all of his gear. *"Klebold is getting dressed and he puts on his long black trench coat and says, 'I'm fat on this side,' and then he begins talking about how he looks 'fat with all the stuff on.'"*[677]

Brian Sargent had several alibi witnesses that placed him away from the school grounds on April 20, 1999. There are also more than four dozen people who recognized Dylan Klebold as the trench coat-wearing gunman, contradicting the testimony of the girl who believed she saw Sargent firing upon students near the outside staircase. The evidence exonerating Brian Sargent is overwhelming. He was not involved in the attack on Columbine High School.

Joe Stair = Innocent

Of the suspects identified by name by witnesses of the attack, the case against Joe Stair has always been the weakest. Stair's alibi for the initial part of the assault was also weak, however, which fueled rumors of his involvement. Joe, a former TCM member and 1998 graduate of Columbine, was at home with his mother on the morning of April 20th. In his statement, the investigator wrote *"he woke up at approximately 100 hrs. Stair ate, then played video games at home. At approximately 1200 hrs., his sister,* [name redacted] *Stair, called home and spoke to his mother and that this is when he first heard of the shootings at Columbine.*"[678] It is unclear whether Stair really woke up at 1:00 in the morning, as written in the report, or if this was a typographical error and the detective intended to indicate 10:00 in the morning instead. It is not known if Joe Stair's mother was interviewed by police. No statement can be found in the documents released by investigators. The absence of this interview effectively left Stair without a corroborating alibi at the time the shootings were taking place.

It should be noted that Stair's younger sister attended Columbine and was in the school library during the massacre that occurred there. She escaped uninjured, but a female student hiding beneath the desk next to hers was badly wounded. Stair's sister told investigators that she and the others were able to flee the library "*at or about 11:45 am.*"[679] She was first taken by police to a small maintenance building at Clement Park. "*They remained there for approximately 20 minutes, and were then driven to the public library, where she was able to contact her mother.*"[679] According to this timeline, Joe's sister phoned home shortly after noon, which is consistent with Stair's statement to police. Stair reported that after hearing from his sister, they "*watched the news for an hour or so, then he and his mother responded to the library near Columbine High School*"[678] to pick her up. It is unknown why they waited to retrieve her. Stair told investigators that "*his mother was in no condition to drive because of this event upsetting her so much.*"[541] Police were requesting statements from all available witnesses. Having escaped the school library where the majority of the killing occurred, the girl's testimony was of particular interest. It is unknown whether Stair's sister informed her mother that she needed to talk with an officer prior to being brought home. The girl finished writing her statement at 2:40 pm.[679] When Stair arrived at the public library, students familiar with him and his association with the Trench Coat Mafia pointed him out to police. He was detained, interviewed by law enforcement,[678,680,681] and then transported to the Command Center near the school for further questioning.[680,682] Stair was driven home by police at approximately 3:30 that afternoon and worked his normally scheduled shift that evening.[678]

Of the witnesses who suggested Joe Stair's involvement in the attack, only one told police that she had physically seen him outside the cafeteria. *"Outside, by the corner of the building, I saw a guy I recognized as Joe Stair. He was running, but I couldn't tell where he was running to or from. Stair had his blonde hair down. Its past his shoulders. He's about 6' tall, skinny, he was wearing a long dark trench coat. I saw him from his waste* (sic) *up. I saw nothing in his hands. He was observed a short distance from whatever was going on at the door."*[683] None of the individuals seated at her table got a glimpse of Stair or any other gunman during the shooting and at least 50 other witnesses reported seeing Dylan Klebold in the area near the stairs at this same time (see Appendix A). The girl indicated to investigators that she had never seen Klebold before and after being shown a cafeteria surveillance video still of Dylan, she reported that "*the person she saw in a trench coat standing at the bottom of the cement stairs certainly could have been Dylan Klebold, and not Joe Stair.*"[684] One boy told police that a friend saw Stair "*outside the school on the day of the shooting*"[685] but when interviewed, the friend said he had actually seen a person he believed to be Joe about two weeks prior to the attack.[686] Similarly, a female student informed investigators that her friend saw Stair in the cafeteria shortly before the shooting began[687] but, when interviewed, the friend said that was untrue.[688]

All other suggestions for Stair's involvement came from so-called "ear witnesses". These are individuals that did not actually see him during the assault, but believed they heard the name "Joe" used by one of the gunmen. Several people hiding in classrooms in the science wing indicated to law enforcement that they knew of others who had heard the name spoken by one of the shooters, but a few of these reports were determined to be in error. A student reported that his teacher had heard the name "Joe",[689] but when contacted the teacher did not mention hearing this herself and instead listed three others she thought had.[690] Of the three, only two have interviews included in the publicly released documents and one of them made no mention of it, telling police that while she heard explosions and gunshots near the library, "*she did not witness any of the shooting or see any of the gunmen.*"[691] The second girl and several others did, however, hear someone talking to "Joe" but were unsure if the speaker was out in the hallway or in the Commons area. Two students heard, "*hey Joe,*"[692,693] with one of these telling investigators that he heard the gunmen say, "*Hey Joe, where are you?*"[693] A female student reported hearing one of the "*boy voices*"[694] yelling the name "Joe". "*The statement with the name 'Joe' was made referencing him to come to them or to go.*"[694] Two other girls recalled something to the effect of "*Joe, I have three of them in here*"[695] or "*Joe, where are you, I got three.*"[688] One of these girls is certain that the word she heard was "Joe" and not "Yo", while the second "*stated it was her belief that the individual said 'Joe' but it could have possibly been 'Yo'.*"[688] None of these witnesses got a glimpse of the speaker or the person he was talking to, and none could pinpoint the location from which the voice originated. As such, it is unclear if it came from one of the gunmen, another student, or a member of law enforcement outside assisting students fleeing the school at the southwest side of the building near the Commons area and below the science wing. The name "Joe" could have just as easily referred to an individual in one of the latter groups and is not strong evidence for Stair's participation. For example, a boy hiding behind a trash can in the cafeteria reported "*he heard somebody say, 'Let's shoot up.' He said he does not believe they were referring to narcotics, but rather getting ready to shoot their weapons. He also said he heard the name 'Dominic' mentioned, but he did not know who that might be.*"[696] There was, in fact, a student named Dominic hiding in the kitchen area off the cafeteria with three friends. He was not involved in any way with the gunmen or the destruction they wrought upon Columbine.[697] Most likely, one of his friends called to him, and this is what the other student overheard. Without visual confirmation of a gunman uttering the name "Joe", or proof of Stair's presence at the school, there is no way to know if what these "ear witnesses" heard had anything to do with the shooters. Further investigation by law enforcement failed to connect Stair to the crime.

Approximately three weeks after the attack, Joe Stair was interviewed by police again. At that time, he gave investigators consent to search his computer, providing them with his password and screen name. He also allowed police to search his bedroom. The search yielded some newspaper articles referencing a murder-suicide that had occurred the previous year. The perpetrator had been a friend of Joe's and an associate of the Trench Coat Mafia. Police also collected Stair's trench coat, a newspaper article on Adolf Hitler, "*a notepad that had what appeared to possibly be the beginning of plans for a truck heist,*"[678] and miscellaneous pictures and papers. Among the latter was a yearbook entry by Dylan Klebold that read: "*Yo Joe... Stay different, better than the norm! Jocks suck dick. TCM!! Later <<-VODKA->>*"[678] None of the material obtained linked Stair to the horrific events at Columbine.

Two days later on May 14, 1999, Joe Stair sat for a polygraph examination. Among the questions asked were:

"*Regarding Columbine High School, did you personally participate in planning that armed attack?*"

"On April 20, 1999, did you know for sure that an armed attack would occur at Columbine High School?"

"Regarding Columbine High School, did you knowingly provide any of the weapons used in that armed attack?"[541]

Stair answered "No" to all of the above inquiries. The polygraph examiner wrote in his report that *"the subject's psycho-physiological responses to the foregoing relevant questions were indicative of him answering the questions truthfully"* and *"it is the opinion of the examiner that the subject has told substantially the truth."*[541]

Joseph Stair's lack of an irrefutable alibi hurts his defense somewhat, but the evidence gathered to demonstrate his involvement is equally weak and does not even meet the criteria required of circumstantial evidence. "Ear witnesses" that cannot prove definitively the name "Joe" was spoken by one of the gunmen, or that it referred specifically to Joe Stair, and an eyewitness that placed him in a location where more than 50 others saw Dylan Klebold, do not make for a solid foundation of a case. Moreover, Stair passed a polygraph test and the search warrant executed for his room provided nothing to tie him to the crime. It would appear that Joe Stair was yet another person unjustly accused because of a prior relationship with Harris and Klebold.

Multiple Shooters = No supporting evidence

In the chaos that surrounded the events of April 20, 1999, there were dozens of reports of multiple gunmen and bombers. Perry, Morris, Sargent, and Stair were the names most often bandied about, but other witnesses believed there were additional, unidentified shooters involved. Perhaps some of the most often cited testimony for this theory came from survivors of the library attack. In reality, of the 44 library victims who gave statements to police, only five indicated that they thought they heard explosions or gunshots occurring in other parts of the school while Eric and Dylan were still in the library. Three of those witnesses based their belief that the explosions had to be coming from the Commons area below the library by how much the library floor shook when the bombs went off.[532,698,699] Two others indicated that they heard blasts in other areas, but did not specify what gave them the impression that they came from elsewhere.[700,701] One of these five also told police he thought he heard shooting coming from different parts of the school but was unable to determine the location because "*noises in the school tend to funnel to the library.*"[699] All of those who believed sounds were coming from areas other than the library were hiding with fellow students, none of whom indicated to police that they felt the noises originated somewhere else. In addition to the shaking of the floor, which would be expected if the bombs were detonated inside the library, the inability to determine their location may be, as one student explained, the result of "*the echoing of the explosions within the library*"[702] that made it difficult for him to tell from which direction they came.

Several other students told investigators that there were more than two people involved in the shooting. Many of these eyewitnesses have been cited on web pages that promote a multiple shooter scenario. Many of these reports, however, can be easily dismissed with just a little further reading. Two of the witnesses listed as having knowledge of more shooters actually told police that while they did not see a third gunman, they either had a *"feeling that there was a third person there"*[703] or that they believed this due to the number of gunshots and explosions.[704] A library witness also thought the amount of noise indicated three gunmen but reported that she never saw any suspects because *"I didn't want to move and was only able to see shadows."*[705] Another often cited witness, who was inside the cafeteria at the time of the attack, gave a clothing description of one of the gunmen that did not fit either Klebold or Harris.[706] Upon review of the cafeteria surveillance video stills, however, she recognized Eric and Dylan as the shooters she saw that day.[707] The attire she had attributed to Harris was actually worn by faculty members running through the cafeteria trying to get students to safety.[708] Yet another girl told police that as she was hiding in one of the science classrooms she observed Dylan Klebold and a second gunman, whom she described as a man in his thirties with short, spiky blond hair.[709] Her observations on that day must be questioned, however, because she also reported that between 11:05-11:10 that morning she had spoken to Eric Harris at the "smoker's pit". The girl said, "*she made a remark about having a bad day to the students at the pit and that Eric said something like, 'Not only are you having a bad day, it's Hitler's birthday.'*"[709] She claimed that she specifically remembered this conversation because Eric usually did not talk to her. She named Brooks Brown, one of the murder victims, and another student as being present at the smoker's pit that morning. A detailed timeline of events clearly showed that this interaction with Harris could not have occurred because Eric was not at the smoker's pit at any time on the morning of the attack. Moreover, neither Brooks Brown nor the other student named indicated that they saw Harris there that day, with Brown specifically stating that he did not see Eric until immediately before the start of the attack.[710,711]

Another often mentioned "third gunman" was an unidentified individual seen near Harris and Klebold when they initially began shooting at the top of the stairs outside. He was described as wearing a white T-shirt and blue jeans. Some witnesses observed this individual with both Eric and Dylan,[377,675,712,713,714] while others saw only two people: one in a T-shirt, the other in a trench coat.[715] Most of those who saw this "third gunman" with the two trench-coated shooters told police they did not see this individual with a weapon, but a few observed a person in a white T-shirt throw something onto the roof of the school.[654,713,714,715] In addition, one boy told police that the person in the white tee yelled "Go, Go!" and then the two males in trench coats began firing.[714] However, further evaluation of reports from all witnesses who observed the outside portion of the attack puts the existence of this third gunman into doubt. One of the witnesses who reported observing this third suspect throwing bombs onto the roof later identified Eric Harris from the cafeteria surveillance video stills as the person he saw.[654] In addition, a female student reported that just prior to Harris and Klebold opening fire, *"she observed the suspects look at each other and 'nod.'* [She] *explained at the time she observed the above behavior she thought to herself it was somewhat 'strange.'* [She] *related after seeing the suspects nod to each other it was then she realized they were 'armed.'* [She] *explained she next observed the taller of the two suspects fire several rapid rounds in an easterly direction."*[487] The girl indicated that it was the nod between the two boys that initiated the attack and she did not hear anyone yell "Go! Go!" prior to the start of the shooting. Another student informed police that he saw a sophomore he knew *"standing near by a male party in a trench coat and another party wearing a white shirt that had black straps going across his lower chest."*[716] Harris wore a black bandolier atop his shirt to carry his ammunition. The boy told investigators that this sophomore *"took off running yelling a warning for everybody to get-a-way or something like that."*[716] Perhaps this is when the words "Go! Go!" were overheard. Instead of the statements coming from the assailants, they may have actually originated with a fellow student trying to save his classmates. In interviews with the sophomore, who was mentioned by name in the report, he did not discuss any words of caution he might have shouted to those around him. The girl who observed the assailants nodding to one another also told police that she only saw two gunmen, which she identified as Harris and Klebold. In total, 30 witnesses indicated that they, too, observed only two individuals shooting and throwing bombs during the outside assault (see Appendix C).

This discrepancy in accounts suggests that the individual in the white T-shirt could have either been an innocent bystander or Eric Harris after he had removed his trench coat. While it might seem odd that someone would be standing near the two boys when they started shooting, witness testimony suggests it may have been because many did not consider that the attack was real at first. More than 100 individuals reported to police that they were not initially concerned because they believed it was nothing more than a senior prank (see Appendix B). In fact, the sophomore seen near the gunmen told investigators he thought *"this was all some sort of video situation and the firecrackers were sound effects"*[717] and that even after seeing them fire upon and hit other kids, *"he still thought that this was all possibly a paint ball incident."*[717] A male student described *"one kid running backwards up the hill with a smile on his face. He said that the kid was wearing a white shirt and faded blue jean shorts, and he just sort of stopped to watch. [He] said that he doesn't think that the kid was a part of anything, just that at first, they thought it was a joke. He said that he saw other people running that were smiling."*[718] Could this have been the presumed third gunman? Two others that fit the description include a boy with *"short blond hair wearing a white t-shirt and blue jeans"*[719] who appeared to be injured, and a heavyset boy in a white T-shirt *"running toward the soccer field."*[720] Could one of these individuals have been confused for a third gunman? Or perhaps when Harris shed his trench coat[721,722,723] it led witnesses to believe he was an entirely different person. One student explained that this did confuse him. He reported that he initially believed he saw three shooters, but after viewing the cafeteria surveillance video stills realized that the person he saw in the trench coat and the one he observed a short while later in a white shirt were actually both Eric Harris.[724]

Eyewitness testimony is extremely important to any investigation, but police know that it is not infallible. Although the autopsy report, cafeteria surveillance footage, and Harris's death scene photos clearly show that Eric was wearing a white T-shirt and black BDU's on April 20, witnesses variously reported him wearing a white T-shirt, gray T-shirt, black T-shirt, a green-colored shirt, or a light-colored shirt——that was possibly tan. His pants were described as dark pants, black pants, blue jeans, army pants, army camo pants, or olive-colored pants (see Appendix C). Harris was positively identified by these witnesses yet, due to the chaos of the moment, many had difficulty recalling exactly what he wore.

Much of the multiple gunmen confusion follows a similar vein, and to explore every single conspiracy theory is outside the realm of this book. It is quite easy to see how those who look at only portions of the available evidence could arrive at the conclusions they do. In order to build a legitimate and responsible case for a particular theory, however, picking and choosing only that which supports the theory is not—and should not be—an option. Ignoring contradictory evidence prevents us from gaining any insight or understanding into this tragedy by directing focus elsewhere and distracting us from the wealth of information that helps us get closer to some semblance of an answer.

Chapter Ten

Were They Mentally Ill?

Countless experts in law enforcement and the psychiatric field have presented posthumous diagnoses of the mental states of Eric Harris and Dylan Klebold. These professional opinions vary widely despite access to much of the same information. One group of experts highlight certain facets of the boys' behavior and minimize others, while the next group claims that what was minimized was actually vitally important. The only thing this really serves to illustrate is that it is impossible to diagnose what cannot be examined. How can there be certainty regarding an individual's mental condition or thought processes if that person cannot be engaged in a dialogue? How can the assumption of manipulation, lack of empathy or feeling, or any number of complex emotional states be made without the ability to ask specific, probing questions designed to elicit the most revealing and direct answers? Quite simply, it cannot.

There is a reason that a valid doctor-patient relationship is both legally and ethically required before a person can receive a proper diagnosis, counseling, and therapy. Such a relationship cannot be cultivated from journal writings or videos, nor from evaluation of one's friends or family. This might allow for the development of a working hypothesis, but without access to the patient it is merely a hypothesis nonetheless. Definitive knowledge of particular psychiatric disorders driving Eric and Dylan in their murderous rampage is impossible because no one had the benefit of interviewing either boy on the matter. Without access to Harris or Klebold, even the most experienced professionals can only offer an opinion and nothing more. As such, pronouncements of Harris as a psychopath with Klebold as his depressive follower cannot— and should not be— promoted as fact. It is both misleading and potentially dangerous to imply Eric's homicidal and Dylan's suicidal urges were inevitable and unpreventable. This blanket declaration not only closes the door blindly on all of the life experiences that created these two boys, but it also frees us as a society from recognizing the role that we play in the lives of others. It sends the message that what a person becomes is either predetermined at birth or evolves independently from all of the influences around them. Nature rules all and nurturing has nothing to do with it. Eric Harris was not destined to kill. Dylan Klebold's self-hatred did not develop in a vacuum. To suggest as much could prevent us from recognizing other young people who are struggling—who are trying to find a purpose for themselves but are on the verge of giving up or lashing out because they cannot navigate their way.

The objective of this book, as a whole, is to present only the known, documented, and factual evidence to help clear up two decades of misunderstanding about this case. This chapter, however, represents nothing more than the author's hypotheses on whether Eric and Dylan were truly beyond hope. There will be no proclamations that this book holds the answers to "what were they thinking?" and "why did they do it?" Those answers, if even they had them, died in the school library with Harris and Klebold. However, there are aspects of their personalities revealed in their journals, school work, personal interactions, and videos that have not been widely discussed. It is the feeling of this author that a presentation of these facets may allow others to draw their own conclusions about Eric and Dylan. The intent is to inform, not to influence, but the author's opinions will be freely expressed herein.

It does not require an in-depth analysis of Dylan's writing to realize that, in many ways, he was profoundly unhappy and harbored deep feelings of self-loathing. Dylan's journal entries date back more than two years before the attack, and from the very first his despair is palpable. Klebold detailed his reflection on the past, wondering *"how/when i got so fucked up w. my mind, existence, problem-when Dylan Benet Klebold got covered up by this entity containing Dylan's body... "*[195] and how he now lacked *"the true human nature that Dylan owned."*[195] In a poem, Dylan wrote of his "godliness" but said that what he wanted more than anything was the humanity that was denied him: *"being made a human without the possibility of BEING human, the cruelest of all punishments."*[725] Klebold viewed himself as completely different from all others, expressing appreciation for his intellect and ability to understand existence and reality but lamenting his inability to connect with his peers. He wrote that *"thinking of suicide gives me hope, that ill be in my place wherever i go after this life. that ill finally not be at war w. myself, the world, the universe- my mind, body, everywhere, everything at PEACE... me- my soul (existence). & the rotine* (sic)*- is still monotonous, go to school, be scared & nervous, somewhat hoping that people can accept me... that i can accept them."*[195]

Through much of Dylan's writing, he expressed how hard it was for him to relate to other people. As detailed in chapter seven, virtually all who knew Klebold described him as a shy individual. "Shy" is often the misused generic term to describe a person who has trouble opening up to others in social situations. There are varying degrees of shyness; the most severe of which are, these days, characterized as psychological disorders. Given what we have learned about Dylan through interviews with friends and family, and from his own writings, his shyness appears to have been quite a significant factor in his life. The extent to which this affected his self-esteem comes across, to a degree, in his journal entries. Individuals blessed with an extroverted personality, or only mild or situational bashfulness, cannot appreciate how profound "shyness" as a condition can be for a person suffering from it. For most of those afflicted, social interactions are filled with tension and fear. Finding the right words to say, or any words at all, becomes very difficult. The internal dialogue only makes things worse: "what if I say something stupid?", "Come on, say something, they'll think I'm a freak!", or "I can't believe I said/did that, I'm such an idiot!" Dylan expressed it simply as, "*i never know what to say or do.*"[196] On an intellectual level, a sufferer may understand that the anxiety is unfounded, but such an understanding does little to quell the physiologic reactions that occur within the body. Elevated heart rate, a queasy stomach, shortness of breath, and racing thoughts are not the easiest to reign in, even when one realizes the stimulus should not warrant such a response. In fact, the knowledge may only compound the issue as the shy person berates himself for being unable to control his emotions in a seemingly benign situation. Being incapable of handling what others give no thought to can be a real blow to the sufferer's self-confidence. Dylan was often critical of himself in his writing, struggling to figure out why he behaved as he did and why others did not respond to him in the way he wanted. Recounting why he hated his life, Klebold wrote: "*nobody accepting me even though i want to be accepted, me doing badly & being intimidated in any & all sports, me looking weird & acting shy- BIG problem."*[196]

Dylan apparently tried to deal with his feelings through writing and poetry. According to a journal entry, he also tried to relieve his pain through cutting. *"Anyway... I was Mr. Cutter tonight- I have 11 depressioners on my right hand now, & my fav. contrasting symbol, because it is so true & means so much- The battle between good & bad never ends."*[196] It is unclear how many people were aware of this behavior, but even kids who were not friends with Klebold seemed to know about it. A witness to the shootings, when questioned on the day of the attack, told police that the assailants were seniors at the school and that *"one carved his arm with a razor."*[726]

Klebold viewed himself as wholly separate and apart from all other people. He represented his perception of existence as a box divided by walls he called *"limitations."*[727] The majority of people existed in only a small portion of the box, while none were found in the outermost fringe. Dylan placed himself completely outside of it, all alone.[727] In one of his last journal entries, Dylan wrote: *"I know that i am different, yet i am afraid to tell the society. The possible abandonment, persecution is not something I want to face, yet it is so primitive to me."*[728] In recent years, it has been reported that Klebold and Harris had a lot of friends and that their portrayal as outcasts was inaccurate. Dylan's own writing, however, contradicts such claims. He did have acquaintances, people he spoke with at school and work, or saw at group gatherings on weekends, but Klebold indicated quite clearly in his journal that he had few real or close friends. In listing what was good in his life he penned, *"a couple good friends,"* and when detailing the bad he wrote, *"no girls (friends or girlfriends), no other friends except a few, nobody accepting me even though i want to be accepted."*[196] In fact, Dylan lamented that he had only ever truly connected with one person. Dylan's best friend was not Eric Harris; he was the third member of the Rebel Clan. On July 23, 1997 Klebold wrote, *"My best friend ever: the friend who shared, experimented, laughed, took chances with, & appreciated me more than any friend ever did has been ordained... 'passed on'... in my book. Ever since* [redacted] *(who i wouldnt mind killing) has loved him... thats the only place hes been: with her... If anyone had any idea how sad I am... I mean, we were the <u>TEAM</u>. When him & I first were friends, well I finally found someone who was like me: who appreciated me & shared very common interests. Ever since 7th grade, ive felt lonely... when* [redacted] *came around, I finally felt happiness (sometimes). We did cigars, drinking, sabotage to houses, EVERYTHING for the first time together & now that he's 'moved on' i feel so lonely, w/o a friend."*[446] Several months later when Eric, too, began dating a girl, Klebold's misery deepened even further. *"Some god i am... All people i ever might have loved have abandoned me, my parents piss me off & hate me... want me to have fuckin ambition! How can i when i get screwed and destroyed by <u>everything</u>? I have no money, no happiness, no friends..."*[447] In August 1998, Dylan continued to express his frustration and sadness over his relationships with those closest to him: "*my friends (at my choice) are depleting & collapsing under each other (Eric &* [redacted]*) like i thought they would.*"[729]

People left to themselves to deal with extreme emotional states cope with their feelings in all sorts of ways. Some may turn their anger inward, believing that they are not deserving of happiness, blaming themselves for everything negative that happens. Some turn things outward, accusing others of unfairness or cruelty while failing to realize or acknowledge the role they may play in their own situation. Individuals, especially those with more than an average intellect, may also ponder the meaning or purpose of their pain. Consider what happens when an event occurs to shake your confidence and self-esteem. How long do you linger over it? Dylan spent a lot of time pondering things. In his journal he wrote, "*i think a lot. Think… think… thats all my life is, just shitloads of thinking… all the time… my mind never stops.*"[194] How many times do you replay the situation over in your mind— how it could have gone differently, what you wished you had done? How do you resolve your feelings of embarrassment, sadness, humiliation, or anger? Most people are unable to just "let it go" and need to rationalize some sort of mental compromise as a way to make themselves feel better and, perhaps, lessen their own responsibility to some extent by placing blame elsewhere. These are normal human mechanisms for coping with a difficult or unpleasant situation. Otherwise, we could not move on to face the next set of challenges. What about those individuals whose take on a situation after they have spent time mulling it over seems a bit extreme given the circumstances? Each of us knows that person who always seems to take a common event and blow it out of proportion. Everyone can think of several friends, co-workers, relatives, or neighbors who share this tendency. Are all of those people exhibiting abnormal behavioral traits? Do all of those people have an underlying psychological disorder?

It would seem from the examination of both Dylan's and Eric's journal writings that their perceptions of life events, as well as their methods of rationalizing those events, tended to be more extreme. It seems likely that the two boys discussed such things amongst themselves, thereby reinforcing their own beliefs and adding legitimacy to their interpretation of things. Without someone to help them reign in their views, they were free to spin from reality to fantasy and to ever increasing levels of anger over their situations. Their relationship allowed each boy to feed off of the negativity of the other, a dynamic that is probably best demonstrated through their conversations in the "Basement Tapes." It allowed each of them to go further than either may have gone alone. It allowed each of them to justify their actions and their status as above all others. Much has been made of Eric Harris and his presumed Malignant Narcissism. Klebold expressed similar views regarding his self-perceived superiority over others. Yet, this has seemingly been downplayed, especially in recent years. Perhaps this was done to not distract from the predominant psychological "depressive" profile that has been proffered as the reason for his participation in the attack. It has been suggested that Dylan's expressions of anger and disdain for others and society came about only in the months before the assault. Again, his journal entries do not bear this out. Two years before the shootings, Klebold was articulating his feelings about the "morons" and "zombies", about his god-like state, his rage at being an outcast, and the unfairness of not possessing the happiness that others have.

Throughout Klebold's writing, he refers to his ability to see and understand what others cannot. Dylan explained that the experiences of the masses, although he wants them for himself, lack depth and meaning because the masses do not possess his superior intellect and comprehension of the world and reality. He expressed this belief through a poem written in April 1997, more than two years prior to the attack:

Existence... what a strange word. He, set out by determination & curiosity, knows no existence, knows nothing realevant to himself. The petty destinations of others & everything on this world, in this world, he knows the answers to. Yet they have no purpose to him. He seeks knowledge of the unthinkable, of the indefineable, of the unknown. He explores the everything... using his mind, the most powerful tool known to him. Not a physical barrier blocking the limits of exploration, time thru thought thru dimensions... the everything is his realm. Yet, the more he thinks, hoping to find answers to his questions, the more come up. Amazingly, the petty things mean much to him at this time, how he wants to be normal, not this transceiver of the everything. Then, ocurring to him, the answer. How everything is connected yet seperate. By experiencing the petty others' actions, reactions, emotions, doings, and thoughts, he gets a mental picture of what, in his mind, is a cycle. Existence is a great hall, life is one of the rooms, death is passing thru the doors, & the ever-existant compulsion of everything is the curiosity to keep moving down the hall, thru the doors, exploring rooms, down this never-ending hall. Questions make answers, answers conceive questions, and at long last he is content.[730]

He also wrote of his disdain for those who lacked his level of awareness. *"I think, too much, I understand, I am <u>GOD</u> compared to some of these un-existable, brainless zombies. Yet, the actions of them interest me, like a kid w. a new toy. Another contrast, more of a paradox, actually, like the advanced go for the undevelopeds realm, while <u>some </u>of the morons become everything dwellers- but, exceptions to every rule, & this is a BIG exception- most morons never change- they never decide to live in the 'everything' frame of mind.*[731]

There is no question that Dylan Klebold was suicidal. He mentioned it often, almost blissfully at times. He expressed feelings of self-doubt, self-hatred, and chastised his own shortcomings. But throughout his writings, from early 1997 until his death, there should also be no doubt that Dylan was full of anger and jealousy. He blamed himself, yes, but he blamed others as well. Dylan considered himself a victim, someone who suffered while others less deserving prospered, sometimes at his expense. Klebold convinced himself that his mind, his thoughts, and his understanding were light-years ahead of everyone else. Given the total of his writings, this was likely a coping mechanism—a method of dealing with his shattered self-esteem. He often wrote of his intellectual superiority, of his godlike comprehension of the world and man, however, throughout Klebold's journal there is always an undercurrent of pain and self-loathing. Left to his devices, without commiseration from Eric Harris, perhaps Dylan would have killed only himself and ended his pain. Or, as he wrote, he might have gone on his own "*killing spree*"[201] before taking his own life. It is also plausible that Klebold, like so many who suffer through a turbulent and difficult adolescence, would have come to terms with who he was and would have learned to channel his feelings, creativity, and intelligence in a more positive direction.

Despite reports to the contrary, the same themes of self-doubt and low self-esteem are evident in the writings of Eric Harris. Harris's journals are notorious for the vitriol and rage they contain. While he may have managed to keep most of his anger and hostility hidden from friends and family, Eric poured out his hatred in his private writings. Virtually every article penned about Harris included an excerpt or two from his journal to illustrate his deep-seated wrath. Eric has been labeled, posthumously, as a psychopath with Malignant Narcissism. Essentially, if this diagnosis is to be believed, there was never a chance for Harris to be anything other than a killer. His only interest was himself. He had little empathy or feelings for the wants or needs of anyone else. Eric was born to murder—it was inevitable. On the surface, there is evidence to support such claims. As with most things, however, the surface does not represent the entire story. When Harris's life is viewed in total, when all of the available evidence is examined, there are clear indications that Eric was not destined for the path he chose.

It should be noted that psychopathy is not recognized as a disorder unto itself by any organized body of psychiatric or psychologic medicine, even though the terminology is used quite frequently within the field of law enforcement. Characteristics of psychopathy are identified as an offshoot under the umbrella of the clinically recognized Antisocial Personality Disorder (ASPD).[732,733] The differentiation between ASPD and psychopathy lies in the ability of the affected individual to feel remorse or empathy. A person affected by ASPD is capable of those emotions but may subdue them in order to behave the way they wish. A psychopath would be unable to experience said emotions or feel them only superficially. Clinically, it is impossible to demonstrate that an individual is incapable of feeling, as emotion cannot adequately be subjected to diagnostic testing. As such, psychopathy can be suspected but never proven.

The basis for identifying Eric Harris as a psychopath lies in the works of psychiatrist Hervey Cleckley and psychologist Robert Hare. Hare built upon Cleckley's works of the 1940's and developed a *Psychopathy Checklist*, later revised, that has since been applied to Harris. The checklist consists of twenty factors that can each receive a score ranging from zero to two, *"for which 0 indicates that it definitely does not apply, 1 that it applies somewhat or only in a limited sense, and 2 that it definitely does apply to the person."*[732] Individuals receiving a score of 30 or higher would fit the psychological profile of a psychopath, although Hare reported that *"some investigators have obtained good results with cutoff scores as low as 25."*[732] The twenty factors on the list are:

> Glibness/superficial charm
> Grandiose sense of self-worth
> Pathological lying
> Cunning/manipulative
> Lack of remorse or guilt
> Emotionally shallow
> Callous/lack of empathy
> Failure to accept responsibility for own actions
> Need for stimulation/proneness to boredom
> Parasitic lifestyle
> Lack of realistic, long-term goals
> Impulsivity
> Irresponsibility
> Poor behavioral controls
> Early behavioral problems
> Juvenile delinquency
> Revocation of conditional release
> Criminal versatility
> Many short-term marital relationships

Promiscuous sexual behavior[732]

In an attempt to determine how closely Eric Harris fits the diagnosis of a psychopath, each trait will be examined individually. The author claims no psychiatric training. This exercise should be viewed as the author's opinion only and not a professional psychiatric evaluation.

Glibness/superficial charm—Score: 1 (mid-range)

Many people who knew Harris described him as clever with a sharp wit. Socially, he often made light of a situation through the use of humor and he was usually able to convince others, particularly those in authority, to see things his way. However, Harris had a great deal of difficulty using that charm to win girls. He made attempts, but they were usually unsuccessful. If he did get a girl's attention, he quickly lost it (see Chapter Six). In addition, it is well documented that Eric would often not approach a girl directly but would speak with her friends first in order to gauge her interest in him. Harris even put a student up to asking a girl to the Prom for him,[382] something a bonafide psychopath seems unlikely to do. Psychopaths are risk takers and feel anxiety and fear much less intensely than others. The prospect of rejection is not likely to significantly thwart the desire of the psychopath.

Grandiose sense of self-worth—Score: 1 (mid-range)

In his journal, Eric repeatedly referred to himself as a god, remarking on his superior intellect, self-awareness, as well as mocking others for their inability to think for themselves or do more than act like a flock of sheep. However, he also stated quite plainly that he hated the way he looked, his awkwardness with girls, and his inability to gain respect.[177,190,191,192] While Harris may have possessed traits common to those with narcissism, narcissists seem to lack the ability to admit their flaws or to acknowledge their fragile self-esteem. Like Dylan, Harris's proclamations of self-importance may have been a mechanism for coping with his poor self-image, but he was not incapable of understanding that much of his anger originated from it.

Pathological lying—Score: 0 (lowest)

By definition, a "pathological liar" is *"an individual who habitually tells lies so exaggerated or bizarre that they are suggestive of mental disorder."*[734] Harris lied and, according to him, he lied a lot.[735] However, his lies were not without reason nor were they extravagant. Eric's lies were self-serving to get himself out of trouble and to make others, particularly his parents, believe that he was not doing anything inappropriate. Much is made of Harris bragging about being able to lie himself out of situations. They cite this trait as duping delight, a hallmark of psychopathy. However, true duping delight involves not just the pleasure taken from lying successfully, but also the risk the liar has taken in telling the lie in the first place. Eric's lies had a specific purpose, they were not done for sport to entertain himself.

Cunning/manipulative—Score: 2 (highest)

Harris was able to convince his parents, teachers, co-workers, and his Diversion counselor that he was walking the straight and narrow all the while he was secretly planning a large-scale assault on his high school. Along with Klebold, he talked a friend into attending a gun show with them so that they could obtain weapons. Eric knew how to handle people without arousing suspicion to get the things that he wanted. It is worth noting that Klebold possessed some skills in this area, too, although this is rarely addressed. Dylan participated in the planning for "NBK" for at least a year and never tipped his hand to anyone. In the "Basement Tapes," Dylan thanks Mark Manes and Phil Duran, from whom the boys were able to secure Klebold's TEC-DC9. He says, *"We used them. They had no clue, if it hadn't been them, it would have been someone else over 21."*[736]

Lack of remorse or guilt—Score: 1 (mid-range)

Harris did not appear to exhibit remorse for the people he killed, wounded, or terrorized. Eight months prior to the assault, however, he did write of how he would steel himself against any emotion in order to be able to go through with his crime. *"someones bound to say, 'What were they thinking?' when we go NBK or when we were planning it, so this is what I am thinking, 'I have a goal to destroy as much as possible so I must not be sidetracked by my feelings of sympathy, mercy, or any of that, so I will force myself to believe that everyone is just another monster from Doom like FH or FS or demons, so It's either me or them. I have to turn off my feelings. "*[737] A person lacking the ability to feel remorse for his actions or empathy for the pain of others would have no need to make such a plan to guard his emotions. Eric also apologized, repeatedly, in both his journal and in the "Basement Tapes" to his parents and tried to reassure them that they were not at fault and could not have prevented what he was going to do. These statements of contrition, because they are out of the norm for a psychopath's behavior, have been claimed disingenuous and another form of manipulation by those wishing to promote this diagnosis for Harris. What they fail to address is the purpose for such a manipulation. If a psychopath has only his own self-interest in mind and is unconcerned about how his actions affect others, why would he go to the trouble to address his parents multiple times in such a manner? He fully expected to be killed in the attack and would never be facing his parents again. In that situation, any pretense for caring for them, their feelings, or how he would be remembered by them would then be wholly unnecessary to the true psychopath. In a "Basement Tape" video, *"Harris begins discussing his mother and father and the cops who may want to have his 'parents pay.' Harris describes his parents as the 'best parents' and states that anything they would have tried to do this past year he would have gotten around it. Harris states, 'There is no one else to blame but me and Vodka.'"*[738] Eric's statement, and ones similar to it, cannot be considered self-serving because he would have nothing to gain from them. How can it be considered manipulation when he apologized and readily admitted his crimes would leave his mother and father *"just like fucking shocked beyond belief"*?[390] The pathology comes from Harris continuing to move forward with the heinous plan despite the pain he knew it would cause those close to him. His ability to go through with the attack, in spite of the devastation to his loved ones, in no way negated that love. Nor did it indicate that they were just pawns in his game. How often do people put their own desires above those they care about, even when there is reasonable certainty for the incalculable suffering of those left behind? Most could not fathom hurting the ones that are most dear to them, but just because someone makes the choice to do so, can we prove that means the individual never cared in the first place?

Emotionally shallow—Score: 1 (mid-range)

Scoring for this trait is, by necessity, a guess because it does not seem possible to determine how deeply another person can feel an emotion. As such, a one is given only because a great depth of emotion cannot be proven based on available evidence. Eric, himself, reported having only one close friend (Klebold).[293] It is conceivable that this could be due to an inability to connect on a personal or emotional level with his peers, but it is unknown if it was because he was incapable of deep feeling or because he guarded his emotions so closely. In the author's opinion, videos that Eric made for class, his personal writings, and statements from his friends seem to indicate that he could experience genuine happiness, excitement, compassion, and tenderness towards others, especially his family. These feelings were not limited to people, as Harris also expressed an appreciation and love of animals, albeit through threats of violence towards those who would hurt them[739] and even took steps to have Dylan cover a shift at work so that he could stay home to care for his ailing dog.[308] In addition, during one of the "Basement Tapes," Eric appeared to become emotional when reminiscing about old friends in Michigan. He was observed crying just before he shut off the video recorder.[410]

Callous/lack of empathy—Score: 1 (mid-range)

It should be repeated that Eric's actions on April 20, 1999 were incredibly callous and that he showed neither empathy nor mercy for his victims. In other aspects of his life, however, he did show concern for the feelings and well-being of others. As mentioned previously in his writing and on the "Basement Tapes," Harris repeatedly expressed his love for his parents and his regret for the pain and trouble his actions would cause them. He voiced his love and admiration for his older brother and apologized to friends for any trouble they might encounter as a result of what he was to do. When writing of the gun show at which he and Dylan had obtained some of their weapons, Eric conveyed his disappointment at not being able to share the venue with his father. "*You know, its really a shame. I had a lot of fun at that gun show, I would have loved it if you were there dad. we would have done some major bonding. would have been great.*"[409] Harris also reportedly made a concerted effort not to bond further with his family in the weeks prior to the attack. In the "Basement Tapes," "*Harris states he is not spending time with his family, so there won't be any 'bonding' and 'this won't be harder to do.'*"[736] Such statements would be superfluous for someone who had little feeling for others. If his parents had served their purpose to him, he would not care how they would cope with the aftermath or how they would feel about him after he was gone. It would be utterly unnecessary for him to deliberately avoid spending time with his family if Eric did not really care for them.

Failure to accept responsibility for own actions—Score: 2 (highest)

While publicly Harris put on a face of contrition for his transgressions, privately he seemed willing to blame others as much, if not more, than he blamed himself. Whether it be the feud with Brooks Brown, the locker incident for which he was suspended, or the van break-in, Eric's writings always seemed to diminish his responsibility, focus the blame elsewhere and, in some cases, point to himself as a victim more than a perpetrator.

Need for stimulation/proneness to boredom— Score: 1 (mid-range)

Individuals fitting this trait often lack self-discipline and have trouble holding a job or completing assignments because they get bored of them. Harris, on the other hand, appeared to be quite disciplined, dependable, and did well in school and at work. However, the author has allotted a one specifically for the "missions" that Eric, Dylan, and a friend carried out over several months in 1997.

Harris described these excursions as revenge for wrongs done to them. The excitement he expressed when detailing the "missions" suggested that, to some extent, Eric participated for the sake of the thrill and danger. Whether this represented a true need for stimulation or if this is closely correlated with typical thrill-seeking activities expected of a normal adolescent male is unknown.

Parasitic Lifestyle- Score: 0 (lowest)

All indications are that Eric Harris worked hard in school, at home, and at his job. He earned good marks in class, helped his parents around the house,[740] and was held in high esteem by his employers for being dependable and hard-working.[275,276,741]

Lack of realistic, long term goals—Score: 1 (mid-range)

By all indications, Harris did not make plans for his life beyond high school. Eric did not begin discussions with a Marine Corps recruiter until early April 1999, a time when his plans and commitment to "NBK" were all but finalized. Harris appeared to be engaging the recruiter only to appease his parents, who were concerned about his lack of preparation for his future. In the "Basement Tapes" he says, *"his parents have been on his 'back for putting things off' such as 'insurance, and the Marine Corp.'"* He then discusses, *"this is my last week on earth."*[738] Disturbingly, however, Eric and Dylan did spend an entire year devising, financing, constructing, and ultimately orchestrating the attack on Columbine. This degree of preparation is troubling testimony to Harris's ability to put a long-term goal into action.

Impulsivity—Score: 0 (lowest)

Aside from the van break-in, which both Harris and Klebold admitted was unplanned, Eric appears to have been the one to thoroughly plan his actions and he rarely gave in to impulsivity.

Irresponsibility—Score: 0 (lowest)

As outlined above, Eric worked hard in school, helped out at home, and exhibited a strong work ethic at his job.

Poor behavioral controls—Score: 2 (highest)

Harris managed to keep himself out of trouble for the most part, but he did acknowledge during his Diversion assessment that he was quick to anger over even the smallest things. One of Eric's parents told the assessment counselor that *"Eric seems to suppress his anger, then 'blow up' and hit something or verbally lash out. He hasn't done this at home but has done it at school and work."*[338]

Early behavioral problems—Score: 0 (lowest)

This trait refers to problems that occur prior to the age of thirteen. There is no evidence to suggest that Eric exhibited any behavioral issues prior to the eighth grade when he, Dylan, and several other boys sent a threatening letter to a female classmate.[221]

Juvenile delinquency—Score: 2 (highest)

Harris participated in computer hacking, vandalism, bomb-making, terroristic threats, and theft prior to the attack.

Revocation of conditional release—Score: 0 (lowest)

This factor is not applicable to Harris because he was never incarcerated. Eric completed the requirements of the Juvenile Diversion Program and was granted early termination. There were no terms set for revocation of release from the program if he re-offended.

Criminal versatility—Score: 2 (highest)

Harris's list of crimes included: computer hacking, vandalism, theft, bomb-making, terroristic threats, and eventually assault and murder.

Many short-term marital relationships—Score: 0 (lowest)

This trait illustrates the inability of the psychopath to commit to a long-term relationship. Obviously, Harris was never married. However, the few dating relationships he did have were likely comparable to those of most teenage boys (see Chapter Six). In addition, it appears that in all cases it was the girl, not Eric, who initiated the break up and that Harris, in several cases, made attempts to continue the relationship despite the girl's lack of interest (see Chapter Six).

Promiscuous sexual behavior—Score: 0 (lowest)

By all accounts, it is most likely that Eric Harris died a virgin (see Chapter Six).

The tally for Harris's *Psychopathy Checklist—Revised* scores sum to seventeen—, which is far below the requirement for classification as a psychopath. According to Hare, Eric would also fall below the average *Psychopathy Checklist—Revised* score for non-psychopathic criminals, but within the standard deviation for the latter criminal type. It has been determined that *"mean PCL-R scores in North American male and female offender populations typically range from about 22 to 24, with a standard deviation of from 6 to 8."*[733]

If the standard by which Harris has been diagnosed a psychopath is Hare's *Psychopathy Checklist—Revised*, and Eric failed to attain a requisite score of 25-30, how can a diagnosis be assigned? Moreover, how can an investigator give more weight to one aspect of Harris's writing and behavior (e.g., his hatred for people and desire to kill) and discount other aspects (e.g., his expressions of low self-esteem and remorse for the pain caused to his family) as manipulation? When the subject is not available for questioning and evaluation, there is no way that such a determination can be made. Instead, all available evidence should be given equal weight and any assumptions should be clearly identified as such. Professionals, in particular, need to be especially careful that they do not promote something as fact when no such fact can be proven. A statement of professional opinion should be presented as opinion and not touted as a certainty.

It is clear that Eric Harris possessed a good number of undesirable behavioral traits. In addition to being quick to anger, Eric was very slow to forgive.[118] Harris himself wrote, "*I dont forget people who wronged me*."[342] He appeared to be especially sensitive and had a long memory for perceived insults and slights. Even fairly minor transgressions were enough to earn people a place on Harris's "Shit List". Many of those on the list expressed surprise at their inclusion, often telling police they were unaware of any circumstances that could have caused a rift between themselves and Eric. A teacher who might have disciplined Harris while on hall duty,[742] a mother who felt her freshman daughter was too young to date him,[374] and a girl whose only likely "crime" was hanging out with jocks:[743] Eric put each of them on his hit list. Situations that to most people would have been a momentary annoyance or temporary frustration were, to Harris, problems worth killing over. Eric seemed to hold on to every bad thing that happened to him. He allowed all of these perceived injustices to fester and convinced himself that they justified the commission of violence. If Harris had trouble dealing with transient embarrassment, it is no wonder that having balls thrown at his face in gym,[174] getting slammed into lockers,[174,175] being called a faggot,[140,167] having ketchup as well as other objects thrown at him,[166,167,168,176] and being ridiculed almost daily for his fashion choices and taste in music (see Chapter Two) were more than he could handle.

In addition to labeling Eric a psychopath, he has also been deemed a narcissist. In the Diagnostic and Statistical Manual of Mental Disorders (DSM), people with Narcissistic Personality Disorder (NPD) are assigned particular behavioral traits. In the past, diagnosis required that an individual possess at least five of the traits from that list.[744] In 2011, the American Psychiatric Association slightly revised the criteria for NPD in the fifth edition of the DSM, however, Harris's "diagnosis" was made utilizing the traits outlined in DSM-IV. These criteria include:[744]

A grandiose sense of self-importance

A preoccupation with fantasies of unlimited success, power, brilliance, beauty, or ideal love

Belief that he or she is special and unique and can only be understood by other special people

A requirement for excessive admiration

A strong sense of entitlement

Taking advantage of others to achieve his or her own ends

Lacking empathy

Often envious of others or believes others are envious of him/her

Arrogant affect

For the author, if one is to adhere to this list for diagnosis, then it appears to describe both Eric Harris and Dylan Klebold. As mentioned, it is unclear why no one has ever pointed out that Dylan possessed the same narcissistic tendencies. Both boys, through their writings and in the "Basement Tapes," appeared to possess a grandiose sense of self-importance and a strong sense of entitlement. Both believed that only other equally special people (those with self-awareness, other "gods") could truly understand them. In fact, the latter trait was likely the basis for the bond the two boys forged with one another. Klebold, and Harris to a lesser extent, often expressed envy over the lives, relationships, and possessions of peers. While Eric appeared to be preoccupied with fantasies of power over others, Dylan seemed consumed with the notion of attaining a pure and perfect love. Both Harris and Klebold, at least in the last year of their lives during the preparation for the attack on Columbine, took advantage of others in order to achieve their ultimate goal. Of the two, Eric was the one who seemed to most desire admiration from his peers, writing in his journal and in notes to a friend that he was not receiving the respect he deserved.[177,401] Harris certainly appears to fit the majority of criteria for a diagnosis with Narcissistic Personality Disorder, but it should be acknowledged that Klebold's behavior seems equally consistent with the condition. However, there is enough evidence to suggest that neither boy should be classified as such. True narcissists suffer from poor self-esteem, as Dylan and Eric surely did. The true narcissist will do whatever it takes to avoid having to face their weaknesses. They are quite practiced at twisting every situation so that their fragile ego is protected and they are not made to take stock of their failings. Harris and Klebold appear to have lied to themselves and to one another about their superiority, but there is every indication that they did not truly believe in it. It was more likely a method to cope with a world and with people they could not control or make accept them. Both boys in moments of private candor indicated as such, and recognized this poor self-image as a significant factor in their unhappiness and behaviors

No one can know whether Eric and Dylan could have been saved—whether there was some point at which intervention would have altered the course of events and prevented this horrible tragedy. But the information they left behind seems to indicate that the rage and hatred grew from within. Harris and Klebold, through their own individual experiences, seem to have lost hope that they could create the kind of lives that they wanted. Their personalities and co-dependent friendship allowed them to retreat into themselves and each other, and to justify their anger and desire for revenge at their inability to achieve what others had. Perhaps they each suffered from a psychological disorder, or perhaps the combination of their two volatile personalities created a disorder in itself. Harris's reclamation would no doubt have been more difficult because, despite Klebold's obvious despair, Eric appeared to be the one who had truly given up on living. Harris had made the massacre at Columbine and his Doom Tier levels his "life's work."[745] *"THIS is what I am motivated for. THIS is my goal. THIS is what I want to do with my life!"*[409] He did not appear to be able to see beyond high school and allowed himself to be wholly consumed in his hatred. Dylan had made plans for his future. Perhaps this was, in part, to appease his parents. But Klebold, who would sometimes allow himself to dream of a life after Columbine, may have also left that window open in case plans for the attack changed. Dylan often wrote of his anger, jealousy, and wish for revenge. He, with Harris, meticulously planned the assault for almost a year. Despite all of this, Klebold's writing suggests that if he could have been convinced of the possibility of happiness—of love and acceptance—then he might have been persuaded to abandon his course.

Eric was far more jaded, expecting little of other people because he had trained himself to believe that humans, and society as a whole, were incapable of being more than rule-abiding automatons unable to accept those that were different. His experiences as the object of ridicule and scorn likely reinforced these views. Harris's ideas may have developed, in part, from his following of philosophers like Friedrich Nietzche and Thomas Hobbes. Eric believed in moral nihilism: that right and wrong were artificial states created by man to facilitate living together in peace and harmony. *"Only science and math are true, everything, and I mean everyfuckingthing else is Man made."*[342] In his journal he also wrote, *"Fuck mercy fuck justice fuck morals fuck civilized fuck rules fuck laws… DIE manmade words…" "there's no such thing as True Good or True evil, its all relative to the observer. its all just nature, chemistry, and math. deal with it. but since dealing with it seems impossible for mankind, since we have to slap warning labels on nature, then… you die. burn, melt, evaporate, decay, just go the fuck away!"*[746] Harris repeatedly described his belief that in order to conform to society's morals a person had to abandon their individuality and natural instincts. Those that did not do this, like him, were considered outcasts, *"psychos or lunatics or strangers or just plain different. crazy, strange, weird, wild, these words are not bad or degrading... if humans were let to live how we would naturally, it would be chaos and anarchy and the human race wouldn't probably last that long, but hey guess what, thats how its supposed to be! societys and government are only created to have order and calmness, which is exactly the opposite of pure human nature."*[747]

A major flaw with this assessment is that it fails to consider how animal, and even insect, societies are able to coexist without destroying one another. Humans are not the only group to have established set patterns, arrangements, hierarchies or "rules" to facilitate calm and order within the populace. Nature "understands" that without order there is chaos, so even colonies of ants have roles for each of the members to fulfill in order to ensure the success of the group. Worker bees support the queen so that she can lay eggs, lionesses hunt for the pride while the lion protects it, and primates have very well-defined social structures that enable the family group to thrive and peacefully co-exist with others of their kind. Assuming that because humans possess superior intelligence they should somehow be exempt from such a model makes little sense biologically or evolutionarily. Nature teaches that cooperation is key to the longevity and success of all social animals of any species. Harris claimed to believe in nothing but math and science yet seemed unaware of this tenet of biology. In addition, many who study animal behavior—particularly the higher primates—believe that the building blocks for morality have been observed in these species. Frans de Waal and other well-known primatologists have, for years, documented episodes of fair play, empathy, sharing, conflict resolution, guilt, and shame in primates. These observations may suggest that the morality we have come to believe is uniquely human may not be exclusive to our kind, but rather developed in biologically related species millions of years ago.[748] According to de Waal, *"The moral law is not imposed from above or derived from well-reasoned principles; rather it arises from ingrained values that have been there since the beginning of time."*[749] If we are evolutionarily programmed to be moral beings, then the human race could not abandon this trait any more than it could abandon the need for oxygen. Eric's failure to reconcile these theories may have been due to a lack of knowledge or understanding, as illustrated by his statement, *"just because your mommy and daddy told you blood and violence is bad, you think it's a fucking law of nature? Wrong."*[342] Harris did not recognize that the laws of nature may, in fact, indicate that order and morality have an evolutionary basis and are not devised by man.

Eric's philosophies, however, sometimes seemed to contradict his own true feelings. In a note to a friend, Harris spelled out what he felt was wrong with humans and, by extension, society as a whole. He referred to it as *"a trip through the mind of a wise one."*[217]

"ok, time for philosophy: Nihilism, Anarchism, and several others are all wrapped up into 1 ball called my head. society wants to get rid any human instincts we may have, like [teacher's name redacted] *said a few times, the industrial age and factories and shit, all to better the community and lessen the human part of life. sit in order, be respectful, dont talk outloud, drive safely, dont run, dont lie, bla bla dont dont! why the FUCK not! we are humans, we should use our brains for something besides memorizing cube roots. the things that puts us above animals is our brains, and society wants to flatten it out. they dont want thinkers and dreamers, only thinkers and dreamers who think and dream about how to be successful and be a good citizen. anyone who shows more thoughts or emotion than the norm is said to be wierd or crazy, wrong! they are just more in touch w/ their humanity, and people who think they can sum up mankind in simple lame quotes piss me off. like 'there are 2 kinds of people... the quick and the dead... the smart and the dumb... leaders and followers...' well you fucks are wrong! The only 2 kinds of people are male and Female! the rest is B.S. follow your instincts, be free from all, listen to no one, be SELF AWARE! step back and look at what you are doing, do you look stupid? smart? silly? foolish? that's why I acted like I did at After prom, have you ever watched, actually watched, someone dance? it is ridicu.o...lus. people are funny, they want to be accepted. dont be afraid to judge people either. people say you shouldn't judge others because thats not how they are on the*

inside… well oh fucking well and flippin bad, your impression of someone is what they seem like, and if they are to caught up and stupid to have their true self most obvious, then thats their choice. if they look like a lame gothic black devil wannabe then damnit thats what they want you to think and boom, verdict made."[217]

Although Eric espoused these philosophies, it does not appear that he adhered to them entirely. Despite not wanting to conform to society, Harris admitted that he, too, could not help but to fall in line. "*It's a fucking filthy place we live in- all these standards and laws and Great Expectations (webb) are making people into robots even though they might 'think' they arent and try to deny it. no matter how hard I try to NOT copy someone else I still AM!*"[341] He also wrote, "*I always try to be different, but I always end up copying someone else. I try to be a mixture of different things and styles but when I step out of myself I end up looking like others or others THINK I am copying.*"[315] And, despite telling his friend that it was okay to make assumptions about a person's character without getting to know them, Eric expressed resentment that others had done this very thing to him. In his journal he wrote, "*we arent GODS. just because we are at the top of the food chain with our technology doesn't mean we can be 'judges' of nature. sure we can think what we want, but you can 'think' and 'believe' you can judge people and nature all you want, but you are still wrong!*"[737] He did not seem to like others judging him by his appearance, complaining: "*Everyone is always making fun of me because of how I look, how fucking weak I am and shit, well I will get you all back*"[190] and "*no no no don't let the wierd looking Eric KID come along, ooh fucking nooo.*"[192] In November 1998, Eric penned, "*Whatever I do people make fun of me, and sometimes directly to my face. I'll get revenge soon enough. fuckers shouldn't have ripped on me so much huh! HA! then again its human nature to do what you did... so I guess I am also attacking the human race. I cant take it, Its not right... true... correct... perfect. I fucking hate the human equation.*"[401] From these entries, it would seem that despite his proclamations that people should use their free will and label others as they see fit, when his peers actually did this to him it affected him deeply.

Eric wrote of his belief that people, having abandoned their natural instinct and superior brain power that made them human, no longer deserved to exist. He used this rationalization to justify his killing. At some points in his writings, he indicated that only he and those he deemed fit should survive.[342,737] While at others, he included himself amongst those who needed to perish in order to wipe the scourge of humanity off the face of the planet.[341,342,746,750] In both scenarios, he allowed himself permission to participate in the destruction of man. As with many of Harris's statements, this is inconsistent and contradictory. Why, if he was superior to others and an example of what humanity should be, would he need to die too? Eric's journals and videotaped statements often seem to directly oppose one another. This dichotomy of thought is the main reason that interpretation of his true feelings and psychological state is not possible—particularly for those who choose to ignore these types of outliers because they seem to dirty up the neat little package recently presented of Eric's mental state. Evaluation of selective data, rather than all available data, will not bring about understanding of the truth.

Failure to recognize similar behavioral traits in at-risk young men and women will only result in more tragedy. The goal should not be to slap labels on Harris and Klebold to explain how they went so wrong, especially if those doing so are not considering all of the evidence. The opportunity for answers died with Eric and Dylan on April 20, 1999. There can be no definitive closure in this case, and by ignoring aspects of behaviors repeatedly exhibited by both boys simply because they do not tie in with the "accepted diagnoses," we may miss the chance to help— or at least stop—another troubled individual. Our focus needs to be on learning to identify kids like Eric and Dylan and taking a more proactive approach to reach out to those who express tendencies towards self-harm or violence towards others. We need to strengthen the communication between law enforcement agencies and schools so that a youth offender can be properly supervised. We need to strengthen communication between administrators, teachers, and parents so that matters are not "dropped" before they are adequately investigated. Most importantly, we need to educate our kids to recognize that a student that is persistently in trouble or making threats may pose a true safety concern. The children see far more in class, in the hallways, and in the cafeteria than any adult. It is up to us to empower them to take their concerns to the appropriate authorities and make sure those concerns are addressed promptly. No system is likely to be perfect, but if everyone makes it their personal responsibility to intervene when necessary, we will get closer than we have been up to this point.

Appendix A

Note: The *Columbine Report* encompasses pages one through 25889.

<u>Saw Dylan outside walking toward cafeteria from nearby parking lot-</u>

- The *Columbine Report,* pp. 2823, saw Dylan pull out a gun from under his coat and shoot it. Identified Klebold **after the fact** through media photos.
- The *Columbine Report*, pp. 3427-3428, **certain** he saw Dylan in parking lot with a shotgun. **Knew who Dylan was.**
- The *Columbine Report*, pp. 4254-4255, saw Dylan walking from the parking lot carrying shotgun in left hand and semiautomatic in his right hand. Identified as the **possible** shooter **after the fact; picked Klebold out of photo lineup**.

<u>Saw Dylan outside the cafeteria-</u>

- The *Columbine Report*, pp. 3034-3035, saw Dylan with gun walking toward the school. Identified **after the fact but had seen him in school before**. He described Dylan as having a "thin beard," and Dylan's necropsy indicated the presence of a goatee.[747]

- The *Columbine Report*, pp. 3112-3113, saw Dylan outside on the sidewalk with Eric. He was holding a smaller gun (also saw him come into the cafeteria). Identified **after the fact** through media photos.

- The *Columbine Report,* pp. 3531, **certain** he saw Dylan shoot at students and throw a pipe bomb into the parking lot. **Knew Klebold**.

- The *Columbine Report*, pp. 3614-3615, saw Dylan walking down the hill and throwing an object into the parking lot. Identified **after the fact** through media photos. Originally thought it was Perry until she saw the pictures.

- The *Columbine Report*, pp. 3895-3896, **certain** she saw Dylan shooting towards the cafeteria and then walking along the building. **Knew Klebold**.

- The *Columbine Report*, pp. 3973 (duplicate reports on pg. 2519 and pg. 4065), saw Dylan shoot someone in the leg and throw pipe bomb into the parking lot. Identified **after the fact** through media photos.

- The *Columbine Report*, pp. 3982, **certain** she saw Dylan outside on the hill area. **Knew Klebold**.

- The *Columbine Report*, pp. 3343-3344, **certain** she saw Dylan shoot someone on the ground outside the cafeteria; also saw both shooters at the junction of the library hall and the north main hall and identified Dylan again. **Knew who Klebold was**.

- The *Columbine Report*, pp. 945-946, **certain** she saw Dylan at the top of the stairs near building entry just prior to shooting; he moved away and she saw Harris standing in that area. **Knew Klebold**.

- The *Columbine Report*, pp. 3929-3931, saw Dylan shoot at two people, come from the outside steps by the west entrance of the cafeteria and then enter the cafeteria. Identified **after the fact**.

- The *Columbine Report*, pp. 4520, saw Dylan coming down the stairs outside carrying a semiautomatic pistol with a long magazine. Saw him light a pipe bomb and throw it into the parking lot. Identified **after the fact** through media photos **but had seen him before in school**.

- The *Columbine Report*, pp. 3762-3763, saw Dylan outside cafeteria carrying semiautomatic; saw him throw a pipe bomb into the parking lot. Identified **after the fact** through media photos **but had seen him before in school**.

- The *Columbine Report*, pp. 3069, saw Dylan outside the cafeteria. Did not see him throw the bomb into the parking lot but saw the explosion it caused. Identified **after the fact** through media photos.

- The *Columbine Report*, pp. 2275 and 2278-2279, **tentative** ID of Dylan walking past windows of cafeteria holding a gun. **Had seen before in school**. Cafeteria surveillance photo of Klebold "*came closest to the appearance of the person he saw*."

- The *Columbine Report*, pp. 2293, **certain** he saw Dylan walking down stairs outside shooting, saw him shoot student at point blank range. **Knew who Klebold was**.

- The *Columbine Report*, pp. 2413, saw Dylan walking down the stairs outside attempting to hide his gun inside his coat as he walked; he saw two males fall just prior to this. Identified **after the fact** through media photos **but had seen him before in school**.

- The *Columbine Report*, pp. 2542, **certain** she saw Dylan outside nearby one of the female victims. Saw him throw something. **Knew Klebold**.

- The *Columbine Report*, pp. 2627, Dylan had a gun in his left hand going down the stairs outside (also saw him and Eric in the cafeteria, pg. 2628). Identified **after the fact** after viewing photographs.

- The *Columbine Report*, pp. 4379-4380, saw Dylan shoot a victim in the back outside. Identified **after the fact** through media photos.

- The *Columbine Report*, pp. 4545-4548, saw Dylan shoot a boy outside. Identified **after the fact** through media photos **but had seen him before both in school and in his BMW**.

- The *Columbine Report*, pp. 4647, saw Dylan outside on the hill. Identified **after the fact** through media photos.

- The *Columbine Report*, pp. 4677, **certain** he saw Dylan outside the school and coming into the cafeteria. **Knew who Klebold was**.

- The *Columbine Report*, pp. 4772, **reasonably certain she** saw Dylan outside. She worked at Great Clips next to Blackjack Pizza where Eric and Dylan were employed.

- Female student, www.npr.org/templates/story/story.php?storyId=103189913, **certain** she saw Dylan outside shooting near a female victim.

- The *Columbine Report*, pp. 670-671, **certain** he saw Dylan outside when female victim was shot. Identified **after the fact** through pictures on television.

- The *Columbine Report*, pp. 803-804, saw Dylan on hill, then come down hill and shoot victim point blank range, throw bomb into parking lot. **Certain** it was Dylan after seeing cafeteria surveillance photos. Initially thought it was Robert Perry **but only because** he associated the trench coat that the suspect was wearing with Perry. **Knew Klebold**.

- The *Columbine Report*, pp. 815-816, **reasonably sure** (gives it a seven out of ten) that the person he saw outside at the top of the stairs near library entrance with trench coat, TEC-DC9, and baseball cap backwards was Dylan. First thought it was Eric, then thought it was Robert after hearing a rumor that Perry had turned himself in to police.

- The *Columbine Report*, pp. 690, **thinks it was** Dylan he saw outside the cafeteria.

- The *Columbine Report*, pp. 715, saw Dylan walking down the hill outside, by the stairs near the cafeteria. Identified **after the fact** through media photos, **had seen him around school**.

- The *Columbine Report*, pp. 877, **certain** he saw Dylan walking down staircase outside cafeteria and fire at someone. **Knew Klebold**.

- The *Columbine Report*, pp. 888, **certain** he saw Dylan at the top of the staircase and saw him throw pipe bombs and shoot his shotgun. **Knew Klebold**.

- The *Columbine Report*, pp. 922, **certain** he saw Dylan at the top of the staircase outside by the library doors. **Knew Klebold**.

- The *Columbine Report*, pp. 1065, saw Dylan at the top of the staircase outside. Identified Dylan **with certainty** after viewing cafeteria surveillance photos.

Initially thought it was someone else, possibly Morris, based solely on the trench coat and what he thought was a beret. Did not know Klebold prior to the shooting.

• The *Columbine Report*, pp. 1109, **certain** she saw Dylan and Eric at the top of the staircase. Walked past them just before the shooting started and then saw them shooting. **Knew Klebold**.

• The *Columbine Report*, pp. 781, **certain** she saw Dylan and Eric at the top of the staircase. Walked past them just before the shooting started and then saw them shooting. **Knew Klebold**.

• The *Columbine Report*, pp. 1235-1236, saw Dylan move from bottom of stairs up to top outside. Initially identified Brian Sargent, but after viewing cafeteria video stills was **positive** it was Dylan. Did not know Klebold prior to the shooting.

• The *Columbine Report*, pp. 1172, saw Dylan at the top of the stairs. Identified him by name, but report does not specify if she was familiar with him prior to the assault or if she learned his name afterward.

• The *Columbine Report*, pp. 1189, saw Dylan walking down the hill by the stairs. Identified **after the fact** from media photos **but had seen him before in school**.

• The *Columbine Report*, pp. 1214, saw Dylan at the top of the stairs shooting. Identified **after the fact** from media photos **but had seen him before in school**.

- The *Columbine Report*, pp. 1245-1246, saw Dylan running up and down the stairs outside. Identified **after the fact** from media photos **but had seen him before in school**.

- The *Columbine Report*, pp. 1268-1270, saw Dylan at the top of the stairs outside and then go down them with other gunman. Identified **after the fact from photos**.

- The *Columbine Report*, pp. 182, **certain** he saw Dylan at the top of the stairs outside, the west doors near library. **Knew Klebold**.

- The *Columbine Report*, pp. 195-196, saw Dylan and Eric outside at the top of the stairs. Identified **after the fact** from media reports **but had seen them before in school**.

- The *Columbine Report*, pp. 210, **certain** Dylan was the one who shot him outside downstairs by cafeteria. Identified through police photos.

- The *Columbine Report*, pp. 324, teacher **certain** she saw Dylan at the top of the hill, outside the library shooting. **Knew Klebold**.

- The *Columbine Report*, pp. 493, teacher **certain** he saw Dylan at the top of the hill, outside the library shooting. **Knew Klebold**.

- The *Columbine Report*, pp. 522-523, **believes** she saw Dylan at the top of the hill, outside the library near the top of the steps. Saw him throw pipe bomb into the parking lot, then saw him walk down the hill looking like he was going towards entrance to Commons but could not see based on vantage point. Knows that the boy she saw outside and the one she saw in the library were the same person. **Identified through media photos**.

- The *Columbine Report*, pp. 600, **certain** she saw Dylan at the top of the stairs outside, near the fence. **Knew him by sight at school; learned his name through media photos.**

- The *Columbine Report*, pp. 2370, **positively** identified Dylan at the top of the stairs after being shown cafeteria surveillance video photo stills. Initially thought it was Perry. Did not know Klebold.

- The *Columbine Report*, pp. 3944, saw Dylan at the top of the stairs outside. **Identified after the fact** through press coverage.

- The *Columbine Report*, pp. 4301, **positively identified** Dylan at the top of the hill and saw him throw something into the west parking lot. **Had seen him around school and put name to face through media coverage**.

- The *Columbine Report*, pp. 3999, saw Dylan at the bottom of the stairs outside the cafeteria firing a gun towards the ground. Identified **after the fact** by looking at police lineup photos. **Had seen Klebold around school**.

Saw Dylan in the cafeteria-

• The *Columbine Report*, pp. 2628, coming down the stairs with Eric, walking around shooting and throwing bombs. Also saw Dylan going down the stairs outside. Identified **after the fact** after seeing photographs.

• The *Columbine Report*, pp. 3113, saw Dylan enter into the cafeteria. Also saw him outside on the sidewalk with Harris. Identified **after the fact** through media photos.

• The *Columbine Report*, pp. 3213, **certain** she saw him enter the cafeteria. Also saw him outside walking towards it. **Knew Klebold**.

• The *Columbine Report*, pp. 2827 and pg. 2837, saw Dylan throw a bomb in the cafeteria. Identified **after the fact** through media photos **but had seen him before in school**.

• The *Columbine Report*, pp. 2888 **certain** she saw Eric and Dylan coming down the stairs in cafeteria firing guns and throwing bombs. **Knew Klebold**.

• The *Columbine Report*, pp. 3140 saw Dylan come into the cafeteria. Identified **after the fact** through media photos and confirmed by looking at cafeteria surveillance stills.

- The *Columbine Report*, pp. 3278-3279, **certain** saw Dylan enter the cafeteria. Also saw him in science hall; he fired into chemistry lab. Identified **after the fact** through media photos.
- The *Columbine Report*, pp. 247, **certain** he saw Dylan enter the cafeteria. **Knew Klebold**.
- The *Columbine Report*, pp. 5914, **certain** he saw Dylan in the cafeteria. **Knew Klebold**.

Dylan exiting building-

- The *Columbine Report*, pp. 1465-1467, **certain** he saw Dylan exit the east doors, south of the main entrance to the school. Initially believed it was Robert Perry, but after speaking with Perry's father and viewing cafeteria surveillance photo stills was sure it was Klebold he saw.

Saw Dylan in the main hallway-

- The *Columbine Report*, pp. 2812, **certain** she saw Harris with Dylan; Dylan shot in her direction. Saw gun hanging near his waist and saw him holding the TEC-DC9. **Knew Klebold**.
- The *Columbine Report*, pp. 1683, **certain** she saw Dylan running east down the main hallway area toward the front office. Saw him firing his gun (he held it in his right hand

although he was left-handed). Report does not make clear whether she knew of him prior or identified him after the fact.

• The *Columbine Report*, pp. 6001, she saw Dylan near gym down main hallway, identified **after the fact** through media photos **but had seen him before in school**.

Saw Dylan in library hall-

• The *Columbine Report*, pp. 2944 and 2947, **possibly** saw Dylan near the double doors from the west side before the doors into the library. **Identified by viewing cafeteria surveillance stills**. Told interviewer she had some concern with ID because she thought shooter had long black hair. In a previous interview, she described shooter as having dark brown hair.

• The *Columbine Report*, pp. 5874 and 5878, teacher **certain** he saw Dylan coming out of the library (he observed a second male with him but did not see him well enough to recognize him). **Knew Klebold; both Eric and Dylan had been to his house**.

Saw Dylan in science hall-

• The *Columbine Report*, pp. 3278-3279, **certain** he saw Dylan in the science hall and fire at the chemistry lab. Also saw him in the cafeteria. Identified **after the fact** through media photos.

- The *Columbine Report*, pp. 1766, saw Dylan in the science hall. Identified **after the fact**, report does not specify how, **but had seen him before in school**. In this student's written statement, he said he was almost positive he saw the same man on TV news acting worried. In his typed statement, he said he did not see Klebold again after Dylan tried to gain entry into the classroom where he and others were hiding.

- The *Columbine Report*, pp. 2185, **certain** she saw Dylan in the science hall. **Knew who Klebold was**.

- The *Columbine Report*, pp. 2222, saw Dylan in the science hall. Identified **after the fact** through media photos **but had seen him before in school**.

- The *Columbine Report*, pp. 5926 and 5932, teacher **certain** she saw Dylan in the science hall and believed the other gunman was Eric. While talking to 911 from her classroom, she gave them Klebold's name. **Knew Klebold, had him in class**.

- The *Columbine Report*, pp. 5603, **thinks he saw** Dylan shooting down hallway from just inside the west doors (he was standing near the tech lab when he saw Dylan). **Knew who Klebold was,** identified Dylan in **cafeteria surveillance stills**.

- The *Columbine Report*, pp. 5625, saw Dylan in the hallway loading his weapon (he was standing near the tech lab when he saw Dylan). Identified Klebold **with certainty** after looking at **cafeteria surveillance photos** but had initially thought the suspect was Robert Perry. He did not know Klebold; he remarked that Klebold and Perry look alike.

Saw Dylan in band hallway outside auditorium-

- The *Columbine Report*, pp. 3920, saw suspect running behind them and **it appeared to be Dylan**. **Knew Klebold**. Student thought he had a ski mask on; hair was sticking out and she thought based on this and his dress that it was Klebold.

Appendix B

Listing of people who thought it was a senior prank, from the *Columbine Report*:

Pages 104, 135
Pages 318, 324, 347, 370, 383, 386
Pages 402, 427, 443, 477
Pages 513, 538, 577, 593
Pages 629, 688
Pages 1053, 1056, 1082
Pages 1109, 1119
Pages 1203, 1210, 1226, 1252, 1255, 1284
Page 1341
Pages 1437, 1447
Pages 1511, 1519
Page 1672
Pages 1740, 1759, 1785
Pages 1853, 1899
Pages 1909, 1926, 1948, 1972
Pages 2006, 2025, 2041, 2045, 2099
Pages 2103, 2107, 2143
Pages 2201, 2217, 2243, 2287
Page 2513
 Pages 2617, 2663, 2675, 2679
Pages 2740, 2756, 2790

Page 2806
Pages 2927, 2955, 2962, 2988
Pages 3050
Page 3112
Pages 3222, 3248, 3288
Page 3401
Pages 3525, 3567
Page 3668
Page 3868
Page 3962
Pages 4053, 4057, 4078, 4082
Pages 4107, 4114
Page 4309, 4349
Pages 4404, 4408, 4419, 4424
Pages 4504, 4565
Pages 4608, 4649
Page 4706
Page 5143
Pages 5428, 5445
Page 5506
Pages 5610, 5627, 5646
Page 5794
Pages 5853, 5864, 5871, 5876
Pages 5934, 5959, 5964, 5985, 5989
Page 6034
Page 7363

Appendix C

<u>Saw only two gunmen outside—could not identify either or identified only one-</u>

- The *Columbine Report*, pp. 4254-4255 saw two gunmen dressed in black. **Identified Klebold** as possibly one of the gunmen, only got a glimpse of the other and could not identify.
- The *Columbine Report*, pp. 3112-3114, saw two gunmen and **positively identified Klebold**, but could not be sure that Harris was the other shooter.
- The *Columbine Report*, pp. 801-802, saw two gunmen. **Identified Klebold**.
- The *Columbine Report*, pp. 879, **identified Klebold** but heard a second gunman firing as well.
- The *Columbine Report*, pp. 1063-1065, saw two gunmen wearing all black. **Identified**

Klebold but did not see other gunman well enough to identify.

• The *Columbine Report,* pp. 206-207, saw two gunmen. **Identified Klebold**.

• The *Columbine Report*, pp. 939-940, saw two gunmen: one in a trench coat, the other in a white T-shirt and blue jeans.

• The *Columbine Report*, pp. 765, saw two gunmen: one in a white T-shirt, the other in a trench coat.

• The *Columbine Report*, pp. 1044, saw two gunmen: one in a white T-shirt and jeans, the other in a trench coat. Observed the former throwing bomb on roof.

• The *Columbine Report*, pp. 1051, saw two gunmen: one in a gray T-shirt, the other in a trench coat.

• The *Columbine Report*, pp. 1094, saw two gunmen outside near the stairs. **Identified Klebold after viewing more recent photos**, pp. 1099, initially thought it was Perry. Both suspects wore black pants.

• The *Columbine Report*, pp. 1114, saw two gunmen outside near stairs. Both in trench coats, then one took off his trench coat. Thought the one who removed coat wore light gray T-shirt and olive-colored pants (pp. 1119).

• The *Columbine Report*, pp. 1180, saw two gunmen: one wore a trench coat, the other wore a white T-shirt.

• The *Columbine Report*, pp. 1269-1270, saw two gunmen on the stairs outside.

Identified Klebold; the other shooter wore a white T-shirt.

- The *Columbine Report*, pp. 2791-2792, saw two gunmen in trench coats. Could not identify them.
- The *Columbine Report*, pp. 3424-3425, saw two gunmen outside. **Identified Harris**, said he was wearing a black T-shirt and black pants.

Saw two gunmen and could identify both-

- The *Columbine Report*, pp. 670-671, **saw only Harris and Klebold; identified after the fact** through media coverage.
- The *Columbine Report*, pp. 699, saw only two gunmen; in audio diary for NPR **identified Harris and Klebold**. www.npr.org/templates/story/story.php?storyId=103189913
- The *Columbine Report*, pp. 888, **saw only Harris and Klebold** at the top of the staircase.
- The *Columbine Report*, pp. 1109, **saw only Klebold and Harris** at the top of the staircase. Walked past them just before the shooting started and then saw them shooting.
- The *Columbine Report*, pp. 781-782, **saw only Klebold and Harris** at the top of the staircase. Harris was possibly wearing a green shirt.

• The *Columbine Report*, pp. 1172, **saw only Harris and Klebold** at the top of the stairs.

• The *Columbine Report*, pp. 1212-1214, **saw only Harris and Klebold** at the top of the stairs shooting. Described Harris as wearing army camo pants and a white T-shirt.

• The *Columbine Report*, pp. 1236, saw only two gunmen and **believed them to be Harris and Klebold**. Harris was wearing a white T-shirt and black pants (pg. 1227).

• The *Columbine Report*, pp. 1249-1250, initially believed he had seen three gunmen outside. After seeing cafeteria surveillance footage **believed he had seen Harris twice**, once with his trench coat on and then with it off, and thought he was two different people. Also **identified Klebold**. Described Harris in a white T-shirt and black pants.

• The *Columbine Report*, pp. 182-183, **saw only Harris and Klebold** at the top of the stairs outside. Harris wearing a white T-shirt and black BDU's.

• The *Columbine Report*, pp. 195, saw only two shooters at the top of the stairs outside. **Identified them as Klebold and Harris through media reports and friends; had seen them around school but did not know their names at the time**.

• The *Columbine Report*, pp. 599-600, **saw only Harris and Klebold** at the top of the stairs outside. Described Harris's shirt as light-colored, possibly tan.

- The *Columbine Report*, pp. 922, **saw only Harris and Klebold** at the top of the stairs. Saw Eric throwing bombs on roof. Said Harris wore a black T-shirt and black pants

References

Note:

The *Columbine Report* encompasses pages 1 through 25889.

The "Columbine Documents" encompass pages 25923 through 26859.

Duplicate page numbers exist in The *Columbine Report*, where pertinent this is indicated by noting the block/range of pages in which the reference cited can be located.

1. Brown, Brooks and Merritt, Rob. *No Easy Answers: The Truth Behind Death at Columbine.* New York: Lantern Books, 2002; pp. 231.

2. The *Columbine Report*, a statement by Clement Park Sports and Athletics Supervisor, pp. 1176.

3. The *Columbine Report,* a salesman touring Clement Park, pp. 1060.

4. The *Columbine Report*, an officer taking statements at scene, pp. 9819-9823.

5. The *Columbine Report*, a teacher reporting TCM to 911, pp. 8895.

6. The *Columbine Report*, a ninth-grade student wounded during attack designated TCM, pp. 8759.

7. The *Columbine Report*, a library witness designated shooters TCM, pp. 9828.

8. The *Columbine Report*, a reporter designated shooters TCM based on student reports, pp. 9831.

9. The *Columbine Report*, a student named Dylan and identified him as TCM member, pp. 9790.

10. The *Columbine Report*, a student identified gunmen as TCM, pp. 8923.

11. The *Columbine Report*, an officer identified TCM as responsible, pp. 8834.

12. The *Columbine Report*, a student relayed learning of TCM involvement from another student, pp. 8839.

13. The *Columbine Report*, an FBI agent assigned to look into the TCM, pp. 8736-8743.

14. The *Columbine Report*, police questionnaire with specific inquiries about TCM, pp. 809.

15. The *Columbine Report*, police quickly learned limited scope of TCM, pp. 13609.

16. The *Columbine Report*, a victim told to avoid TCM in middle school, pp. 209-210.

17. The *Columbine Report*, middle school students told to avoid TCM by CHS students, pp. 1601.

18. The *Columbine Report*, middle school students told to avoid TCM by CHS students, pp. 3460.

19. The *Columbine Report*, a friend told boy not to look TCM in the eye, avoid at all costs; was teased by the TCM once, pp. 3051.

20. The *Columbine Report*, a girl thought TCM members were all bisexual, pp. 1074.

21. The *Columbine Report*, a boy thought TCM members were gay so did not hang around them, pp. 1498.

22. The *Columbine Report*, a boy heard TCM members were bisexual, pp. 4561.

23. The *Columbine Report*, a boy believed TCM members were either gay or bisexual; saw jocks call TCM names, fights between two groups; some TCM wore white makeup, pp. 6612.

24. The *Columbine Report*, a boy heard TCM members were gay; also said they secluded themselves, pp. 6743.

25. The *Columbine Report*, a boy heard through the rumor mill that TCM members were gay, pp. 7470.

26. The *Columbine Report*, a girl heard that TCM members were gay, pp. 2980.

27. The *Columbine Report*, a girl believed the TCM all had sex together and were Satanic, pp. 1419-1421.

28. The *Columbine Report*, a girl believed the TCM had sex initiation requirements; also saw Chris Morris returning to school at 12:15 pm, pp. 5225-5226.

29. The *Columbine Report*, a girl heard that to join the TCM people had to have sex with guy

who wore beanie with propeller, pp. 3525.

30. The *Columbine Report*, a former TCM member said to join people had to be liked by other TCM; Harris and Klebold were TCM members, pp. 10656.

31. The *Columbine Report*, an associate of the TCM said they treated each other as family, hugged; at lunch with Brian Sargent that day; Dylan seemed to ignore teasing, pp. 7412-7413.

32. The *Columbine Report*, the school dean indicated Stair greeted male friends with kiss; incident in which he and friend "harassed" the jocks by kissing, pp. 1090- 1091.

33. The *Columbine Report*, a student said TCM members would make out in halls, provoke other students to call them names, pp. 7379.

34. The *Columbine Report*, a student said if TCM members kissed they were called fags, pp. 13153.

35. The *Columbine Report*, the school dean indicated two TCM kissed to make jocks angry, they were disciplined;

Eric and Dylan complained about a kid parking too close, mouthing off, pp. 5708.

36. The *Columbine Report*, a girl witnessed incident where TCM called fags for kissing in cafeteria; saw one telling kids, "Satan loves you," pp. 1011-1012.

37. The *Columbine Report*, a TCM associate dispelling rumors about group sex, pp. 8796.

38. The *Columbine Report*, a girl believed that the TCM were devil worshipers, pp. 1652.

39. The *Columbine Report*, a boy thought that the TCM were devilish, pp. 1754.

40. The *Columbine Report*, a boy thought that the TCM were Satanic, pp. 1365.

41. The *Columbine Report*, an associate of the TCM said that she and others were called "Satan"; also said TCM had disintegrated the previous year, pp. 7309.

42. The *Columbine Report*, a boy thought a game the TCM played, Magic, was about the devil and power, pp. 1475.

43. The *Columbine Report*, a girl thought the TCM were Satanic, never saw them harass anyone, pp. 6821.

44. The *Columbine Report*, a boy mentioned book Stair called the *Devil's Bible*, pp. 4054.

45. The *Columbine Report*, a girl said Stair discussed not believing in God, pp. 4073.

46. The *Columbine Report*, an associate said that the TCM largely disbanded in 1998, pp. 1303.

47. The *Columbine Report*, a boy said the TCM was more prevalent the year before, pp. 4123.

48. The *Columbine Report*, 1998-1999 yearbook dedication to the TCM, pp. 10101.

49. The *Columbine Report*, a TCM girl said that Eric and Dylan were members of the group, pp. 10776.

50. The *Columbine Report*, Perry said that Eric and Dylan were members of the TCM, pp. 10857.

51. The *Columbine Report*, Brian Sargent said that Eric and Dylan were members of the TCM, pp. 8784-8785.

52. The *Columbine Report*, a former TCM member said that Eric and Dylan were part of the group, pp. 1410.

53. The *Columbine Report*, Robyn Anderson said that Eric and Dylan were involved with the TCM, pp. 10620.

54. The *Columbine Report*, a former TCM member said that Eric and Dylan were part of the group, pp. 10867.

55. The *Columbine Report*, a former TCM member said that Eric and Dylan were part of the group, pp. 9823.

56. The *Columbine Report*, a TCM associate said that Eric and Dylan were part of the group, pp. 10770.

57. The *Columbine Report*, a TCM associate said that Eric and Dylan were part of the group; Eric teased over clothing, small size, musical taste; Eric punched in the face, pp. 10717-10720.

58. The *Columbine Report*, a friend said that Eric and Dylan were TCM members, pp. 10755.

59. The *Columbine Report*, a boy said that the TCM intimidated people and retaliated against those who insulted them, pp. 10909.

60. The *Columbine Report*, people avoided Eric and Dylan because they were different; saw Eric and Dylan in the main hallway, pp. 2811-2813.

61. The *Columbine Report*, Robyn Anderson said that Chris Morris felt Eric and Dylan were not TCM members, pp. 10635.

62. The *Columbine Report*, a boy said that Eric was not a TCM member, pp. 5085.

63. The *Columbine Report*, a friend said that Eric and Dylan were not TCM members, pp. 5239.

64. The *Columbine Report*, Klebold's father said that Dylan told him people called him and his friends TCM, pp. 10514.

65. The "Columbine Documents," Eric's planner with "Trench Coat Mafia Hit-Men For Hire" reference, pp. 26274.

66. The "Columbine Documents," Eric's grade sheet for "Trench Coat Mafia Hit-Men For Hire", pp. 26112.

67. The "Columbine Documents," Eric's cover page for "Trench Coat Mafia Hit-Men For Hire", pp. 26598.

68. The "Columbine Documents," Eric made reference to "us" as TCM in his "Trench Coat Mafia Hit-Men For Hire"" paper, pp. 26600.

69. "Columbine Massacre CCTV," YouTube video, 1:06-1:27, posted by "Cabanaman", 18 February 2006, http://www.youtube.com/watch?v=MP eWxR4J8RM&search=Columbine. (accessed 28 August 2013).

70. "Columbine, Wayne Harris 911 Phone Call" YouTube video, 0:07-0:11, posted by "Extraterrestrial Laboratory", 21 October 2017,

https://www.youtube.com/watch?v=fUucL 2xfowc (accessed 19 January 2019).

71. The *Columbine Report*, a girl said people called TCM members freaks, pp. 1018.

72. The *Columbine Report*, a boy said people thought of TCM as a joke, pp. 1489.

73. The *Columbine Report*, a girl said that the TCM were social outcasts, pp. 1300.

74. The *Columbine Report*, a boy said that the TCM were outcasts, pp. 2720.

75. The *Columbine Report*, a boy said that the TCM were outcasts, pp. 3532.

76. The *Columbine Report*, a girl said that the TCM were thought of as a joke, pp. 4404-4405.

77. The *Columbine Report*, a boy said that the TCM were social outcasts, pp. 4650.

78. The *Columbine Report*, a boy did not know TCM members but knew they were a joke, pp. 4527.

79. The *Columbine Report*, a boy said that the TCM were a group of weird kids, pp. 4875.

80. The *Columbine Report*, a girl did not associate with the TCM but knew they were all mean, strange, and weird, pp. 2671.

81. The *Columbine Report*, a girl knew of problems between jocks and the TCM, pp. 831.

82. The *Columbine Report*, a boy said that the jocks picked on the TCM, pp. 763.

83. The *Columbine Report*, a boy said that the TCM and the jocks insulted each other, pp. 3151.

84. The *Columbine Report*, a teacher said that the TCM exiled themselves from the student body, pp. 4851.

85. The *Columbine Report*, a boy heard of jocks picking on the TCM, pp. 7229.

86. The *Columbine Report*, a girl said that the jocks were mean to the TCM but that the TCM did not retaliate; Harris picked on frequently by jocks, pp. 7530-7531.

87. The *Columbine Report*, a former TCM member said that he received abuse from staff and students, pp. 10685.

88. The *Columbine Report*, a boy said that the jocks' teasing created the term "Trench Coat Mafia", pp. 1538.

89. The *Columbine Report*, a boy said that the jocks' teasing created the term "Trench Coat Mafia"; Harris and Klebold were picked on by jocks, pp. 1102.

90. The *Columbine Report*, a former TCM member said that the jocks' teasing created the term "Trench Coat

Mafia"; Eric and Dylan picked on a lot, pp. 10868.

91. The *Columbine Report*, a jock teased Eric and Dylan about clothing and bowling skills, pp. 7260-7261.

92. The *Columbine Report*, a boy said that the jocks' teasing created the term "Trench Coat Mafia", pp. 7051.

93. The *Columbine Report*, a TCM member said that the jocks always gave the TCM crap, pp. 8784.

94. The *Columbine Report*, a TCM member said that the jocks made fun of the TCM, pp. 10885-10886.

95. The *Columbine Report*, a boy reported jocks harassing a TCM member, pp. 905.

96. The *Columbine Report*, a girl confirmed identity of TCM member from "Reference 95", pp. 926.

97. The *Columbine Report*, a former TCM member said that the TCM received harassment daily, pp. 10873.

98. The *Columbine Report*, an athlete said that the jocks would harass the TCM on a daily basis, pp. 6135.

99. The *Columbine Report*, an athlete said that the football players picked on the TCM all the time; Eric and Dylan spoke of blowing up the school, pp. 7515.

100. The *Columbine Report*, a boy said that he heard athletes gave TCM crap, TCM did not like jocks because of it; Dylan

quiet and did not make friends in class, pp. 4806-4807.

101. Brown, Brooks and Merritt, Rob. *No Easy Answers: The Truth Behind Death at Columbine.* New York: Lantern Books, 2002; pp. 68.

102. The *Columbine Report*, a boy relayed details of confrontation with the TCM, pp. 14976- 14977.

103. The *Columbine Report*, a boy relayed details of confrontation with the TCM, pp. 763.

104. The *Columbine Report*, a boy alleged Morris pulled a knife during a fight, pp. 10284.

105. The *Columbine Report*, a boy alleged Morris pulled a knife during a fight, pp. 10202.

106. The *Columbine Report*, Perry alleged Morris threatened him with violence, pp. 10854.

107. Gibbs, Nancy and Roche, Timothy. "The Columbine Tapes." *TIME,* December 20, 1999.

108. The *Columbine Report*, a girl felt intimidated by the TCM because they gave her dirty looks, pp. 885.

109. The *Columbine Report*, a boy said that the TCM harassed people; he and Dylan almost got into a physical fight, pp. 1069-1070.

110. The *Columbine Report*, a girl saw the TCM harassing people, pp. 5117.

111. The *Columbine Report*, a boy saw the TCM harassing jocks in the cafeteria, pp. 5907.

112. The *Columbine Report*, a substitute teacher said that after the incident three black students complained of TCM harassment, pp. 5554.

113. The *Columbine Report*, a football player said that the TCM cursed at him, broke antenna, pp. 8841

114. The *Columbine Report*, a wrestler argued with the TCM over a parking space, pp. 10544.

115. The *Columbine Report,* a boy said that the TCM would back each other in disputes, pp. 483.

116. The *Columbine Report*, Robyn Anderson spoke of a fight between the TCM and freshmen, pp. 12271 within page block 12238-12292.

117. The *Columbine Report*, former boss spoke of a fight between the TCM and other group, pp. 10160.

118. The *Columbine Report*, former boss said Harris, Klebold, and Morris went to fight but other kids ran off, pp. 10170.

119. The *Columbine Report*, a boy heard Eric and Dylan talk of revenge for mistreatment, told all jocks to stand up, pp. 8925-8926.

120. The *Columbine Report*, a girl heard Eric and Dylan mention revenge for mistreatment, told all jocks to stand up, pp. 642.

121. The *Columbine Report*, a boy heard Eric and Dylan tell jocks to stand up, pp. 615.

122. The *Columbine Report* a boy heard Eric and Dylan tell jocks to stand up, pp. 565-567.

123. The *Columbine Report*, a boy heard Eric and Dylan tell jocks to stand up, they had waited to do this for a long time, pp. 578-579.

124. The *Columbine Report*, a girl heard Eric and Dylan mention revenge for mistreatment, told jocks to stand up, pp. 547.

125. The *Columbine Report*, a girl heard Eric and Dylan mention revenge for mistreatment, told jocks to stand up, pp. 524-527.

126. The *Columbine Report*, a boy heard Eric and Dylan tell jocks to stand up, pp. 355.

127. The *Columbine Report*, a girl heard Eric and Dylan mention being made fun of by jocks, waited to do this for a long time, pp. 384.

128. The *Columbine Report*, a boy heard Eric and Dylan mention revenge for mistreatment, pp. 348.

129. The *Columbine Report*, a boy heard Eric and Dylan mention revenge for mistreatment, told jocks to stand up, pp. 152.

130. The *Columbine Report* a boy heard Eric and Dylan mention revenge for mistreatment, told jocks to stand up, pp. 41.

131. The *Columbine Report*, a girl heard Eric or Dylan mention revenge, told jocks to stand up, pp. 514.

132. The *Columbine Report*, a boy heard Eric and Dylan mention revenge for mistreatment, wanting to kill jocks, wanting to do this for a long time, pp. 403.

133. The *Columbine Report* a boy heard through a library window the gunmen say they always wanted to do it, pp. 671.

134. The *Columbine Report*, a girl heard Eric and Dylan mention always wanting to do this, pp. 630.

135. The *Columbine Report*, a girl heard gunman say it was revenge, pp. 1785.

136. The *Columbine Report*, a bullied girl who thought Eric and Dylan were heroes, pp. 15556.

137. The *Columbine Report*, people avoided Eric and Dylan because they were different; saw Eric and Dylan in the main hallway, pp. 2812-2813.

138. The *Columbine Report*, Dylan said few people ever talked to him, pp. 5205.

139. The *Columbine Report*, a girl told not to talk to Eric because he was weird, pp. 3886.

140. Huerter, Regina. "The Culture of Columbine." "Columbine Commission Interviews," 1 December 2000.

141. The *Columbine Report* a boy said everyone picked on the shooters, pp. 9832.

142. The *Columbine Report*, Eric and Dylan teased over clothing and bowling stances; saw both boys at upper west entrance before attack began, pp. 785.

143. The *Columbine Report*, Dylan teased over his clothing, pp. 556.

144. The *Columbine Report*, Dylan and Eric teased in bowling class and over clothing, pp. 18882.

145. The *Columbine Report*, Dylan and Eric teased in bowling class; teased a lot more the previous year, pp. 16418.

146. The *Columbine Report*, Eric was picked on because of his small size, pp. 10834-10835.

147. The *Columbine Report*, Eric and Dylan picked on constantly, never accepted, pp. 10726.

148. The *Columbine Report*, a boy said he teased Eric about his appearance all the time, pp. 10273.

149. The *Columbine Report*, Eric received verbal teasing, pp. 4454.

150. The *Columbine Report*, Eric and Dylan teased about their appearance, pp. 6813.

151. The *Columbine Report*, Eric and Dylan teased about their clothing, pp. 2961.

152. The *Columbine Report*, everyone made fun of Eric and Dylan, pp. 3106.

153. The *Columbine Report*, jocks would harass Eric and Dylan sometimes, pp. 3896.

154. The *Columbine Report*, jocks verbally harassed Eric and Dylan, they retaliated, pp. 13173.

155. The *Columbine Report*, Eric and Dylan told co-worker they were teased at school, pp. 18743.

156. The *Columbine Report*, a jock teased Eric and Dylan about clothing and bowling skills, pp. 7260-7261.

157. The *Columbine Report*, everyone made fun of Dylan in gym class, pp. 736.

158. The *Columbine Report*, people made fun of Dylan in gym class, pp. 4827-4828.

159. The *Columbine Report,* people made fun of Dylan in gym class; he seemed to ignore it, pp. 4350.

160. The *Columbine Report*, Dylan told friend the jocks were giving him trouble, pp. 770.

161. The *Columbine Report*, Dylan teased about his clothing, pp. 5701-5702.

162. The *Columbine Report*, Dylan teased about his clothing, pp. 1865.

163. The *Columbine Report*, Dylan got in an argument with a wrestler about his clothing, pp. 7343.

164. The *Columbine Report*, Dylan was the brunt of jokes; Dylan was a follower, pp. 6974.

165. Salazar, Ken (Attorney General). "Report of the Investigation into the 1997 Directed Report and Related Matters Concerning the Columbine High School Shootings in April 1999." State of Colorado Department of Law Office of the Attorney General. 26 February 2004; Appendix 1-pp. 8.

166. The *Columbine Report*, Harris constantly picked on, had food thrown at him, pp. 10853.

167. Erickson, William. "The Report of Governor Bill Owens' Columbine Review Commission," May 2001; pp. 91.

168. Solomon, Andrew. *Far from the Tree: Parents, Children, and the Search for Identity*. New York: Scribner, 2012; pp. 590.

169. The *Columbine Report*, Eric's friends would engage in teasing him as well, pp. 6881.

170. The *Columbine Report*, friends would also tease Dylan and Eric; in class

the two spoke of killing and shooting people, pp. 6576.

171. The *Columbine Report*, Eric upset at friend who was making fun of him, pp. 6196-6197.

172. The *Columbine Report*, a friend taunted Eric so both the boy and his friend were put on his "Shit List", pp. 10265.

173. The *Columbine Report*, a student was relentless in abuse of Eric during gym; the entire class made fun of Eric, pp. 10264.

174. The *Columbine Report*, Eric purposely hit in the face with balls in gym, shoved into lockers by multiple jocks, pp. 1290.

175. The *Columbine Report*, Eric and Dylan slammed into lockers by jocks, pp. 4650.

176. Brown, Brooks and Merritt, Rob. *No Easy Answers: The Truth Behind Death at Columbine*. New York: Lantern Books, 2002; pp. 108.

177. The *Columbine Report*, Eric wrote how someone could get off his "Shit List"; wrote how he yelled at someone who constantly mocked his clothes, pp. 12995-12996.

178. "Eric Harris Inside Columbine (Full Video)," 00:00-00:26, YouTube video, posted by "ColumbineArchives1," 24 August 2012 http://www.youtube.com/watch?v=s-

l90HbShgM (accessed 24 September 2013).

179. The *Columbine Report*, jocks routinely blocked hall, forcing kids to go around them, pp. 4980.

180. The *Columbine Report*, Eric confronted a kid teasing him about Rammstein, pp. 903-904.

181. The *Columbine Report*, Eric teased about his clothing, he told them to shut up, pp. 4788.

182. The *Columbine Report*, Eric got aggressive with a kid who bumped into him in the hall, pp. 2038.

183. The *Columbine Report*, Eric picked fights and wanted Morris to back him up, pp. 10837- 10838.

184. The *Columbine Report*, the jocks picked on Eric constantly because he was small, pp. 9823.

185. Eric Harris Juvenile Diversion Program documents, Eric lied about his height, pp. 19.

186. Eric Harris Autopsy Report, *A Columbine Site*, http://www.acolumbinesite.com/autopsies/eric2.gif (accessed 27 September 2013).

187. The *Columbine Report*, Dylan told his father that Eric was picked on, pp. 10509.

188. The *Columbine Report*, Eric's medical records regarding pectus excavatum, pp. 10094-10095.

189. Brown, Brooks and Merritt, Rob. *No Easy Answers: The Truth Behind Death at Columbine*. New York: Lantern Books, 2002; pp. 51.

190. The "Columbine Documents," Eric wrote of being made fun of and his low self-esteem, pp. 26014.

191. The "Columbine Documents," Eric wrote of being made fun of and hating the human equation, pp. 26015.

192. The "Columbine Documents," Eric wrote of being left out, thought of as weird; tried to get a gun for Dylan; tried to get sex, pp. 26018.

193. The *Columbine Report*, Eric argued with a kid who bumped into him, alluded to April 20, pp. 7198-7199.

194. The "Columbine Documents," Dylan wrote of someone from gym that worried him, pp. 26388.

195. The "Columbine Documents," Dylan wrote of being scared, wanting to be accepted, pp. 26389.

196. The "Columbine Documents," Dylan wrote of wanting to be accepted, being hated and ignored, pp. 26390.

197. The "Columbine Documents," Dylan wrote of being an outcast and people conspiring against him, pp. 26392.

198. The "Columbine Documents," Dylan wrote of being hated, pp. 26396.

199. The "Columbine Documents," Dylan wrote of his failed relationship and being rejected for hating jocks, pp. 26398.

200. The "Columbine Documents," Dylan wrote of hating the happiness of the jocks, pp. 26405.

201. The "Columbine Documents," Dylan wrote about a killing spree and that the "meak" are trampled, pp. 26400-26401.

202. The "Columbine Documents," Dylan wrote about going "NBK" with someone other than Eric, pp. 26404.

203. The "Columbine Documents," Dylan wrote of "NBK" in Eric's 1998 yearbook, pp. 26241.

204. The "Columbine Documents," Dylan wrote of "NBK" in Eric's 1998 yearbook, pp. 26237.

205. The "Columbine Documents," Dylan wrote of the zombies causing pain and teaching them a lesson, pp. 26485-26486.

206. Dylan Klebold Autopsy Report, *A Columbine Site*, http://www.acolumbinesite.com/autopsies/dylan2.gif (accessed 3 September 2013).

207. The *Columbine Report*, one of the gunmen—likely Dylan—heard

screaming "I hate you" during attack, pp. 963-964.

208. The *Columbine Report*, the display case in the library was shot out, pp. 11149.

209. "columbine fire department video.wmv," YouTube video, 13:27-13:39, posted by "ToxicKlay," 2011. http://www.youtube.com/watch?v=xPUZ_R0mpz4 (accessed 24 September 2013).

210. Bingham, Janet; Callahan, Patricia; and Olinger, David. "School's opening day a bittersweet event." *Denver Post (Denver)*, 17 August 1999. http://extras.denverpost.com/news/shot081 7a.htm (accessed 25 May 2013).

211. The *Columbine Report*, Eric and Dylan felt administration favored the jocks, pp. 5276.

212. The *Columbine Report*, Eric and Dylan felt they were treated unfairly by the administration, pp. 16607-16608.

213. The *Columbine Report*, Dylan told the dean he was upset with how the administration handled people that picked on him and others, pp. 5707.

214. The *Columbine Report*, teachers would not intervene when Eric and Dylan were harassed, pp. 6577.

215. The *Columbine Report*, the teachers would unjustifiably pick on Eric and Dylan, pp. 7356-7357.

216. The *Columbine Report*, a teacher would pick on Eric and others in class, pp. 1152.

217. The *Columbine Report,* Harris did not like a teacher he felt picked on him, pp. 12993.

218. The *Columbine Report*, a list of computers and other damage caused by Eric and Dylan, pp. 11944.

219. The *Columbine Report*, a list of damage to the front office caused by Eric and Dylan, pp. 12539-12540.

220. Erickson, William. "The report of Governor Bill Owens' Columbine Review Commission," May 2001; pp. 98-99.

221. The *Columbine Report*, Eric, Dylan, and five others sent a threatening letter in eighth grade, pp. 17957.

222. The *Columbine Report*, in eighth grade Eric told a kid he did not like him, pp. 777.

223. Salazar, Ken (Attorney General). "Report of the Investigation into the 1997 Directed Report and Related Matters Concerning the Columbine High School Shootings in April 1999." State of Colorado Department of Law Office of the Attorney General. 26 February 2004; Appendix 1, pp. 7.

224. Brown, Brooks and Merritt, Rob. *No Easy Answers: The Truth*

Behind Death at Columbine. New York: Lantern Books, 2002; pp. 74.

225. Brown, Brooks and Merritt, Rob. *No Easy Answers: The Truth Behind Death at Columbine.* New York: Lantern Books, 2002; pp. 68.

226. The "Columbine Documents," the snowball incident with Brooks Brown, pp. 25924.

227. Brown, Brooks and Merritt, Rob. *No Easy Answers: The Truth Behind Death at Columbine.* New York: Lantern Books, 2002; pp. 77-78.

228. The "Columbine Documents," snowball incident; Eric denied drinking, pp. 25926.

229. The "Columbine Documents," Eric requested mediation with Brooks, pp. 25925.

230. Salazar, Ken (Attorney General). "Report of the Investigation into the 1997 Directed Report and Related Matters Concerning the Columbine High School Shootings in April 1999." State of Colorado Department of Law Office of the Attorney General. February 26, 2004; pp. 14.

231. The "Columbine Documents," no one pressed charges for the vandalism, pp. 25928.

232. The "Columbine Documents," the Browns believed that Eric damaged a tree on their property, pp. 25929.

233. Salazar, Ken (Attorney General). "Report of the Investigation into the 1997 Directed Report and Related Matters Concerning the Columbine High School Shootings in April 1999." State of Colorado Department of Law Office of the Attorney General. 26 February 2004; pp. 11-12.

234. The "Columbine Documents," Harris's father wrote of Eric being blamed unfairly, pp. 25930.

235. Salazar, Ken (Attorney General). "Report of the Investigation into the 1997 Directed Report and Related Matters Concerning the Columbine High School Shootings in April 1999." State of Colorado Department of Law Office of the Attorney General. 26 February 2004; Appendix 1, pp. 3-4.

236. Salazar, Ken (Attorney General). "Report of the Investigation into the 1997 Directed Report and Related Matters Concerning the Columbine High School Shootings in April 1999." State of Colorado Department of Law Office of the Attorney General. 26 February 2004; Appendix 1, pp. 1.

237. Salazar, Ken (Attorney General). "Report of the Investigation into the 1997 Directed Report and

Related Matters Concerning the Columbine High School Shootings in April 1999." State of Colorado Department of Law Office of the Attorney General. 26 February 2004; pp. 7.

238. Salazar, Ken (Attorney General). "Report of the Investigation into the 1997 Directed Report and Related Matters Concerning the Columbine High School Shootings in April 1999." State of Colorado Department of Law Office of the Attorney General. 26 February 2004; pp. 36.

239. Salazar, Ken (Attorney General). "Report of the Investigation into the 1997 Directed Report and Related Matters Concerning the Columbine High School Shootings in April 1999." State of Colorado Department of Law Office of the Attorney General. 26 February 2004; pp. 9.

240. The *Columbine Report*, Eric, Dylan, and a friend hacked into a computer for locker combos, pp. 323.

241. The *Columbine Report*, Eric, Dylan, and a friend hacked into a computer for locker combos, pp. 10754.

242. The *Columbine Report*, Eric, Dylan, and a friend hacked into a computer for locker combos, pp. 8200.

243. The *Columbine Report*, left threatening note in a boy's locker; one of the boys called teacher a dumb bitch, pp. 497.

244. The *Columbine Report*, Eric, Dylan, and a friend suspended for threatening notes and hacking, pp. 5749.

245. The *Columbine Report*, Eric, Dylan, and a friend suspended for threatening notes and hacking, pp. 5706.

246. Salazar, Ken (Attorney General). "Report of the Investigation into the 1997 Directed Report and Related Matters Concerning the Columbine High School Shootings in April 1999." State of Colorado Department of Law Office of the Attorney General. 26 February 2004; pp. 19-20.

247. The *Columbine Report*, Eric's life philosophy, pp. 10415.

248. Salazar Ken (Attorney General). "Report of the Investigation into the 1997 Directed Report and Related Matters Concerning the Columbine High School Shootings in April 1999." State of Colorado Department of Law Office of the Attorney General. 26 February 2004; pp. 13-14.

249. Salazar Ken (Attorney General). "Report of the Investigation into the 1997 Directed Report and Related Matters Concerning the Columbine High School Shootings in April 1999." State of Colorado Department of Law Office of the

Attorney General. 26 February 2004; pp. 28.

250. The *Columbine Report*, Brooks Brown received a threatening e-mail, pp. 10369.

251. Salazar, Ken (Attorney General). "Report of the Investigation into the 1997 Directed Report and Related Matters Concerning the Columbine High School Shootings in April 1999." State of Colorado Department of Law Office of the Attorney General. 26 February 2004; pp. 20-21.

252. The *Columbine Report*, Judy Brown warned neighbor about Eric, pp. 2306.

253. The *Columbine Report*, friend was present when paintball shot through Brown's window, pp. 5024-5025.

254. Salazar, Ken (Attorney General). "Report of the Investigation into the 1997 Directed Report and Related Matters Concerning the Columbine High School Shootings in April 1999." State of Colorado Department of Law Office of the Attorney General. 26 February 2004; pp. 17.

255. Brown, Brooks and Merritt, Rob. *No Easy Answers: The Truth Behind Death at Columbine*. New York: Lantern Books, 2002; pp. 93.

256. The *Columbine Report*, Eric stared at and intimidated a classmate, pp. 6140

257. The *Columbine Report*, a boy accused Eric of stealing his Discman, pp. 10299.

258. The "Columbine Documents," Dylan wrote of dubbing freshmen in Eric's yearbook, pp. 26235.

259. The "Columbine Documents," Dylan wrote of dubbing "frisbee fags" in yearbook, pp. 26238.

260. The *Columbine Report*, Dylan bullied a boy with special needs, pp. 247-249.

261. The *Columbine Report*, Dylan bullied a boy with special needs, pp. 8673.

262. The *Columbine Report*, Dylan called a girl a bitch in gym class, pp. 7416.

263. The *Columbine Report*, a boy threatened Dylan for calling his girlfriend a bitch, pp. 7380.

264. The *Columbine Report*, Dylan called a girl a bitch in gym class, pp. 10286.

265. The *Columbine Report*, Eric and Dylan would give a teacher dirty looks when she asked them to turn down music, pp. 13334-13335.

266. Dylan Klebold Juvenile Diversion Program documents Dylan vandalized a student's locker, pp. 17.

267. The "Columbine Documents," Dylan wrote of talking to the dean about vandalized locker, pp. 26456.

268. The *Columbine Report*, Dylan was disruptive in French class, pp. 5036.

269. The *Columbine Report*, Dylan was disruptive in French class, pp. 7214-7215.

270. The *Columbine Report*, Dylan had a bad temper and was very critical of French teacher, pp. 8888.

271. The *Columbine Report*, Dylan was openly disrespectful to a teacher; he swore in class, pp. 8892.

272. The *Columbine Report*, Dylan would intentionally slam the chemistry teacher's door, pp. 5931.

273. The *Columbine Report*, Dylan was usually late to calculus or slept in class, pp. 10542.

274. The *Columbine Report*, Dylan laughed at and intimidated a teacher, pp. 5179.

275. The *Columbine Report*, Eric was a model employee, pp. 10177.

276. The *Columbine Report*, Eric was a model employee; his female supervisor communicated with him online, pp. 13307-13308.

277. The *Columbine Report*, Dylan hit his female supervisor at work; both Eric and Dylan spoke of killing jocks and blowing up the school, pp. 10150.

278. The *Columbine Report*, arresting deputy's report of van break-in, pp. 10321-10324.

279. The *Columbine Report*, police report of van break-in, pp. 10314.

280. The *Columbine Report*, value of and list of items stolen during van break-in, pp. 10331.

281. The *Columbine Report*, police report of an interview with Dylan after van break-in, pp. 10333.

282. The *Columbine Report*, Dylan's written confession to the van break-in, pp. 10329.

283. The *Columbine Report*, Eric's written confession to the van break-in, pp. 10328.

284. The "Columbine Documents," Eric's writing about the Diversion Program in father's journal, pp. 25933.

285. The "Columbine Documents," Harris's father calling psychologists, pp. 25934-25936.

286. The "Columbine Documents," the Harris family's notes about the Diversion Program, pp. 25938-25943.

287. Eric Harris Juvenile Diversion Program documents, program requirements, pp. 7.

288. The *Columbine Report*, formal charges filed against Eric and Dylan, pp. 10345-10348.

289. The *Columbine Report*, Eric and Dylan stole computer parts from school; Dylan was shy, pp. 10697.

290. Eric Harris Juvenile Diversion Program documents, listed his past misdeeds, pp. 14-15.

291. Eric Harris Juvenile Diversion Program documents, Eric said he was looking forward to Diversion; he listed Dylan as his best friend, pp. 20.

292. Eric Harris Juvenile Diversion Program documents, Eric's punishment at home for theft; interviewer recommended Eric for program; Eric said he was not in a relationship and had never been sexually active, pp. 3.

293. Eric Harris Juvenile Diversion Program documents, Eric indicated he had only one close friend, pp. 28.

294. Dylan Klebold Juvenile Diversion Program documents, Dylan called Eric a "very good friend," pp. 22.

295. Dylan Klebold Juvenile Diversion Program documents, Dylan wrote that he had three close friends, pp. 30.

296. Eric Harris Juvenile Diversion Program documents, Eric's acceptance date into program; counselor's program release comments pp. 39.

297. Dylan Klebold Juvenile Diversion Program documents, Dylan's punishment at home for theft, pp. 2.

298. Dylan Klebold Juvenile Diversion Program documents, Dylan said he was never sexually active, pp. 30.

299. Dylan Klebold Juvenile Diversion Program documents, Dylan's past misdeeds, pp. 15-16.

300. Dylan Klebold Juvenile Diversion Program documents, parents said he was angry and intolerant of others, pp. 18.

301. Dylan Klebold Juvenile Diversion Program documents, Dylan denied he needed therapy, pp. 25.

302. Dylan Klebold Juvenile Diversion Program documents, Dylan denied depression and suicidal thoughts, pp. 73-76.

303. Dylan Klebold Juvenile Diversion Program documents, Dylan's most traumatic experience, pp. 26.

304. The *Columbine Report*, Dylan's letter to his crush also detailed his despair over the van break-in arrest, pp. 26408-26409.

305. The *Columbine Report*, Dylan cursed Deputy Walsh, pp. 10378.

306. Erickson, William. "The Report of Governor Bill Owens' Columbine Review Commission." May 2001; pp. 21.

307. Dylan Klebold Juvenile Diversion Program documents, interviewer's recommendation, pp. 3.

308. Solomon, Andrew. *Far from the Tree: Parents, Children, and the Search for Identity*. New York: Scribner, 2012; pp. 595.

309. Eric Harris Juvenile Diversion Program documents, report by Community Service supervisor, pp. 71.

310. The "Columbine Documents," Eric described trouble completing community service, pp. 26190.

311. Eric Harris Juvenile Diversion Program documents, Eric's speeding ticket, pp. 49-50.

312. Eric Harris Juvenile Diversion Program documents, handed in his apology letter; discussed changing medication, pp. 48-49.

313. The "Columbine Documents," Eric's apology letter, pp. 26525.

314. The "Columbine Documents," teacher's response to Eric's paper, pp. 26116.

315. The "Columbine Documents," Eric's feelings about the van break-in; was trying to be original, pp. 26005.

316. Dylan Klebold Juvenile Diversion Program documents, Dylan late to fulfill his community service requirements, pp. 50.

317. Dylan Klebold Juvenile Diversion Program documents, Dylan's community service hours, pp. 79.

318. Dylan Klebold Juvenile Diversion Program documents, struggled in school, pp. 52-53.

319. Dylan Klebold Juvenile Diversion Program documents, Discovery class a waste of Dylan's time, pp. 70.

320. Dylan Klebold Juvenile Diversion Program documents, counselor's program release comments, pp. 40.

321. Eric Harris Juvenile Diversion Program documents, suffered from depression, pp. 51.

322. Eric Harris Juvenile Diversion Program documents, JDP had access to Eric's therapy records, pp. 29.

323. Eric Harris Juvenile Diversion Program documents, interviewer noted depression, anger, and Zoloft, pp. 2.

324. Eric Harris Juvenile Diversion Program documents, interviewer noted three to four weeks of usage of Zoloft, pp. 5.

325. Eric Harris Juvenile Diversion Program documents, interviewer noted Zoloft usage, pp. 38.

326. Drug Information Sheet for Zoloft (Sertraline HCl), www.zoloft.com/#isi Follow "About"

link for full Prescribing Information. (accessed 19 January 2019).

327. Furberg, Curt D.; Glenmullen, Joseph; and Moore, Thomas J. "Prescription Drugs Associated with Reports of Violence Towards Others." *PLoS ONE*, 2010. www.plosone.org/article/info%3Adoi%2F 10.1371%2Fjournal.pone.0015337 (accessed 21 June 2013).

328. FDA-Approved Medication Guide. Chapter 17.10, "Medication Guide Luvox CR (LOO Vox CR) (Fluvoxamine Maleate) Extended-Release Capsules." Revised October 2012.

329. Skolek, Marianne. "Part 2-FDA's Continual Responsibility for Making Our Children Into a Nation of Drug Addicts!" *Salem-News.com*, 28 March 2011. www.salem-news.com/articles/march282011/child-addicts-ms.php (accessed June 21, 2013).

330. "GWU Investigation of PhD Awarded to Ann Blake Tracy." George Wythe University. https://www.gw.edu/_elements/userfiles/fil e/documentation/GWU_Investigation_Ann Tracy.pdf

331. "George Wythe Foundation Board of Trustees Cleanup Documentation." George Wythe University. http://www.gw.edu/board/history_docume ntation/ (See Degree Revocation Files).

332. "History of SSRI's Prozac LSD PCP and the effects-Ann Blake-Tracy" YouTube video, 0:52-1:00, 22 June 2009, posted by "DrugAwareness.org," www.youtube.com/watch?v=7uC1ef86 Lek (accessed 22 June 2013).

333. Bollyn, Christopher. "Anti-Depressant Drugs-Weighing in at Columbine." *Education Reporter*, no. 246 (July 2006).

334. Dylan Klebold Autopsy Report. *A Columbine Site.* www.acolumbinesite.com/autopsies/dyl an8.gif (accessed 1 September 2013).

335. Solomon, Andrew. *Far from the Tree: Parents, Children and the Search for Identity.* New York: Scribner, 2012; pp. 595.

336. Pankratz, Howard. "Drug Firm Settles with Columbine Victim." *Denver Post (Denver)*, 6 February 2002.

337. Eric Harris Juvenile Diversion Program documents, Eric filled out the mental health assessment, pp. 23.

338. Eric Harris Juvenile Diversion Program documents, Eric's parents filled out the mental health assessment, pp. 16.

339. The *Columbine Report*, Eric ranted about killing, including Brooks Brown, pp. 10361.

340. The *Columbine Report*, the "Writings of God" pp. 10383.

341. The "Columbine Documents," Eric hated the world; HOE and self-awareness; failing to be original; everyone, including him, will die, pp. 26003-26004.

342. The "Columbine Documents," Eric's first "NBK" reference; morals are manmade; doctor wanted him on medication; Eric would choose who lives, pp. 26006-26007.

343. Mark Taylor's statement to the FDA, 13 September 2004. ecommerce.drugawareness.org/home.html (accessed 2 September 2013).

344. Brooks Brown, Reddit Ask Me Anything, 2011. https://web.archive.org/web/20180125200 623/https://www.reddit.com/r/IAmA/com ments/gulaf/iama_columbine_survivor_na med_brooks_brown_i_was/ (accessed August 20, 2013).

345. The *Columbine Report*, no mention of misuse of medications in the "Basement Tapes" transcripts, pp. 10374-10483.

346. United States Court of Appeals, Tenth Circuit. *Rohrbough v. Harris*. 15 December 2008. caselaw.findlaw.com/us-10th-circuit/1393864.html (accessed 20 August 2013).

347. "John DeCamp-Columbine Shooting and Anti-Depressant Medication Lawsuit," YouTube video, 5:40- 5:58, posted by "TheCorsair00," 6 December 2010.

www.youtube.com/watch?v=cQHfkIh8 moQ (accessed 24 September 2013).

348. "John DeCamp-Columbine Shooting and Anti-Depressant Medication Lawsuit," YouTube video, 4:18- 4:30, posted by "TheCorsair00," 6 December 2010. www.youtube.com/watch?v=cQHfkIh8 moQ (accessed 24 September 2013).

349. Breggin, Peter. "CNN's Sanjay Gupta & Former Secretary of Homeland Security Address Psychiatric Drug/Violence Connection in School Shootings." *Natural News*, January 2013. www.cchrint.org/2013/01/14/psychiatri cdrugs-schoolshootings/ (accessed 19 September 2013).

350. Pankratz, Howard. "Columbine Experts Curbed Judge Limits Testimony Suit." *Denver Post (Denver),* 1 November 2003.

351. The *Columbine Report*, statement from girl who dated both Eric and Dylan, pp. 13254

352. The "Columbine Documents," Dylan wrote of his break up and suicide, pp. 26398-26399.

353. The *Columbine Report*, a girl turned down Dylan for a date; they remained friends, pp. 4436.

354. The *Columbine Report*, a girl turned down Dylan for a date, pp. 13268.

355. The *Columbine Report*, a girl turned down Dylan for a date, pp. 926.

356. The *Columbine Report*, a girl thought Robyn Anderson wanted to date Dylan, pp. 1140.

357. The *Columbine Report*, a boy thought Robyn Anderson wanted to date Dylan, pp. 8200.

358. The *Columbine Report*, a girl thought Robyn Anderson wanted to date Dylan, pp. 858.

359. The *Columbine Report*, Dylan did not consider Robyn Anderson a girlfriend; Dylan was very shy, pp. 10508.

360. The *Columbine Report*, Robyn Anderson wrote of her friendship with Dylan, pp. 13280-13281.

361. The *Columbine Report*, Robyn Anderson wrote that she never dated Dylan, pp. 13285.

362. The "Columbine Documents," Dylan wrote of his first love, pp. 26395.

363. The "Columbine Documents," Dylan's second letter to his crush, pp. 26479.

364. The "Columbine Documents," Dylan's last message to his crush, pp. 26485.

365. Blevins, Jason and Simpson, Kevin. "Mystery how team players became loners." *Denver Post (Denver)*,23 April

1999.
extras.denverpost.com/news/shot0423d
.htm (accessed August 14, 2013).

366. The *Columbine Report*, a girl asked Eric to a school dance. pp. 3983.

367. The *Columbine Report*, a girl broke up with Eric because he lived too far away, pp. 13558.

368. The *Columbine Report*, Eric insulted an ex-girlfriend in a friend's yearbook, pp. 960.

369. The *Columbine Report*, a girl met Eric at a soccer match, pp. 10277.

370. The *Columbine Report*, a girl met Eric at a soccer match, pp. 10280.

371. Lowe, Peggy. "Killer's Hatred Shows in Vitriolic 'Film Festival'." *Denver Post (Denver)*, 14 December 1999.

372. Erickson, William. "The report of Governor Bill Owens' Columbine Review Commission." May 2001; pp. 22.

373. The *Columbine Report*, a freshman girl Eric took on one date in February 1999, pp. 1221.

374. The *Columbine Report*, a freshman girl's mother put a stop to her dating Eric, pp. 1223.

375. The *Columbine Report*, a friend said that a freshman girl thought Eric was weird, pp. 5319.

376. The *Columbine Report*, a freshman girl's mother would not let her go to the Prom with Eric, pp. 4289.

377. The *Columbine Report*, a freshman girl and friends went to lunch with Eric a few weeks before, pp. 3131.

378. The *Columbine Report*, a teacher said that a freshman girl wrote fondly of Eric; she had a crush, pp. 1575.

379. The *Columbine Report*, a girl never called Eric after he left his number for her; she saw him at the top of the stairs prior to attack, pp. 5526-5527.

380. The *Columbine Report*, Eric was repeatedly turned down by a co-worker, pp. 3607.

381. The *Columbine Report*, Eric was repeatedly turned down by a girl, pp. 10215.

382. The *Columbine Report*, Eric was turned down for the Prom, pp. 7358.

383. "Did prom rejection push killer over the edge?" *Deseret News*, 3 May 1999

384. The *Columbine Report*, Eric was turned down for the Prom, pp. 17761.

385. The *Columbine Report*, Eric's friends tried to get him a date for the Prom, pp. 10836.

386. The *Columbine Report*, a girl's mother said that Eric sounded angry on the phone, pp. 6195.

387. The "Columbine Documents," Eric wrote of wanting to get laid before "NBK", pp. 26024.

388. The "Columbine Documents," Eric wrote of wanting to get laid before "NBK", pp. 26018.

389. The *Columbine Report*, Eric's last date, pp. 6195-6199.

390. The *Columbine Report*, Eric willed a CD to a girl, pp. 10376.

391. Keefe, Shannon. "Columbine remembers through words and images." *Denver Post (Denver)*, 19 April 2000. http://extras.denverpost.com/life/col041 9.htm (accessed 11 September 2013).

392. The *Columbine Report*, a 23-year-old woman made claims of knowing Harris, pp. 10844.

393. The *Columbine Report*, a 23-year-old woman claimed to have a picture and recording of Harris; claimed to have met Brooks Brown through Eric, pp. 10846.

394. Brooks Brown, Reddit, Ask Me Anything 2011 https://web.archive.org/web/201801252 00623/https://www.reddit.com/r/IAmA/ comments/gulaf/iama_columbine_survi vor_named_brooks_brown_i_was/ (accessed 20 August 2013).

395. Brown, Brooks and Merritt, Rob. *No Easy Answers: The Truth*

Behind Death at Columbine. New York: Lantern Books, 2002; pp. 106-107.

396. The *Columbine Report*, Brown met the 23-year-old after April 20, 1999; reported her to police as a possible threat, pp. 12252-12253 within the block of 12238-12292.

397. The *Columbine Report*, a 23-year-old woman could not identify Eric's distinguishing physical characteristics, pp. 10845.

398. The *Columbine Report*, Eric's medical records regarding pectus excavatum, pp. 10094-10095.

399. Eric Harris Autopsy Report, *A Columbine Site*, http://www.acolumbinesite.com/utopsies/eric3.gif (accessed 24 September 2013).

400. The *Columbine Report*, Eric's chest scar is described, pp. 10325.

401. The "Columbine Documents," Eric wrote of wanting to get laid; he hated the "human equation"; he wanted respect and was not judged fairly, pp. 26015.

402. "Devon Adams and Brooks Brown edit - from the Columbine Killers Pt 1," YouTube video, 3:27- 3:41, posted by "Miss Everlasting," 16 August 2016. https://www.youtube.com/watch?v=v3Pz6djJgWQ (accessed 13 January 2019).

403. The *Columbine Report*, a 23-year-old woman's phone number was not found

in phone records of the case, pp. 25802-25803.

404. The *Columbine Report*, a 23-year-old woman mentioned killing government people, pp. 12255-12256.

405. The *Columbine Report*, a 23-year-old woman mentioned sneaking into the library, detonating pipe bombs, and a thirteen-gunshot salute for Dylan's birthday, pp. 12256- 12258.

406. The *Columbine Report*, a 23-year-old woman said that she was supposed to participate in the attack, pp. 12260.

407. The *Columbine Report*, a 23-year-old woman said that she was to meet with Eric at a bus stop, pp. 12263-12265.

408. The *Columbine Report*, a 23-year-old made claims of her participation on a second message board, pp. 10850-10851.

409. The "Columbine Documents," Eric wrote that the carbine and one of the shotguns were his; wished his father had gone to the gun show with him; the massacre was his life's work, pp. 26016.

410. The *Columbine Report*, Eric spoke in the "Basement Tapes" of being dead in two and a half weeks, pp. 10375.

411. The "Columbine Documents," Dylan referenced being dead in 26.4 hours, pp. 26486- 26487.

412. The "Columbine Documents," Dylan penned an itinerary of the massacre in Eric's planner, pp. 26313.

413. The "Columbine Documents," Dylan wrote an itinerary of the massacre in his journal, pp. 26490.

414. The *Columbine Report*, a 23-year-old said that she was in the room with Dylan's ghost, pp. 12267-12269.

415. The *Columbine Report*, a man sent threatening messages to the 23-year-old, pp. 15264-15267.

416. The *Columbine Report*, the 23-year-old relayed how she met the man who threatened her, pp. 15247.

417. The *Columbine Report*, aunt of the 23-year-old said that she was obsessed with Columbine, pp. 15249.

418. The *Columbine Report*, a boy said that Dylan was shy, pp. 7044.

419. The *Columbine Report*, a girl said that Dylan was shy, pp. 10677.

420. Brown, Brooks and Merritt, Rob. *No Easy Answers: The Truth Behind Death at Columbine*. New York: Lantern Books, 2002; pp. 30.

421. The *Columbine Report*, a girl said that Dylan was shy, pp. 10529.

422. The *Columbine Report*, a boy said that Dylan was very shy, pp. 5282.

423. The *Columbine Report*, a boy said that Dylan did not interact with others in class, pp. 5100.

424. The *Columbine Report*, a girl said that Dylan did not interact with others in class, pp. 5197.

425. The *Columbine Report*, a boy said that Dylan did not interact with others in class, pp. 5285.

426. The *Columbine Report*, a girl said that Dylan did not interact with others in class, pp. 6172

427. The *Columbine Report*, a girl said that Dylan did not interact with others in class, pp. 6287.

428. The *Columbine Report*, a boy said that he could not get Dylan to talk in class, pp. 6117.

429. The *Columbine Report*, a teacher said that Dylan lacked social skills, pp. 5558.

430. The *Columbine Report*, a boy said that Dylan was a follower, pp. 10149.

431. The *Columbine Report*, a boy said that Dylan was a follower, pp. 10188.

432. The *Columbine Report*, a boy said that Dylan was a follower, pp. 3531.

433. The *Columbine Report*, a boy said that Dylan was a follower, pp. 4650.

434. The *Columbine Report*, a girl said that Dylan was a follower, pp. 5027.

435. The *Columbine Report*, a girl was surprised Dylan would participate in the massacre, pp. 6207.

436. The *Columbine Report*, a boy was surprised Dylan would participate in the massacre, pp. 6281.

437. The *Columbine Report*, a girl was surprised Dylan would participate in the massacre but was not surprised that Eric would, pp. 1140.

438. The *Columbine Report*, a boy was surprised Dylan would participate in the massacre, pp. 3420.

439. The *Columbine Report*, a boy was surprised Dylan would participate in the massacre but was not surprised that Eric would, pp. 5946.

440. The *Columbine Report*, a girl said that Dylan was a follower, pp. 10636.

441. The *Columbine Report*, a girl was not surprised Eric was involved in the massacre; Dylan a follower; Eric spoke of blowing up a store, pp. 10616-10618.

442. The *Columbine Report*, a boy said that Dylan was gentle, a follower, and would not do it on his own, pp. 1779-1780.

443. The *Columbine Report*, Dylan's father said that Eric would occasionally get mad at Dylan if he screwed something up; Eric had not been at their home for six months but was there in the week before the attack, pp. 10512-10513.

444. The *Columbine Report*, a boy said that Dylan was a follower, pp. 1828.

445. Solomon, Andrew. *Far from the Tree: Parents, Children, and the Search for*

Identity. New York: Scribner, 2012; pp. 595.

446. The "Columbine Documents," Dylan was jealous of his best friend's girlfriend and wanted to kill her, pp. 26394.

447. The "Columbine Documents," Dylan wrote of going on a killing spree by himself in November 1997, pp. 26400.

448. The *Columbine Report*, Rebel Missions may have been Dylan's idea, pp. 13852.

449. The *Columbine Report*, Dylan gave Eric the *Anarchist's Cookbook*, pp. 8199.

450. The *Columbine Report*, Dylan could stand up to Eric, pp. 6977.

451. The "Columbine Documents," Dylan considered not going through with it in January 1999, pp. 26415.

452. The *Columbine Report*, items were removed from Dylan's house, pp. 10606-10611.

453. The "Columbine Documents," hand signals found at Dylan's house, pp. 26508.

454. *The Columbine Report*, hit list found at Dylan's house, pp. 10284.

455. The "Columbine Documents," hit list found at Dylan's house, pp. 26370.

456. The "Columbine Documents," Dylan's plan for nicotine poison, pp. 26361.

457. The "Columbine Documents," list of things Dylan wanted to buy for "NBK", pp. 26369.

458. The *Columbine Report*, Dylan had a friend buy him fireworks the previous summer, pp. 957.

459. The *Columbine Report*, Eric's neighbors said that Dylan was often at his house, pp. 10249-10255.

460. The *Columbine Report*, items seized from Eric's house, pp. 10225-10229.

461. The *Columbine Report*, Robyn Anderson stated that Dylan bought his own gun and ammunition, pp. 10625-10627.

462. The *Columbine Report*, Mark Manes witnessed Dylan purchase ammunition at a gun show and stated that Dylan arranged a meeting and purchased the TEC-DC9 from him, pp. 8239-8240.

463. The *Columbine Report*, witness saw Dylan when he bought a gun from Mark Manes, pp. 8183-8184.

464. The *Columbine Report*, witness saw Dylan when he bought a gun from Mark Manes, pp. 8186-8187.

465. The *Columbine Report*, contents of backpacks containing the diversionary bombs, pp. 14954.

466. The *Columbine Report*, witness described location of diversionary bombs;

why they were moved by surveyors; open pocket with Walk Man, pp. 14963-14964.

467. The *Columbine Report*, witness described backpacks containing diversionary bombs; confirmed one pack had open pocket, pp. 14965.

468. The *Columbine Report*, site of diversionary bombs saw heavy foot traffic, pp. 14982.

469. The *Columbine Report*, a homeowner said the site of diversionary bombs was heavily traveled, pp. 14978.

470. The *Columbine Report*, Dylan suggested the location for the diversionary bombs, pp. 10380.

471. The *Columbine Report*, witnesses saw Eric and a taller boy, possibly Dylan, near the diversionary bomb site the day before the attack, pp. 14970-14976.

472. The *Columbine Report*, a boy saw Eric at the top of the stairs putting on fingerless gloves, pp. 680.

473. The *Columbine Report*, a girl saw Eric at the top of the stairs just prior to shooting, pp. 894.

474. The *Columbine Report*, a girl saw Eric and Dylan at the top of the stairs just prior to shooting, pp. 1109.

475. The *Columbine Report*, a boy saw Eric shooting and Dylan surveying the damage, pp. 917.

476. The *Columbine Report*, a girl saw Eric shooting and Dylan surveying the damage, pp. 1094-1099.

477. The *Columbine Report*, a boy saw both gunmen shooting towards the soccer field, pp. 661.

478. The *Columbine Report*, a boy saw the taller gunman shooting towards the soccer field, pp. 667.

479. The *Columbine Report*, a boy saw both gunmen shooting towards the soccer field, pp. 765.

480. The *Columbine Report*, a boy saw Eric and Dylan shooting towards the soccer field, pp. 922.

481. The *Columbine Report*, a boy saw trench-coated gunman fire towards the soccer field, pp. 940.

482. The *Columbine Report*, a boy saw Dylan rapid fire his TEC-DC9 and replace its magazine, pp. 670-671.

483. The *Columbine Report*, a teacher saw Dylan fire his TEC-DC9 and replace its magazine, pp. 493.

484. "Interdynamic KG-9 and Intratec TEC DC-9 'assault' pistol USA". *World Guns*.world.guns.ru/handguns/hg/usa/intra tec-dc-9-e.html (accessed 24 September 2013).

485. The *Columbine Report*, a boy saw Dylan spraying bullets everywhere outside, pp. 689.

486. The *Columbine Report*, a boy saw Dylan fire at doors, windows, and two different groups of students with his TEC-DC9, pp. 1180-1181.

487. The *Columbine Report*, a girl saw Dylan firing several rapid shots towards the school, pp. 703- 704.

488. The *Columbine Report*, a boy saw both gunmen firing at doors of the school, pp. 196.

489. The *Columbine Report*, a girl saw Dylan load a gun three or four times, pp. 1172.

490. The *Columbine Report*, a boy saw a student shot at point blank range, pp. 2291.

491. The *Columbine Report*, a boy saw Dylan shoot a student at point blank range, pp. 2909- 2911.

492. The *Columbine Report*, a boy saw a student shot at point blank range; saw same gunman fire at another group of students, pp. 3256-3258.

493. "Reinvestigation into the Death of Daniel Rohrbough at Columbine High School on April 20, 1999 Executive Summary." El Paso County Sheriff's Office, pp. 28.

494. The *Columbine Report*, a boy saw both Eric and Dylan fire at group with two injured victims, pp. 1213.

495. The *Columbine Report*, an injured student unsure who shot him, pp. 225-229.

496. Erickson, William. "The report of Governor Bill Owens' Columbine Review Commission." May 2001; pp. 36.

497. The *Columbine Report*, a police officer said an injured student named Eric Harris, pp. 8120.

498. The *Columbine Report*, a boy saw the trench-coated gunman shoot two of the injured outside, pp. 758.

499. The *Columbine Report*, a boy saw the trench-coated gunman shoot two of the injured outside, pp. 17953-17954.

500. The *Columbine Report*, a girl saw Dylan shoot at a group two injured students were part of, pp. 782.

501. The *Columbine Report*, a girl saw Dylan shoot a female student in the ankle, pp. 9807.

502. The *Columbine Report*, a wounded girl said she was shot by a nine-millimeter; she believed it was Dylan's TEC-DC9, pp. 255.

503. The *Columbine Report*, list of victims murdered by each boy, pp. 11868.

504. The *Columbine Report*, analysis showed a victim died from wounds in upper back that were inflicted by Klebold, pp. 12249.

505. The *Columbine Report*, a girl reported a victim died after Dylan shot him in the head, despite a police report

indicating both Eric and Dylan were responsible for killing him, pp. 109.

506. The *Columbine Report*, School Resource Officer said that Dylan was not outside during his gun battles with Eric, pp. 8072-8074.

507. The *Columbine Report*, Campus Supervisor said Dylan was not outside during gun battles with Eric, pp. 996.

508. "Reinvestigation into the Death of Daniel Rohrbough at Columbine High School on April 20, 1999 Executive Summary." El Paso County Sheriff's Office, pp. 7.

509. The *Columbine Report*, School Resource Officer heard explosion deeper in school as Eric stepped outside, pp. 11211.

510. The *Columbine Report*, a student attempted to contact his police officer father; saw Dylan enter cafeteria and throw a bomb, pp. 2836-2837.

511. The "Columbine Documents," JC-001-012976 to JC-001-015627. Additional Investigation Files/ Dispatch Tape/CS, time 7:18-7:42.

512. "The Columbine High School Shootings-Narrative Time Line of Events-11:10 am to 11:59 am." *CNN*. www.cnn.com/SPECIALS/2000/colum bine.cd/Pages/NARRATIVE.Time.Lin e.htm (accessed 23 September 2013).

513. The *Columbine Report*, deputy did not see Dylan outside during second gun battle with Eric, pp. 8112.

514. The *Columbine Report*, a girl said that Dylan was laughing during the attack, pp. 9151.

515. The *Columbine Report*, a boy said that Dylan was laughing during the attack, pp. 9152.

516. The *Columbine Report*, a girl said that Dylan was smiling and laughing during the attack, pp. 526.

517. The *Columbine Report*, a girl said that Dylan was laughing during the attack, pp. 10.

518. The *Columbine Report*, a boy said that Dylan was laughing during the attack, pp. 53.

519. The *Columbine Report*, a teacher said that Dylan had a smirk on his face during the attack, pp. 324.

520. The *Columbine Report*, a girl said that Dylan had a smirk on his face during the attack, pp. 444.

521. The *Columbine Report*, a boy said that Dylan was laughing during the attack, pp. 889.

522. The *Columbine Report*, a boy said that Dylan appeared nonchalant during the attack, pp. 873.

523. The *Columbine Report*, a boy said that Dylan appeared nonchalant during the attack, pp. 571.

524. The *Columbine Report*, a boy said that Dylan appeared nonchalant during the attack, pp. 19.

525. The *Columbine Report*, a victim said that Dylan looked right at him, smiled, and shot him, pp. 157-158.

526. The *Columbine Report*, Dylan confronted a student in the library, pp. 173-174.

527. The *Columbine Report*, a girl heard one gunman ask the other if they were still going to go through with the attack, pp. 62.

528. The *Columbine Report*, a girl said that Eric seemed in charge during the attack; Dylan tried to impress Eric, pp. 2628.

529. The *Columbine Report*, a girl said that Eric seemed in charge during the attack, pp. 2888.

530. The *Columbine Report*, a girl said that Eric seemed in charge during the attack, pp. 4702.

531. The *Columbine Report*, a boy heard Eric and Dylan shout orders to each other, pp. 2826.

532. The *Columbine Report*, a girl heard both Eric and Dylan directing the other, pp. 314.

533. The *Columbine Report*, Eric told a boy he wanted to blow up his school, pp. 13633.

534. The *Columbine Report*, a girl heard Eric and Dylan speak of blowing up the school, pp. 6642.

535. The *Columbine Report*, Eric wrote of killing in friend's yearbook, pp. 6776.

536. The *Columbine Report*, Eric asked a student to buy him a gun, pp. 10202.

537. The *Columbine Report*, Eric spoke of blowing up the school; Eric and Dylan spoke of shooting up the school on dirt bikes, pp. 10646-10647.

538. The *Columbine Report*, a boy saw Eric and Dylan with pipe bombs; he knew Dylan had a shotgun and knew of Eric's interest in making napalm, pp. 10763-10765.

539. The *Columbine Report*, Eric and Dylan spoke of bombing and killing, pp. 10780-10781.

540. The *Columbine Report*, Eric and Dylan spoke of wanting all the jocks dead, pp. 10727.

541. The *Columbine Report*, Eric and Dylan spoke of killing people, blowing up the school; Joe Stair's polygraph results; Stair's alibi, pp. 10895-10896.

542. The *Columbine Report*, Harris spoke of killing jocks and blowing up the school, pp. 10841.

543. The *Columbine Report*, Eric and Dylan spoke of guns, bombs, and killing people, pp. 5027.

544. The *Columbine Report*, Eric spoke of bombs and asked a boy to buy a gun for him, pp. 2232.

545. The *Columbine Report*, Eric asked a co-worker to buy a gun for him, pp. 10144-10146.

546. The *Columbine Report*, Eric spoke of bombing a school, pp. 13547.

547. The "Columbine Documents," Dylan's essay about a killer and his teacher's response, pp. 26522-26523.

548. The *Columbine Report*, a statement by Dylan's teacher regarding his essay, pp. 3437.

549. The *Columbine Report*, Dylan's teacher told his parents of a disturbing story he wrote, pp. 10463.

550. Klebold, Susan. "I Will Never Know Why," *O Magazine (Chicago)*, November 2009.

551. The *Columbine Report*, Dylan's guidance counselor made no mention of his killer essay, pp. 5660-5661.

552. The "Columbine Documents," Dylan wrote from the point-of-view of a gun, pp. 25996.

553. The "Columbine Documents," Eric wrote from the point-of-view of a gun, pp. 26174.

554. The "Columbine Documents," Eric wrote of the 25 things that made him different, pp. 26187-26188.

555. The *Columbine Report*, a statement about the defaced prom posters, pp. 13128.

556. The *Columbine Report*, a statement about the defaced prom posters, pp. 6985.

557. The *Columbine Report*, a statement about the defaced prom posters, pp. 16408.

558. The *Columbine Report*, a statement about the defaced prom posters, pp. 2596.

559. The *Columbine Report*, a statement about the defaced prom posters, pp. 1531.

560. The *Columbine Report*, a statement about the defaced prom posters, pp. 6113.

561. The *Columbine Report*, police statement regarding picnic table carving, pp. 11764.

562. The *Columbine Report*, a statement regarding picnic table carving, pp. 13554.

563. The "Columbine Documents," Eric wondered if anyone would write a book about him, pp. 26017.

564. The *Columbine Report*, a boy was mistaken regarding the "Thought of the Day", pp. 49.

565. The *Columbine Report*, a girl was mistaken regarding the "Thought of the Day", pp. 124.

566. The *Columbine Report*, a boy was mistaken regarding the "Thought of the Day", pp. 155.

567. The *Columbine Report,* a boy was mistaken regarding the "Thought of the Day", pp. 230.

568. The *Columbine Report*, a boy was mistaken regarding the "Thought of the Day", pp. 281.

569. The *Columbine Report*, a boy was mistaken regarding the "Thought of the Day", pp. 2529.

570. The *Columbine Report*, a boy was mistaken regarding the "Thought of the Day", pp. 4337.

571. The *Columbine Report*, author of the "Thought of the Day" for 20 April 1999, pp. 10914.

572. "Weather History for Denver, CO-Tuesday, April 20, 1999." *Wunderground.* www.wunderground.com/history/airport/KDEN/1999/4/20/DailyHistory.html (accessed 28 May 2013).

573. The *Columbine Report*, a boy confirmed the actual "Thought of the Day", pp. 9097.

574. The *Columbine Report*, a girl confirmed the actual "Thought of the Day", pp. 1232.

575. The *Columbine Report*, a girl confirmed the actual "Thought of the Day", pp. 4513.

576. The *Columbine Report*, a teacher confirmed the actual "Thought of the Day", pp. 2072.

577. The *Columbine Report*, Harris told a wounded girl to "quit your bitching," pp. 122.

578. Dylan Klebold's Autopsy report describing his head wound. *A Columbine Site*. www.acolumbinesite.com/autopsies/dylan 7.gif (accessed 28 August 2013).

579. The *Columbine Report*, Dylan's TEC-DC9 found in his right hand, pp. 12302.

580. The *Columbine Report*, bloodstain on Eric's left knee and a skull fragment beside it, pp. 12321-12322.

581. The *Columbine Report*, location of Dylan's head in line with Eric's left knee, pp. 12303.

582. The *Columbine Report*, coroner moved Klebold's body prior to photographer snapping circulated suicide photos, pp. 7823.

583. Dylan Klebold's Autopsy report indicating he aspirated blood. *A Columbine Site*. www.acolumbinesite.com/autopsies/dylan 5.gif (accessed 28 August 2013).

584. The *Columbine Report*, Dylan may have been capable of involuntary movement, pp. 12309.

585. "Carbines." *Hi-Point Firearms*. https://web.archive.org/web/20130915155 407/www.hi-pointfirearms.com/carbines/carbines_9mm .html (accessed 13 September 2013).

586. The *Columbine Report*, no blood in the barrel of Eric's 9 mm carbine, pp. 12111-12112.

587. The *Columbine Report*, only Eric's DNA found on 9 mm carbine, pp. 12137.

588. "Manual: TEC-9, TEC-9 Mini, TEC-9 Stainless." *Nazarian Army Store*. www.nazarian.no/images/wep/205_tec 9.pdf (accessed 13 September 2013).

589. Babu S Suresh; Mohanty, SP; and Nair, N Sreekumaran. "The use of arm span as a predictor of height: A study of South Indian women." *Journal of Orthopedic Surgery* 9, no. 1 (2001); pp. 19-23.

590. Becquemin, M-H; Berkani, M.; Capderou, A.; and Zelter, M. "Reconsidering the arm span-height relationship in patients referred for spirometry." *European Respiratory Journal* 37, no. 1 (January 1, 2011); pp. 157-163.

591. Matsuse, Takeshi; Ouchi, Yasuyoshi; and Teramoto, Shinji. "Substitution of arm span for standing height is important for the assessment of predicted value of lung volumes in elderly people with osteoporosis." *Chest* 116, no. 6 (1999); pp. 1837-1838.

592. The *Columbine Report*, police had received information from witnesses about Eric and Dylan's

involvement within the first hour of the attack, pp. 9739.

593. The *Columbine Report*, Robert Perry fought with Morris, dropped out, worked at Safeway, last spoke with Eric and Dylan in January 1999, pp. 10853-10854.

594. The *Columbine Report*, a girl believed Perry was friends with Eric; saw Perry at the public library, pp. 5189.

595. The *Columbine Report*, a girl believed Perry was "probably friends" with Eric and Dylan, pp. 6275-6276.

596. The *Columbine Report*, Perry's best friend said Klebold did not like Perry; Perry visited Columbine by bus, pp. 5633-5634.

597. The *Columbine Report*, Perry lived 2.18 miles from the school, pp. 10859.

598. The *Columbine Report*, Perry left to find his sister and met up with his Dad; friend called, pp. 10856.

599. The *Columbine Report*, a statement from Perry's mother, pp. 10864-10865.

600. The *Columbine Report*, a statement from Perry's grandmother, pp. 25763-25764.

601. The *Columbine Report*, a car belonging to Perry's father, pp. 10859.

602. The *Columbine Report*, a boy saw Perry flag down his father's car, pp. 2731.

603. The *Columbine Report*, a boy saw Perry get into father's car; the boy knew partial plate number, pp. 8675.

604. The *Columbine Report*, a friend of Perry's went to his house that day, pp. 10898.

605. The *Columbine Report*, a boy did not know why Perry would be at the public library, pp. 4202.

606. The *Columbine Report*, a teacher thought a student had seen Perry with Eric and Dylan on April 20, pp. 4537-4538.

607. The *Columbine Report*, a student did not see Perry with Eric and Dylan on April 20, pp. 6274.

608. The *Columbine Report*, a girl saw Perry at the public library, pp. 1861.

609. The *Columbine Report*, a girl saw Perry at the public library around 1:00 pm, pp. 1936.

610. Denver Dispatch Tapes, Tape 2, Side A, mentioned time Perry left the public library.

611. The *Columbine Report*, a girl described the physical similarities between Perry and Dylan, pp. 4827.

612. The *Columbine Report*, a girl described the physical similarities between Perry and Dylan, pp. 3143.

613. The *Columbine Report*, a boy thought the tall kid he saw by Dylan's car was Perry, pp. 4454-4455.

614. The *Columbine Report*, a boy said that he saw Perry throwing pipe bombs outside, pg. 8793; described seeing a person who resembled the gunman a month earlier and felt intimidated by him, pp. 2683-2687.

615. The *Columbine Report*, a girl said Perry was on outside stairs, pp. 1032.

616. The *Columbine Report*, a girl thought she saw Perry next to the stairs, pp. 840-844.

617. The *Columbine Report*, a girl thought she saw Perry at the bottom of the stairs, pp. 1017-1023.

618. The *Columbine Report*, a boy thought he saw Perry near the stairs, pp. 801-802.

619. The *Columbine Report*, a girl initially thought she saw Perry, then thought it could have been Dylan, pp. 4083-4087.

620. The *Columbine Report*, a girl initially thought she saw Perry but was certain it was Dylan after viewing cafeteria surveillance video stills, pp. 963-975.

621. The *Columbine Report*, a girl saw Dylan on the hill, pp. 1005-1006 and www.scholastic.com/teachers/article/i-survived-columbine-high-school-shooting (accessed 24 June 2013).

622. The *Columbine Report*, a boy saw Dylan on the stairs, pp. 1244-1245.

623. The *Columbine Report*, a boy saw Dylan walking down the stairs, pp. 1207.

624. The *Columbine Report*, a girl initially claimed Perry spoke to her in the cafeteria and then began shooting, later recanted her story, pp. 4470-4475.

625. The *Columbine Report*, a girl's friend told her she saw Perry in the cafeteria and he spoke to her before he started shooting, pp. 1503.

626. The *Columbine Report*, a boy thought he saw Perry in the cafeteria and hall, but identified Dylan through cafeteria surveillance video stills, pp. 5623-5625.

627. The *Columbine Report*, a girl thought the gunman she saw in the main hallway could have been Perry, pp. 5031.

628. The *Columbine Report*, a girl was certain she saw Dylan in the main hallway, pp. 1683.

629. The *Columbine Report*, a girl saw Dylan in the main hallway, pp. 6001.

630. The *Columbine Report*, a girlfriend of former TCM member saw the gunman; after describing him to her boyfriend he determined it was Perry although he did not see him, pp. 2144.

631. The *Columbine Report*, a teacher identified Dylan in the science

hall and relayed it to the 911 operator, pp. 5926.

632. The *Columbine Report*, a boy said that he saw Perry in a Red Geo, passenger had a gun, pp. 1699-1700.

633. The *Columbine Report*, the Perry family's second car was a Plymouth Grand Voyager, pp. 10858.

634. The *Columbine Report*, a girl said that the passenger in the Red Geo had a video camera, pp. 5924.

635. The *Columbine Report*, a search warrant served against Perry, items reviewed by police, pp. 25758-25772.

636. The *Columbine Report*, a girl confirmed Morris was in bowling class that day, pp. 2150.

637. The *Columbine Report*, a girl confirmed Morris was in bowling class that day, pp. 1922.

638. The *Columbine Report*, a boy confirmed Morris was in bowling class that day, pp. 2086.

639. The *Columbine Report*, a boy confirmed Morris was in bowling class that day, pp. 6233.

640. The *Columbine Report*, a boy confirmed Morris was in bowling class that day, pp. 10694.

641. The *Columbine Report*, Morris skipped fourth hour that day; he owned a Red Dodge Lancer, pp. 10802-10806.

642. "Chris Morris friend of Eric Harris and Dylan Klebold," ABC Nightline interview, Air date 15 May 2000. YouTube video, 6:25-7:12, posted by "TornFromTheMap", 26 February 2010. https://www.youtube.com/watch?v=coq TejlF6Ac (accessed 19 January 2019).

643. The *Columbine Report*, a girl confirmed Morris had been skipping fourth hour for weeks, pp. 1751.

644. The *Columbine Report*, a boy saw Morris leaving school around 10:18 am, pp. 1117.

645. The *Columbine Report*, a girl saw Morris leaving the teachers' lot around 10:20 am, pp. 7024.

646. The *Columbine Report*, a girl saw Morris leaving the teachers' lot around 11:40 am, pp. 7324.

647. The *Columbine Report*, a girl made no mention of seeing Morris that day, pp. 6365.

648. The *Columbine Report*, a deputy began blocking road access to the school at 11:27 am, pp. 8084.

649. The *Columbine Report*, a teacher directed traffic away from the school, pp. 5576.

650. The *Columbine Report*, a girl saw Morris at his girlfriend's house around 12:20 pm, pp. 3235.

651. The *Columbine Report*, search warrant executed at Morris's home on April 20, 1999, pp. 10808-10809.

652. The *Columbine Report*, a boy initially thought he saw Morris on the outside stairs but realized it was Dylan after viewing cafeteria surveillance video stills, pp. 1063-1065.

653. "Columbine Eyewitness Reports Three Individuals--One Arrested," CBS4 interview, Air Date 20 April 1999. YouTube video, 1:22-2:00, posted by "MDJarv", 20 April 2009. www.youtube.com/watch?v=RHefZGoJz2 4&index=6&list=PLD0AEDCE7ABDC68 CF (accessed 23 September 2014).

654. The *Columbine Report*, a boy initially thought he saw Morris outside but realized it was Dylan after viewing cafeteria surveillance video stills, pp. 1261-1266.

655. The *Columbine Report*, a boy identified the shooter in the library hall as Morris based on height and clothing; he only partially saw the shooter's face, pp. 5964-5966.

656. The *Columbine Report*, a teacher identified Dylan as one of the shooters in the library hall, pp. 5877-5878.

657. The *Columbine Report*, a girl identified Dylan as the shooter in the library hall via cafeteria surveillance video still, tentative ID because she thought the

shooter had black hair, pp. 2940-2944; pp. 2947.

658. The *Columbine Report*, a ninth-grade girl identified Morris as the hallway shooter, pp. 5248-5249.

659. The *Columbine Report*, the ninth-grade girl said Morris was shorter and scrawnier than Dylan, pp. 5251-5253.

660. The *Columbine Report*, Morris was as tall as Dylan and thirty pounds heavier, pp. 10798.

661. The *Columbine Report*, a girl who accompanied the ninth-grader identified Dylan, pp. 3343-3344.

662. The *Columbine Report*, a boy said he saw Sargent and five to six TCM members in Blazer at Burger King, pp. 6611.

663. The *Columbine Report*, a boy did not mention seeing Sargent or other TCM in Blazer, pp. 7119-7121.

664. The *Columbine Report*, Sargent gave a boy a ride fifteen minutes into the attack, pp. 3997-3998.

665. The *Columbine Report*, Sargent gave a girl a ride away from the school around 11:30- 11:40 am, pp. 2571-2572.

666. The *Columbine Report*, a girl went to lunch with Sargent, pp. 6317

667. The *Columbine Report*, Sargent went to Burger King with two friends then to a parking lot to smoke; he picked

up three kids when shooting started, pp. 10887.

668. The *Columbine Report*, a girl picked up by Sargent was not interviewed regarding what she did upon escaping the school; she did mention she was with other party who rode with Sargent, pp. 3293.

669. The *Columbine Report*, a girl thought Sargent was outside shooting students, pp. 1122- 1124.

670. The *Columbine Report*, a girl initially thought Sargent was the outside gunman but realized it was Dylan after viewing cafeteria surveillance video stills, pp. 1235-1236.

671. Barr, Zachary. "Sisters See Columbine Anniversary As Turning Point." *NPR*, 18 April 2009. www.npr.org/templates/story/story.php?st oryId=103189913 (accessed 26 September 2013).

672. The *Columbine Report*, a boy thought the gunman had a round face, was not Eric or Dylan, pp. 719.

673. The *Columbine Report*, a boy identified Dylan as the gunman on and near the stairs outside, pp. 1270.

674. The *Columbine Report*, a boy thought the gunman on the outside stairs was either Perry or Dylan, pp. 25615.

675. The *Columbine Report*, a boy relayed he was too far away to identify anyone, pp. 660.

676. The *Columbine Report*, a girl said that she saw Harris with a big, fat guy, pp. 1167-1170.

677. The *Columbine Report*, Dylan commented that he looked fat with all of his gear on, pp. 10376.

678. The *Columbine Report*, Stair was at home with his mother, list of items seized with search warrant, pp. 10892-10893.

679. The *Columbine Report*, Stair's sister escaped Columbine's library around 11:45 am, pp. 590-594.

680. The *Columbine Report*, police interviewed Stair and transported him to the command center, pp. 10890.

681. The *Columbine Report*, a boy saw police detain Stair at the public library, pp. 1198.

682. The *Columbine Report*, a girl saw Stair speaking to police at Clement Park command center, pp. 2145.

683. The *Columbine Report*, a girl said she saw Stair outside the cafeteria as the shooting began, pp. 3828-3829.

684. The *Columbine Report*, the girl who thought she saw Stair said it could have been Dylan after viewing cafeteria surveillance video stills, pp. 3840.

685. The *Columbine Report*, a boy mistakenly thought his friend had seen Stair at school on the day of the attack, pp. 4363.

686. The *Columbine Report*, a boy had seen Stair about two weeks prior to the attack, pp. 761.

687. The *Columbine Report*, a girl mistakenly thought her friend had seen Stair in the cafeteria right before the shooting, pp. 1984.

688. The *Columbine Report*, a girl did not see Stair in the cafeteria before the shooting; she heard someone talking to "Joe", pp. 2941-2945.

689. The *Columbine Report*, a boy thought his teacher heard a gunman say the name "Joe", pp. 2051.

690. The *Columbine Report*, a teacher did not hear "Joe" but named three others she thought had, pp. 2258.

691. The *Columbine Report*, a girl listed by the teacher made no mention of hearing the name "Joe", pp. 1939.

692. The *Columbine Report*, a girl said that she heard, "hey Joe," pp. 5862-5863.

693. The *Columbine Report*, a boy said that he heard, "hey, Joe, where are you?" pp. 2156.

694. The *Columbine Report*, a girl heard the name "Joe" being told to come or go, pp. 2046.

695. The *Columbine Report*, a girl heard "Joe, I have three of them in here," pp. 1928.

696. The *Columbine Report*, a boy heard the gunmen talking and heard the name Dominic, pp. 3164.

697. The *Columbine Report*, a boy named Dominic was not involved in the massacre in any way, pp. 2850.

698. The *Columbine Report*, a boy in the library thought the explosions originated in the Commons because of how badly the floor shook, pp. 350.

699. The *Columbine Report*, a boy in the library thought the explosions originated in the Commons because of how badly the floor shook; thought he heard gunfire outside the library, pp. 482.

700. The *Columbine Report*, a girl in the library thought the explosions originated in the Commons, pp. 380.

701. The *Columbine Report*, a girl in the library thought the explosions originated elsewhere, pp. 365-366.

702. The *Columbine Report*, a boy in the library could not determine which direction the explosions came from, pp. 409.

703. The *Columbine Report*, a boy had a feeling there were three shooters, pp. 263.

704. The *Columbine Report*, a boy thought there had to be more than two shooters due to the number of

explosions and amount of gunfire, pp. 2789.

705. The *Columbine Report*, a girl thought there had to be more than two shooters due to the amount of gunfire, pp. 334.

706. The *Columbine Report*, a girl mistook faculty members for gunmen, pp. 3007.

707. The *Columbine Report*, a girl identified Eric and Dylan as the gunmen she saw in the Commons, pp. 3017-3018.

708. The *Columbine Report*, a girl mistook staff members for gunmen, pp. 3015.

709. The *Columbine Report*, a girl described an older man with short, spiky hair; said she spoke with Harris in Smoker's Pit that morning, pp. 2183-2185.

710. The *Columbine Report*, a girl did not report seeing Eric Harris in the Smoker's Pit that morning despite another student claiming he was there at the same time this girl was, pp. 1416.

711. The *Columbine Report*, Brooks Brown reported not seeing Eric Harris that day until immediately before the shooting began, pp. 10670.

712. The *Columbine Report*, a girl observed someone in a white T-shirt and jeans near Eric and Dylan outside, pp. 830.

713. The *Columbine Report*, a boy observed two assailants, describing one

was in a white T shirt and jeans, throw something on the roof, pp. 4677.

714. The *Columbine Report*, a boy heard a person in a T-shirt and jeans say "Go" and the shooting began; saw a person in a T-shirt throw something on the roof, pp. 750.

715. The *Columbine Report*, a boy saw a person in a T-shirt and jeans throw a bomb on the roof, pp. 656.

716. The *Columbine Report*, a boy saw a sophomore warning others away from danger, pp. 766.

717. The *Columbine Report*, a sophomore initially thought the attack was for a video class or some kind of senior prank, pp. 1118-1119.

718. The *Columbine Report*, a boy saw a kid in a white T-shirt smiling during initial part of the attack, pp. 919.

719. The *Columbine Report*, a girl saw a kid in a white T-shirt and jeans bleeding, pp. 4185.

720. The *Columbine Report*, a boy saw a kid in a white T-shirt fleeing the gun fire, pp. 4455.

721. The *Columbine Report*, a boy saw Harris take off his trench coat, pp. 1114.

722. The *Columbine Report*, a boy saw Harris take off his trench coat, pp. 755.

723. The *Columbine Report*, a man saw Harris take off his trench coat, pp. 1194.

724. The *Columbine Report*, a boy realized that he thought Harris with a coat and Harris without a coat were two different people, pp. 1250.

725. The "Columbine Documents," Dylan lamented he was denied humanity, pp. 26397.

726. The *Columbine Report*, a boy told police that one of the shooters was a cutter, pp. 1115.

727. The "Columbine Documents," Dylan's Existence box, pp. 26387.

728. The "Columbine Documents," Dylan wrote he was different and could not face society's rejection, pp. 26416.

729. The "Columbine Documents," Dylan lamented the loss of his friends, pp. 26412.

730. The "Columbine Documents," Dylan's poem about seeking answers, pp. 26391.

731. The "Columbine Documents," Dylan wrote of his disdain for the morons, pp. 26393.

732. Hare, Robert D; Harpur, Timothy J; and Hart, Stephen D. "Psychopathy and the DSM-IV criteria for antisocial personality disorder." *Journal of Abnormal Psychology* 100, no. 3 (August 1991); 391-398.

733. Cooke, David J.; Forth, Adelle E.; and Hare, Robert D., eds. "Psychopathy: Theory, Research, and Implications for Society." Proceedings of the NATO Advanced Study Institute on Psychopathy. Series D: Behavioural and Social Sciences, Vol. 88. Alvor, Portugal, 27 November-7 December 1995; pp. 4.

734. Definition for "pathological liar". *Merriam-Webster.* http://www.merriam-webster.com/medical/pathological%201iar (accessed August 3, 2013).

735. The "Columbine Documents," Eric wrote of how much he lied and why, pp. 26013.

736. The *Columbine Report*, Dylan said that they used others to get what they needed/wanted, pp. 10377.

737. The "Columbine Documents," Eric wrote of how he would handle his emotions during the attack and that he would help annihilate mankind, pp. 26011-26012.

738. The *Columbine Report*, Eric stated his parents were great and could not have prevented things, pp. 10382.

739. The *Columbine Report*, Eric threatened to hurt anyone who hurt animals, pp. 10414.

740. The *Columbine Report*, neighbors said that Eric often helped with yard work, pp. 10249.

741. The *Columbine Report*, Eric's former boss said that he was a good employee, pp. 10158.

742. The *Columbine Report*, a teacher on Eric's hit list may have run in with him or Dylan on hall duty, pp. 18931.

743. The *Columbine Report*, a girl on the hit list may have been on it for her friendship with jocks, pp. 19093.

744. American Psychiatric Association. "301.81 Narcissistic Personality Disorder." In *Diagnostic and Statistical Manual of Mental Disorders Fourth Edition*, edited by Michael B. First and Ruth Ross, 658-661. Washington, DC: American Psychiatric Association, 1994. http://justines2010blog.files.wordpress.com/2011/03/dsm-iv.pdf (accessed 4 August 2013).

745. The *Columbine Report*, Eric described his DOOM tier levels as his "life's work", pp. 10381.

746. The "Columbine Documents," Eric wrote that good and evil was manmade, he wanted everyone to die, pp. 26010.

747. The "Columbine Documents," Eric believed that society and government are designed to maintain calm and order, pp. 26008 (paperwork is mislabeled as page number '6008').

748. de Waal, Frans. *The Bonobo and the Atheist: In Search of Humanism among Primates.* W.W. Norton & Co., Inc., 2013.

749. Dye, Lee. "Do We Need God to be Moral?" *World News*, 7 April 2013. http://abcnews.go.com/Technology/god-moral/story?id=18898993 (accessed 25 June 2013).

750. The "Columbine Documents," Eric wrote that all mankind—including himself—should die, pp. 26009.